The ILP on Clydeside, 1893–1932

The ILP on Clydeside,
1893–1932: from foundation to disintegration

edited by Alan McKinlay
and R. J. Morris

Manchester University Press
Manchester and New York

distributed exclusively in the USA and Canada by St. Martin's Press

Published by Manchester University Press
Oxford Road, Manchester M13 9PL, UK
and Room 400, 175 Fifth Avenue,
New York, NY 10010, USA

Distributed exclusively in the USA and Canada
by St. Martin's Press, Inc.,
175 Fifth Avenue, New York, NY 10010, USA

British Library cataloguing in publication data
The ILP on Clydeside, 1893–1932: from foundation to
   disintegration.
   1. Scotland, Strathclyde region. Clydeside. Political parties. Independent Labour
   Party. history
   I. McKinlay, Alan II. Morris, R. J. (Robert John), 1943–
   234.24102094141

Library of Congress cataloging in publication data
The ILP on Clydeside, 1893–1932: from foundation to disintegration /
   edited by Alan McKinlay and R. J. Morris.
      p. cm.
      Includes index.
      Includes bibliographical references.
      ISBN 0–7190–2706–3
      1. Independent Labour Party (Great Britain)—History,
   I. McKinlay, Alan, 1957–   . II. Morris, R. J. (Robert John)
   JN1129.I52I47   1991
   324.24107'09—dc20   90–6281

ISBN 0 7190 2706 3 *hardback*

Typeset by Northern Phototypesetting Co Ltd, Bolton
Printed in Great Britain
by Billings & Sons Ltd, Worcester

Contents

Notes on contributors

David Howell is Senior Lecturer in Government at the University of Manchester. The author of the classic *British workers and the Independent Labour Party 1888–1906* (Manchester University Press, Manchester, 1983), his most recent book is *Politics of the NUM: a Lancashire view* (Manchester University Press, Manchester, 1989).

William Knox is Lecturer in Scottish History at the University of St Andrews. His most recent book is *James Maxton* (Manchester University Press, Manchester, 1987).

Alan McKinlay is Colquhoun Lecturer in Business History in the Centre for Business History at the University of Glasgow. He has published widely in business and labour history and corporate strategy.

Joseph Melling is Lecturer in Economic History at the University of Exeter. His many publications on labour history include *Rent Strikes: Peoples' Struggle for Housing in West Scotland 1890–1916* (Polygon, Edinburgh, 1983).

R. J. Morris is Senior Lecturer in Economic and Social History at the University of Edinburgh. His most recent book is *Class, sect and party. The making of the British middle class: Leeds, 1820–1850* (Manchester University Press, Manchester, 1990).

Joan Smith is Senior Lecturer in Sociology at North Staffordshire Polytechnic. She is co-author, with Harry McShane, of *No Mean Fighter* (Pluto, London, 1978).

James J. Smyth is a Research Fellow in the Research Centre for Social Sciences at the University of Edinburgh. He is currently investigating the historical formation of small businesses.

ONE

The ILP, 1893–1932: introduction

R.J. Morris

'. . . if you cannot ride two horses you have no right to be in the bloody circus'.   (James Maxton, 1931)

I grew up in the 1950s in a family which firmly believed itself to be non-political, and if it had been called upon to justify itself, as we are all now required to do by some current political cultures, would have talked about public service, but the preference was really for doing a decent job of work for a fair reward. Gradually I learnt in the gaps between condemnation of all politicians as a burden upon those who worked for a living, that the Attlee government of 1945 was the greatest achievement of the labour movement and possibly of British government. It is fashionable now to downgrade that first Attlee government. Pay-beds, pit closures, the commitment to a nuclear deterrent and a rather vague opportunistic leadership tends to hide the fact that the National Coal Board replaced the coal owners, that the National Health Service replaced the panel doctor and Nye Bevan charmed the most conservative of professions to be staunch defenders of the welfare state, that Palestine never became an Ulster, that a strategy for full employment and for comprehensive welfare benefits was established which lasted thirty years. Would that anyone could confidently say they had such strategies now. Few who grew up under Baldwin and MacDonald would listen to criticisms of Attlee. The 1945 government did not destroy capitalism, but no other government destroyed so many elements of the capitalist economy with such wide-spread national consensus.

Nineteen forty-five is important because it affects the way in which the Independent Labour Party fitted into the traditional histories of the labour movement, the histories of Raymond Postgate, Henry Pelling and Francis Williams. Once upon a time, the story goes, there

1

were fragments: the Social Democratic Federation (marxists), the ILP (socialists), the Lib–Labs (sensible but dull) and the Fabians (middle-class intellectuals and/or gradualist and practical – could you survive an evening with Sidney and Beatrice Webb?). Then followed alliance with the Trades Unions to form the Labour Representation Committee. After a few compromises and a bit of a muddle over the First World War, the Labour Party became a socialist party with the constitution of 1918, but instead of living happily ever after was betrayed by MacDonald and we had to wait until 1945, after another war, after which people swept Attlee and his great men to victory.[1] Which after a pause for superMac and you never had it so good led us to the 1960s when Harold Wilson would finish the job in the white heat of the technological revolution. Thus the ILP was gathered in to the so called 'forward march' picture of labour history. Before 1918 the ILP was part of the heroic pre-history of the Labour Party. After 1918 the ILP was at best marginal, at worst irresponsible. A.J.P. Taylor, who in his spotted bow tie first lectured television audiences on 'English' history, dismissed the ILP with a faint sneer:

> combative working class socialists of the ILP, particularly from Glasgow. They imagined they were about to launch the social revolution . . . David Kirkwood, a shop steward who ended in the House of Lords . . . it (the ILP) became . . . a refuge for middle class idealists.[2]

Henry Pelling – with a little more sympathy – regarded them as an increasing menace to political success which the received wisdom still tells us is based upon unity and moderation. Maxton was 'given to uncompromising utterances'. Most MPs left the ILP because of its 'sectional attitude'. The ILP abandoned its role as 'reconciler of unionism and socialist' and became 'a cave of Adullam for socialists'.[3] This is less crude than the elegant view of the self-confessed outsider Keith Middlemas that the ILP was 'the awkward squad' which 'committed suicide during a fit of insanity'.[4] Pelling gave the restrained judgement; 'the electorate showed little sympathy for splinter groups on the left or for that matter on the right'. Such opinions were a product of the Labour Party's self assurance in the early 1960s.

The theory behind this received wisdom was clearly stated by Professor Bob McKenzie of the London School of Economics, he of the swingometer who guided a generation of television viewers through the general elections of the two party system. The ILP had no place on the swingometer and was put firmly in its place:

> The real problem was that the ILP refused to conform to *British parliamentary practice in the way the Labour party itself had already done* [McKenzie's italics]. The ILP refused to acknowledge the autonomy of its parliamentary party and insisted that its parliamentarians should be subject to the direction of the party organization outside parliament. . . . The Parliamentary Labour Party, although it did not say so in so many words, had accepted all the conventions of Cabinet Government; and, further, it had broken completely with the old, naive view that a parliamentary party should be the servant of the mass movement.[5]

Ralph Miliband provided a perceptive if little read view. ILP history has a continuity in his account, before and after 1918. The ILP in its various phases faced and refaced the problem of creating socialism within a labour movement which is basically not socialist and within a context of democratic culture which is certainly not socialist. The position was recognized early on by Keir Hardie, in *My Confession of Faith in the Labour Alliance*, published in 1910. He claimed that the ILP had lost nothing of its socialist character but reminded members that only himself at West Ham in 1892 had ever won a parliamentary seat without Labour Party backing. He made the important assumption that socialism was not something of the working class, but was being offered to the working class. Hardie believed that as a Labour Party candidate a socialist could get:

> a sympathetic reception for himself and his doctrines because he comes to the average man as the representative of his own party, for which he is paying and over which he exercises control.[6]

It is important to reflect on this account because once the ILP left the Labour Party in 1932 and decided that being a party within a party was no good, there may have been some in the Labour Party who gave a sigh of relief but, as David Howell's essay demonstrates, the Labour Party has continuously had to re-invent the ILP, as Bevanites, the Tribune group, Bennites and others but none has ever seemed able to achieve that breadth of local base and intellectual – cum – parliamentary action group that the ILP claimed before 1932. In the 1920s, the ILP contained both Jimmy Maxton and one C.R. Attlee as members, active in their own different ways for far longer than the historiography would have us believe. Consider the *Notes for Lecturers and Class Leaders, ILP Study Courses No 4, Economic History* prepared by C.R. Attlee, MA, MP:

> Socialism stands for the application of the principle of social justice to the economic organization of society. It claims that the present system of Capitalism has failed to provide the material basis for a good life and that as a phase of industrial evolution it must be replaced by a co-operative commonwealth based upon common ownership and control of the means of life.[7]

Which of us now could begin lectures in that confident manner and follow with a reading list that had the modern equivalents of the Hammonds, the Webbs, Tawney, L.C.A. Knowles, J.A. Hobson and Keynes?

The still influential assumptions of the 1950s and 1960s have formed our views of the ILP and prevented a direct assessment of the contribution which the party made to political life over its long and varied career. Now, after the struggles of the labour movement to reformulate and redirect itself in the uncertain 1970s, the hostile 1980s and the 'new times' of the 1990s, it is time to look more sympathetically at the ILP over the full length of its history. We have chosen to do this through the medium of a series of essays on the ILP in the west of Scotland, especially in Glasgow. There are two reasons for this. In Glasgow the ILP's contribution to British politics was sustained over a longer time period than in any other part of the United Kingdom. Secondly, in the past ten years, it has been in the vitality and variety of local politics that the chief source of innovation and initiative (welcome and unwelcome by the central authorities of the party) has been located. Can we get beyond judgements which are often influenced by the spectacle of a party, which in 1920 contained Maxton, Attlee and MacDonald, breaking up under the twin pressures of being both party within a party, and also of carrying a more radical and decentralised version of socialism than the politicians and trades unionists who dominated the labour movement? Can we get beyond Attlee's characteristically curt and efficient dismissal of the ILP in the 1930s as 'rejoicing in its own irresponsibility' or Gordon Brown's more cautious and kindly 'the rump of a sect of a once great national party'?[8] Is the destiny of the ILP more than an awful warning to those who lead break-away parties? If it is then the answer lies in the west of Scotland, for it was in Glasgow and some of the surrounding constituencies that ILP history followed a distinctive path. The issues of policy and organization which were debated in the ILP were British issues, but increasingly these were debated by Clydeside personalities, and increasingly those personalities got answers which were different from the answers reached by the bulk of the British labour movement.

Our essays show three, perhaps four, phases in the experience of the ILP in Glasgow. In the early years, the subject of Jim Smyth's essay, between its foundation in 1893 and merger with the Scottish Labour Party in 1894, the ILP became an increasingly effective operator in a network of socialist and other working-class organizations. Before 1914, it was relatively weak compared to other parts of Britain, but in 1917 began an expansion which took the ILP in Scotland from 3,000 members in 117 branches to 9,000 in 192 branches by September 1918. It was an expansion which happened nowhere else in Britain and left Scotland with a third of total British ILP membership.[9] For Joan Smith, the notion of the network is important for understanding not just the ILP's role before and during the Great War but also the direction and organizational instincts of the Clydeside ILP leaders in the 1920s and 1930s. It is also important for assessing Glasgow working-class political history during the key years between 1914 and 1922. Lenin's 'Petrograd of the West' label has obscured the debate over the nature of Glasgow's working-class political history in those years for far too long. Such comments have tempted historians to use an overdefinition of 'revolution' which is then used to ask us to 'forget the Red Clyde'.[10] Iain McLean has shown that much of the evidence of class consciousness concerned fragmentary, episodic action which arose from 'craft conservatism'.[11] But while it is true that the people of Glasgow did not storm the Winter Palace every weekend, they did join the ILP in increasingly large numbers and they did vote for ILP candidates in even larger numbers once both the franchise and registration had been sorted out. Much has been made of the gap between the 1918 and 1922 General Election results but it must be remembered that the right to vote in Britain involves both legislation and registration. One of the social processes which drew together the various rent strike committees, the episodic interventions of the Clyde Workers' Committee (CWC), the trades councils and industrial action was the networking activities of the ILP activists. The organisations which drove working class action between 1914 and 1922 were unco-ordinated and often fragile. Each ran their own strikes, demonstrations and meetings, but when the nuts and bolts of each event are examined there was, as Joseph Melling demonstrates, almost always a core of ILP activists involved. John Wheatley helped Kirkwood draft the 1916 dilution agreement for Parkhead as well as persuading him to join the ILP. It was Wheatley again who spoke to the crowd in Shettleston who were defending the McHugh family from eviction.[12] Harry Hopkins of the engineering union and Govan Trades Council also had close links with rent strikers and housing groups. James Messer linked the ILP to the shop stewards at Weirs and the CWC. When Mary Laird organised a meeting of the Glasgow Women's Housing Association in February 1915, the speakers included Hopkins and Patrick Dollan. The ILP was the cement which stuck the fragments together. John MacLean may have criticised the ILP-ers as opportunistic but in Glasgow during those years there were many opportunities.

After 1918 the ILP became a party within a party and with the formation of the Communist Party in 1920 was faced with a rival invested with the political authority of the Russian Revolution. The long-term impact of this double-closure within the British labour movement was devastating: the terms 'revolutionary' and 'reformist' now no longer overlapped but were mutually exclusive. For, as Alan McKinlay shows, this change in political structures was paralleled by the rapid dissolution of the activist networks which had long been the source of the ILP's vitality in Glasgow. In most areas this led to a steady take over of ILP functions by the Labour Party at parliamentary and constituency levels. In west Yorkshire, the ILP rapidly lost its leadership to the constituency Labour Parties. By the mid-1920s, working-class support for the labour movement came through the trades unions and then to the constituency Labour Parties. In Glasgow that process did not take place. Throughout the 1920s, the ILP remained the effective Labour Party on the ground. The ILP style of politics seemed to thrive in areas of relatively weak industrial unionism, hence in the 1880s and 1890s, West Yorkshire rather than Lancashire was the centre of political innovation. By 1920 the initiative had moved to the Clyde.[13] In Glasgow, as in most of Scotland, trade union organisation, where it existed, was sectionalised and co-ordinated through trades councils rather than industrial unions.[14] Even in the third phase when the ILP left the Labour

Party, effective constituency Labour Parties were thin on the ground. Dollan, who wished to retain affiliation, was forced to form the Scottish Socialist Party to ease the transition into the Labour Party for the many ILP-ers who did not follow Maxton. It was this group which created municipal labour Glasgow after 1933.

One central question emerges from this history. What were the features of Glasgow's society and economy upon which its labour movement was built, and which enabled that labour movement to take such a radically different direction from the rest of Britain after 1917? Related to this are supplementary questions about the nature of Glasgow's experience in the 1920s and the importance of powerful personalities such as Maxton, Wheatley and Dollan.

Glasgow was a skilled man's economy. In 1911, the printed census shows that less than 30 per cent of the adult male labour force in Glasgow were in unskilled occupations.[15] Many of these skilled men worked in large units of production like Parkhead Forge in the east end of the city, the railway works at Springburn and the shipyards in the industrial burghs to the west that were acquired by Glasgow in the municipal boundary extensions of 1912.[16] During the rapid expansion of the Clyde shipbuilding and engineering industries after 1860, such men fought for control of their labour through a series of intensely sectional craft unions.[17] They had a specific place in the history of the 'labour aristocracy' which has been the centre of much debate.[18] By the 1850s and 1860s, a characteristic social formation can be observed in many industries. It consisted of men with better pay, more regular earnings, with some control over the pace and organisation of their work, and over entry usually through apprenticeship, to their occupation. Engineers, printers and stonemasons were central to the group whilst older occupations, like flint glass makers and wheelwrights, shared many of these features. The 'labour aristocracy' had their own network of organisations: friendly societies, craft unions, a literary society, a unit of the volunteers, a church or chapel and perhaps a temperance society. Their values were ones of fierce independence, savings and rigid family morality. They were neat in home and dress.[19] Many contemporaries and historians believed that this group and their ideology was a barrier to class formation, class action and any revolutionary challenge to capitalism, hence the link to judgements that the unrest on the Clyde was a matter of 'craft conservatism' and the ILP only an 'artisan' party.[20] Certainly, many of the values and behaviour patterns of this group were congruent with those of the middle classes. The difference came in the aggressive collective defence of craft custom. For the ironmoulder in the west of Scotland, 'it was a union rule to take a rest of fifteen minutes to cool down' after each casting had been completed.[21] The building crafts were involved in a constant running battle for control of the organisation of their work. Richard Price has identified a fluid 'frontier of control', involving resistance to piece rates, payment for walking time, the provision of sheds on site and the pace at which bricks were laid.[22] In politics, the skilled men tended to be Gladstonian liberal, democratic, anti-landlord, anti-despot, fiercely moralistic and often internationalist. Studies of specific localities, notably Edinburgh and Kentish London, and particular trades, such as glassblowing, dominate the literature on the 'labour aristocracy'. Such studies can help us understand the values of skilled people in Glasgow, but not their experience, which differed both in time and place. Throughout this period, incomes were more insecure and subject to large variations. We have an excellent time series for riveting gangs at Charles Connell's shipyard. The leaders of these three-man (and one-youth) gangs could earn between £2 and £6 per week, depending on physical strength, skill, their relationship with yard foremen and the highly cyclical demand for ships. By the 1890s, machine riveting and dilution by apprentices was increasing a core of short-time, low-earning gangs.[23] During the 1914–18 war the income differential between the skilled and unskilled upon which much of their status and distinctive behaviour depended was irreversibly narrowed.[24] Glasgow's housing market also played a part in reducing the social distance between the skilled and unskilled. There was little opportunity for Glasgow's skilled men to own their homes, unlike the urban cottage housing in many parts of England. The fluctuations in earnings meant that the skilled men and their families moved often and achieved less geographical seperation from the unskilled than in the more stable economy of Edinburgh. Some differentiation of experience was created by the yearly lets which skilled people were able to undertake and the weekly or daily lets open to the unskilled and casual labour force.[25] But even this cleavage in tenancy was overlaid by the fact that *all* rents in a given tenement or street were paid to the same factor or housing manager. Clydesiders lived in an urban economy which was lower in wages and, in general, higher in living costs than most of the English industrial centres. The 1905 Board of

Trade enquiry into working-class living standards suggests that the real wages of skilled men in Glasgow were 87 per cent of those in London, Yorkshire, Lancashire and the Midlands. Industrial Glasgow was on a par with the then underdeveloped southern and eastern English counties.[26] Glasgow may have been the skilled man's economy but it provided the skilled man with an insecure and relatively poor standard of living. Here was a culture composed of poverty, skill and insecurity.

The nature of the labour market in Glasgow meant that many skilled men began their working life as boy labour. These were not dead-end jobs leading to a lifetime of casual labour as in London, but were a period of waiting for apprenticeships and learnerships to begin, usually around the age of sixteen.[27] Thus men like Willie Gallacher and Tom Bell experienced the bullying from employers and the powerlessness which was often the lifetime's lot of the unskilled. From this came some of the greater sense of class identity, expressed perhaps in the willingness of many of the ILP to help unionise the unskilled.

The class memory of the skilled contained elements which shaped their politics. The experience of the Highland clearances was a bitter memory and tradition in many families. This anti-landlordism gave them a link with middle-class liberals and with families of Irish origin. It inspired an aggressive suspicion of all owners and together with Glasgow's squalid housing conditions created the perfect environment for the ILP emphasis on housing and the rent strikes of 1915. Communities like Parkhead still held traditions of the displaced hand-loom weavers. For both Kirkwood and Bell this radical tradition of a once high-status occupation which had lost control in the face of deskilling technology and employer exploitation was a significant factor in their personal politics.[28]

The pride and confidence of their culture was based upon two things. The defence of skill and the control of the labour process in physically harsh, noisy and often intimidating environments, and the maintenance of levels of consumption which kept women, especially their own wives, out of the labour market. Although he was never a member of the ILP, Tom Bell's autobiography bears eloquent witness to the cultural importance of these collective experiences and aspirations:

> The conditions under which the moulder worked were vile, filthy and insanitary. . . . Smoke would make the eyes water. The nose and throat would clog with dust. Drinking water came from the same tap as was used

by the hosepipe to water the sand. . . . Every night pandemonium reigned while the moulds were being cast. The yelling and cursing of the foremen; the rattle of overhead cranes; the smoke and dust illuminated by sparks and flames from the molten metal made the place a perfect inferno.[29]

Equally, Bell's account of his parents' wedding illustrated the pride in consumption levels that often involved considerable display.

In those days, the stonemasons, like the miners were the aristocrats of labour. On the occasion of the marriage of my father and mother they were driven to church in a four in hand with a postillion rider in front. As a symbol of affluence my father wore a suit of white moleskins, while my mother wore a brand new Paisley shawl. The wedding supper was held in the public hall to which special invitations were issued to a large circle of friends.[30]

By the 1890s, this conjunction of skill and consumption was under increasing pressure. Semi-automatic machinery threatened the engineer's ability to control the labour process. New methods of management, speed ups, 'Taylorism' and the increased subdivision of labour were equally threatening. John Taylor, boilermaker, wrote in *Forward*, 4 July 1908:

With improved machinery our craft is at a discount, and a boy from school now tends a machine which does the work of three men . . . It is mostly machine minders that are wanted, and a line from some well known liberal or tory certifying that you are not an agitator or a Socialist, is the chief recommendation in the shipbuilding and engineering trades.[31]

The engineering craft society saw the main purpose of the turret lathe, the universal drilling machine and the grinding machine as the reduction of 'the number of highly skilled men, that is the fitters'.

This was a period of rapid change, of fear and continual challenge over the frontier of control. Hence the row over the Ministry of Munitions circular L2 and the Parkhead agreement sanctioned by Kirkwood. Both struck at the basic craft principles of the rate for the job and shopfloor control. Kirkwood sets this out in his account of an earlier personal dispute with a small employer in 1901:

I told the foreman that I would not break the standard rate, and he said he would try and give it to me, though they could not pay it to the other fitters. I refused the preference and left.[32]

'Craft conservatism' was certainly present in abundance but its result was a series of legitimate expectations over rates of pay, pace of work and access to work. If the expectations based upon this moral economy of the skilled man were disappointed then the results were neither stabilising nor conservative. Hence the violent reaction of the shipyard craftsmen to attempts to restrict their freedom of movement during the war. Frequent moves between yards were one way in which the skilled men maintained the free market in labour which liberal common sense taught them was a crucial part of maintaining freedom in their relationships with capital. By 1916, the demands of the craftsmen were bundling government into an involvement with industrial relations and organisation from which it could never quite escape.

The rent strike of 1915 was without doubt the most important and far-reaching achievement of the Glasgow working class during this period. It was an achievement in which the networking and support functions of the ILP were vital. It was an achievement rooted in the social, economic and moral structures of Glasgow. Success was made easier by the ownership structure of urban working-class housing. Success threatened the interests of small investors, shopkeepers, single ladies of independent means, and widows; it did not threaten the interests of the major employers and financiers who had the ear of government. A major relationship of the capitalist economy, the urban rent, received permanent injury because the rent strike hit capitalism at its weakest point – the small property owners and savers.

The rent strike also fitted the anti-landlord element of the old liberal ethic to perfection. The power of the liberal values and politics of late nineteenth-century Scotland had often been cited as a barrier to the development of labour politics before 1914. It was an irony of the early labour movement that many of its leaders were Scottish but they had to move outwith Scotland for success. The rent strike provided a bridge between old liberalism and the underconsumption socialism of the ILP based upon housing and poverty. The rent strike was based upon the moral economy of the late nineteenth century. The moral icon of the 'soldier's wife' featured prominently in the wartime rents campaign. As many writers have pointed out, the majority of the Glasgow working class were patriotic. They joined the forces and made munitions with great eagerness. It was a legitimate expectation that those who fought for their country should have their families protected from eviction by the ruling class. Mrs Crawfurd insisted 'they were

11

asking not for charity, they asked for justice. She respected all law that was just and fair, but she did not ask them to respect the law which allowed increases in rents at the present juncture'.[33]

During the war the rules upon which 'craft conservatism' (or rather liberalism in political terms) was based were being systematically broken. Employers were using war to make excessive profits and break established working practices, restrictions were being introduced on the free market for labour and soldiers' wives were being evicted. Because the revolutionary claims of the rent strike were based upon traditional values, the strike had a unity and consistency of support which proved too formidable for the authorities. In British politics, there are few things more radical than craft conservativism scorned. The result was intermittent industrial action, the rent strikes and a surge in support for the ILP. Socialists often use the term 'alienation' in philosophical debate. The Clyde in wartime saw alienation in action; the failure of social rules to produce expected and just results. From such situations revolutions arise. The destruction of the free market in urban housing and the extension of the community-based politics of the ILP was revolution enough.

Both the rent strike and the dilution crises highlighted the relationship of the men and women of the skilled working class on the Clyde. An account of this relationship is essential for understanding the apparent paradox of the dominant part played by women in the rent strikes and their virtual disappearance from the leading roles in subsequent events. Women were the organizers and initiators amongst the rent strikers because the increase in rents struck at their ability to maintain their household with all the respectability demanded by the skilled working class. Women were leaders because their traditional role allotted them responsibility for managing household spending. In the workplace, women were perceived quite differently. They were a threat to skilled male job security. In August 1915, the ASE executive determined 'that no women shall be put to work on a lathe'.[34]

The reasoning behind this was complex. Men had learnt from long experience that the introduction of women to an occupation was associated with a tendency to lower wages. Although recent research has shown the relationship to be less direct, Scottish trades unionists believed that the introduction of women to the Edinburgh printing trades had resulted in successful strike breaking and wage reductions in 1871-2.[35] The male leaders of the Educational Institute of Scotland believed that their claims for better pay and conditions was hindered by the large numbers of women in teaching.[36] From such a perspective, keeping women out of an occupation was an essential part of defence against increased exploitation by the owners of capital. It was part of defending the family wage, in other words a wage on which a whole family could be maintained. Such a wage enabled women to stay at home and sustain the respectable lifestyle central to the skilled working-class ethic. Women who stayed at home were withdrawn from the labour market, not only reducing the competition for male jobs, but also reducing the harsh and exhausting demands which the combination of paid and domestic work made upon many working-class women.

In the 1950s, Richard Hoggart devoted an important section of his account of the working-class picture of the world to 'me mam'.[37] The biographies of the Clydeside leaders show that many of them learnt some of their first lessons in class relationships from watching mothers battle to keep the family the right side of the poverty line. William Gallacher's early memories included his mother's grey faced exhaustion, and his own pleasure when his sister's and his own earnings enabled her to stop work in the cash economy.[38] John McLean was also influenced by watching his mother's struggles to bring up a family.[39] Kirkwood's memories, which he admitted were rather 'kailyard', were those of the 'ideal' achieved. 'She counted and took care of the scanty wages. She planned out the week's needs. We never wanted. To her, my father's will was her will . . . for her life was perpetual sacrifice'.[40] The gender politics and class politics of the skilled man were bound together by a deeply ingrained logic, which ran thus: keep women out of the labour force, and then earn a family wage to maintain the domestic ideal. The failure to do this was the exhausted nightmare of the working wife. In Glasgow, only 5 per cent of women were recorded as being part of the wage labour force in 1911. In the skilled areas of Partick and Govan, the figure was just over 2 per cent.[41] This conjunction of gender and class was reflected in women's dominance in the rent strikes and their minor part in the bulk of ILP history. It also meant that the apparent lack of organisational coherence between the industrial and housing struggles was irrelevant to an assessment of working-class consciousness in Glasgow between 1914 and 1922. The co-ordination and unity of those struggles was provided by the politics and morality of the working-class family in Glasgow's skilled and insecure economy.

The final break between the Labour Party and the ILP came over standing orders, but behind this lay a long-standing argument over the nature of socialism. For the bulk of the participants socialism meant an attack on poverty motivated by the perceived failures of capitalism. Those failures required a variety of interventions. In the 1920s, the ILP developed a series of policy directions which began with an analysis in which underconsumption was the basis of both poverty and unemployment, hence the importance of minimum wage strategies and housing to both Wheatly and Maxton. The leading members came to believe that 'socialism' could be achieved more rapidly than most Labour Party leaders thought possible and that in the process many more of the rules of liberal capitalism could be broken notably free trade and balanced budgets.

For Alan McKinlay and Jim Smyth these differences were not just a matter of MacDonald and Snowden being incorporated or of Maxton being more radical, they arose from the experience and political traditions of Glasgow since the beginning of the century. Although sectional craft unions had considerable influence in Glasgow, the industrial unions were weak. The Trades Council was the political wing of the trades union movement, hence the political labour movement was not influenced by any of the major exporting industrial unions with a belief in free trade as the basis of their members' prosperity.

Secondly, Wheatley grew up with the experience of an interventionist municipality. The interventions were in the main those which provided infrastructure and services for a thriving liberal capitalist economy, but they worked and it took only a little imagination to see that such interventions could direct consumption towards working-class housing, health and nutrition.

Thirdly, the experience of the Glasgow Labour movement was of thriving community politics. The ILP was a party at the centre of a network, harnessing the energies of everything from Socialist Sunday Schools and Clarion Clubs to the Co-op and Trades Council. Such experience brought a confidence in decentralised socialism which many trades union leaders and London intellectuals did not share. The difference between Attlee and Maxton was not a matter of left and further left but of democratic centralism versus diffused community-based authority. Attlee, the economic historian, gave an account of trades union history which can serve as his metaphor for the history of a well directed political movement 'detachments . . . were welded into regiments and the regiments into armies'.[42] What was lost when Maxton and the ILP tradition faded into the late 1930s was a community-based tradition of 'socialist' politics which gave priority to consumption and decentralised authority and expected decisions over production and centralised bureaucratic power to be dependent.

Third-phase ILP politics is often portrayed as voices crying in the wilderness, with most of those voices belonging to Maxton. If we follow the biblical imagery familiar to the socialists of that generation, then this is a mixed condemnation for in the New Testament, the voice crying in the wilderness was an essential herald of the main event, and many in the 1930s learnt from Maxton that socialism and the attacks on poverty were tightly bound together, even if they ignored his tactics and joined the party that brought Attlee to power in 1945.[43] That government of 1945 made little use of the community-based politics of Glasgow and the ILP. The dominant group in the Labour Party moved towards planning and management, towards central state direction, towards the NHS and the NCB. They lost the Co-op, workplace organisation and the infrastructure of ethical and cultural socialism. They traded the politics of consumption for politics of management. The Co-operative Women's Guild, the Shop Stewards Committees, the Socialist Sunday School and the Worker's Colleges had little part in its plans for education, welfare and the reorganisation of production. The labour movement became encapsulated in the secular trinity of constituency party, Parliamentary Labour Party and trade unions.

That loss made some contribution to the nightmare of 'socialism' in the 1970s and 1980s when Wheatley's cottages had become the high-rise tenements of Red Road in Glasgow, the tenants' groups were directed against the Labour administrations of the great towns, and the *Daily Herald*, once a great popular Labour newspaper was transformed in the *Sun*. There is more to be learnt from the ILP men of Glasgow than a lesson in self-destruction in a two-party parliamentary democracy, or a glimpse of a third way between labourism and Third International communism. Between 1900 and 1930 Glasgow developed a decentralised creative and ill disciplined socialism which saw production and bureaucracy as a servant of consumption and of the attack on poverty of all kinds. Maxton's two horses might be re-named democracy and socialism. They are still very much in the

15

circus.

The essays which follow chart the history of the ILP in the west of Scotland in stages clearly defined by the context within which the party operated. The 1906 election, the war of 1914–18 and, above all, the 1918 Labour Party constitution, all brought about significant changes in the conditions, opportunities and problems facing the ILP. The strategy and identity of the ILP varied with period, personalities and possibilities. The ideology which drove these strategies always involved a broadly based 'socialism'. Socialism was a strategy first and foremost for attacking poverty. The details of policy which were argued over in each period can all be referred to this aim; from the public ownership of housing, mines, or banks, to exchange control, minimum wages and family allowances. The policies and arguments of each period gained with previous experience.

The essays derive their coherence from several features. Above all continuity was provided by the organisation of the ILP itself. The 1918 constitution brought about the collapse and replacement of the ILP in England but not in the west of Scotland. The economic changes of the 1920s replaced the skilled man's economy of Clydeside with an economy of traditional skills and sustained mass unemployment. In regional politics, however, organisational continuities and personalities linked the two periods together. Despite the different context of each period, a political organisation with national and international perspectives was sustained by local political networks and support. The result was a party which became firmly anchored in the politics of collective consumption. Here lies some of the fascination of the story for the current decade, in which 'socialism' has been forced into retreat at national and international levels, and organisational and cultural power has become increasingly centralised but in which poverty though less extensive than in 1900, appears increasingly intensive, divisive and visible, and the politics of consumption have surfaced in a variety of ways which ignore the categories of left and right and create new forms of collective consciousness.

Notes

1 Francis Williams, *Fifty Years March. The Rise of the Labour Party* (Oldham, London, 1951); G.D.H. Cole and R. Postgate, *The Common People, 1746–1946* (Methuen, London, 1946).

2 A.J.P. Taylor, *English History, 1914–1945* (Clarendon Press, Oxford, 1965), pp. 198 and 237.

3 Henry Pelling, *A Short History of the Labour Party* (Macmillan, London, 1961), p. 74.

4 Keith Middlemas, *The Clydesiders: A Left-Wing Struggle for Parliamentary Power* (Hutchinson, London, 1965).

5 Robert McKenzie, *British Political Parties* (Heinemann, London, 1963), p. 445.

6 Ralph Miliband, *Parliamentary Socialism. A Study in the Politics of Labour* (Merlin, London, 1961).

7 C.R. Atlee, *Notes for Lecturers and Class Leaders, ILP Study Notes No. 4, Economic History* (ILP, London, n.d.).

8 C.R. Attlee, *The Labour Party in Perspective* (Victor Gollancz, London, 1937), p. 128. Gordon Brown, *Maxton* (Mainstream, Edinburgh, 1986), p. 254.

9 Ian Donnachie, Christopher Harvie and Ian S. Wood (eds), *Forward! Labour Politics in Scotland 1888–1988* (Polygon, Edinburgh, 1989), p. 24.

10 Christopher Harvie, 'Labour and Scottish Goverment: the Age of Tom Johnson', *Bulletin of Scottish Politics*, 2, spring 1981.

11 Iain McLean, *The Legend of Red Clydeside* (John Donald, Edinburgh, 1983).

12 Joseph Melling, *Rent Strikes. Peoples' Struggle for Housing in West Scotland, 1890–1916* (Polygon, Edinburgh, 1983), p. 36.

13 Patrick Joyce, *Work, Society and Politics. The Culture of the Factory in Later Victorian England* (Harvester, Brighton, 1980), p. 226.

14 W. Fraser, 'Trades Councils in the Labour Movement in Nineteenth Century Scotland', in Ian MacDougall (ed.), *Essays in Scottish Labour History* (John Donald, Edinburgh, 1978), pp. 1–28.

15 J.H. Treble, 'The Market for Unskilled Male Labour in Glasgow, 1891–1914', in MacDougall (ed.), *ibid.*, pp. 115–42.

16 R.J. Morris, 'Urbanisation and Scotland', in W. Hamish Fraser and R.J. Morris (eds), *People and Society in Scotland, 1830–1914* (John Donald, Edinburgh, 1990).

17 John Foster and Charles Woolfson, *The Politics of the UCS Work-In* (Lawrence and Wishart, London, 1986), pp. 132–36.

18 Robert Q. Gray, *The Aristocracy of Labour in Nineteenth Century Britain, c. 1850–1910* (MacMillan, London, 1981) provides the best recent survey.

19 Robert Q. Gray, *The Labour Aristocracy in Victorian Edinburgh* (Oxford University Press, Oxford, 1976); Geoffrey Crossick, *An Artisan Elite in Victorian Society: Kentish London 1840–1880* (Croom Helm, London, 1978); Hugh Cunningham, *The Volunteer Force: A Social and Political History, 1859–1908* (C.R. Hay, London, 1975); Takao Matsumura, *The*

Labour Aristocracy Revisited: The Victorian Flint Glass Makers, 1850–80 (Manchester University Press, Manchester, 1983).

20 Iain McLean, *op. cit.*

21 Thomas Bell, *Pioneering Days* (Lawrence and Wishart, London, 1941), p. 63.

22 Richard Price, *Masters, Unions and Men: Work Control in Building and the Rise of Labour, 1830–1914* (Cambridge University Press, Cambridge, 1980).

23 Sylvia Price, 'Riveters' Earnings in Clyde Shipbuilding, 1889–1913', *Scottish Economic and Social History Journal*, 1981, pp. 42–65.

24 K.G.J.C. Knowles and D.J. Robertson, 'Differences Between the Wages of Skilled and Unskilled Workers, 1880–1950', *Bulletin of the Oxford University Institute of Statistics*, April 1951, pp. 107–27, show that unskilled wages moved from around about 60 per cent of skilled between 1880 and 1914 to around about 70 per cent after 1916.

26 Joseph Melling, 'Clydeside Housing and the Evolution of State Rent Control, 1900–1939', in Joseph Melling (ed.), *Housing, Social Policy and the State* (Croom Helm, London, 1980); David Englander, 'Landlord and Tenant in Urban Scotland: The Background to the Clyde Rent Strikes, 1915', *Scottish Labour History Society Journal*, 15, 1981.

26 Report of an Enquiry by the Board of Trade into Working Class Rents, Housing and Retail Prices . . . in the Principal Industrial Towns of the United Kingdom, Parliamentary Papers, 1908, vol. 108; Richard Rodger, 'The Building Industry and the Housing of the Scottish Working Class', in Martin Doughty (ed.), *Building the Industrial City* (Leicester University Press, Leicester, 1986), p. 171.

27 J.H. Treble, *op. cit.*; Gareth Stedman Jones, *Outcast London: A Study in the Relationship between Classes* (Oxford University Press, Oxford, 1971), pp. 52–98.

28 Harry McShane and Joan Smith, *Harry McShane. No Mean Fighter* (Pluto, London, 1978), pp. 17–18; William Gallacher, *Revolt on the Clyde* (Lawrence and Wishart, London, 1936), p. 1; David Kirkwood, *My Life of Revolt* (Harrap, London, 1935), p. 6; Bell, *op. cit.*, pp. 10–14.

29 Bell, *op. cit.*, pp. 64–5; see Paul Willis, 'Shop Floor Culture, Masculinity and the Wage Form', in John Clarke, Charles Critcher and Richard Johnson (eds), *Working Class Culture: Studies in History and Theory* (Hutchinson, London, 1979).

30 Bell, *ibid.*, p. 14.

31 This is quoted by Joan Smith, 'Commonsense Thought and Working Class Consciousness; Some Aspects of the Glasgow and Liverpool Labour movements in the Early Years of the Twentieth Century' (unpublished PhD thesis, Edinburgh University, 1980). I have received a great deal of

guidance from this work even where my interpretations of the evidence may differ.

32 Kirkwood, *op. cit.*, pp. 73–8.

33 *Glasgow Herald*, 15 November 1915.

34 Quoted by I.S. MacLean, 'The Labour Movement in Clydeside Politics, 1914–1922' (Oxford DPhil thesis, 1971), p. 31.

35 Barbara L. Brady and Anne Black, 'Women Compositors and the Factory Acts', *Economic Journal*, 9, 1899, pp. 261–6; Sian Reynolds, *Britannica's Typesetters: Women Compositors in Edwardian Edinburgh* (Edinbrugh University Press, Edinburgh, 1989).

36 Helen Corr, 'The Gender Division of Labour in the Scottish Teaching Profession, 1872–1914, with particular reference to elementary school teaching' (unpublished PhD thesis, Edinburgh University, 1984).

37 Richard Hoggart, *The Uses of Literacy: Aspects of Working Class Life* (Chatto & Windus, London, 1957), pp. 4–53.

38 Gallacher, *op. cit*, p. 25.

39 Nan Milton, *John MacLean* (Pluto, London, 1973), p. 16.

40 Kirkwood, *op. cit.*, p. 25.

41 Census for Scotland, 1911, Parliamentary Papers, 1912–1913, vol. III, p. 76.

42 C.R. Attlee, *op. cit.*, p. 63.

43 William Knox, *James Maxton* (Manchester University Press, Manchester, 1987).

TWO

The ILP in Glasgow, 1888–1906: the struggle for identity

James J. Smyth

The history of the Independent Labour Party (ILP) in Scotland does not begin with the Bradford Conference of 1893 but with the earlier formation – in 1888 – of the Scottish Labour Party (SLP). Originally titled the Scottish (Parliamentary) Labour Party, the SLP was, in the words of Keir Hardie, 'The Pioneer of the ILP'.[1] Whether or not Hardie's description is strictly accurate, it is unquestionably the case that it is with the formation of the SLP that a Labour political presence was established in Scotland and particularly Glasgow which has continued unbroken to the present day. The SLP can be regarded, or even dismissed, as a relatively insignificant body; it had a small membership, enjoyed no electoral success and eventually subsumed itself within the larger (national) ILP.[2] Yet, it is with the birth of the SLP that Labour politics, as we understand them even today, first emerged.

In seeking to explain why Scotland made this original breakthrough the question of organisation is paramount.[3] This did not mean, however, that Scotland became a bastion of strength for this new movement. Prior to 1914 there were only three Labour MPs elected in Scotland and, overall, Labour's electoral performance was 'relatively weaker' than in England.[4] Yet, there were a number of indicators of a potentially more propitious development: there was the formation of the Scottish Workers Representation Committee (SWRC) prior to the formation of the Labour Electoral Committee (LEC); the creation of the Scottish Trade Union Congress (STUC) in 1897; and the formation of the SLP itself. The existence of such bodies has led David Howell to comment upon the apparent conundrum of how, 'Scottish Labour could claim to be organisationally in advance of its English counterpart . . . [yet] individual prominence and organisational precocity neither indicated nor produced mass support'.[5]

I

In fact, this precocity can be explained in terms of the weakness of the Labour movement in Scotland – due to the lack of a strong trade union base political questions assumed a greater importance than they did in England. Certainly, Scottish trade unions were not as strong as their southern counterparts. The smashing of the Glasgow Cotton Spinners' Association in 1837–8 was a body-blow to Scottish trade unionism which was further debilitated by the depression of the early 1840s.[6] When unions began to re-build in the 1850s they had to do so mainly from scratch and tended to be 'small and localised'.[7] Even where all-Scottish national unions were formed they were, 'federal in structure, with power and financial control remaining firmly in the hands of local societies' – a pattern that was repeated in the 1880s.[8]

Overall, the level of trade unionism in Scotland was lower than in England; the Webbs calculated the proportionate number of trade unionists in the United Kingdom in 1892 as 3.98 per cent of the total population but which for England and Wales was 4.55 per cent and for Scotland 3.64 per cent only.[9] While Scotland shared in the general growth of trade unionism over the following two decades, its level of union membership remained lower than England and Wales.[10]

Another particular aspect of Scottish trade unionism is that it was largely concentrated in the Glasgow area. For 1892 the Webbs deduced that there were 147,000 trade unionists in Scotland – 'two-thirds of the total, indeed, belonging to Glasgow and the neighbouring industrial centres'.[11] As the Webbs were aware, it was not total numbers which gave the trade union movement its significance but, rather, the concentration of members in particular industries and localities.[12] Nevertheless, the 'greater-Glasgow' mass of trade unionists did not overcome Scottish localism but, if anything, exacerbated it.[13] The weakness and localism of Scottish trade unions meant that trades councils played a much more significant role north of the border than they did in England, and they did embrace political matters as well as union affairs.[14] However, while providing a much-needed focus for unity among trades, trades councils could still not play the dominant role of a strong trade union.

The discrepancy between Scotland and England in this respect is most clearly shown in the case of the mining unions. The suffrage and re-distribution reforms of 1884–5 led to a sudden increase in the number of trade union MPs from two to eleven in the General Election of 1885. No union was able to exploit the new situation better than the miners – of the eleven Lib–Labs six were miners representing 'mining' constituencies.[15] The miners did not have to run their candidates in three-cornered contests but used their weight to secure quid pro quo arrangements with the Liberals.[16] There were no such agreements in Scotland where the miners simply did not have sufficient density of numbers in constituencies or the organisational strength to force any recognition from the Liberals.

The build-up of the Scottish mining unions under the leadership of Alexander MacDonald reached a high point in 1874 but thereafter went into a rapid decline and, by 1880, only the Fife and Kinross Miners' Association remained. In 1886 there was a new phase of union growth with 'county' unions established in Ayrshire and for the Forth and Clyde Valley led by Keir Hardie and Chisholm Robertson respectively and, by the end of the year the Scottish Miners' National Federation (SMNF) was formally constituted.[17] The SMNF was by no means a 'national' union however – it had no central authority and real power remained with the localities.[18] Even local organisation remained weak and in its first year the SMNF shrunk from an original twenty-six districts and 23,570 members to fifteen districts and 13,000 members.[19] Within a couple of years the SMNF was defunct. By the late 1880s and early 1890s the mining unions in Scotland were in better shape than they had been in 1880 but, even so, 'only the Fife organisa-tion . . could be called a really established union'.[20]

It is from this perspective – of the general weakness of Scottish trade unionism and the particular vulnerability of the miners – that Hardie's 'independent' challenge to the Liberals at Mid-Lanark and the subsequent formation of the SLP is best understood. It was the inability of Scottish trade unionists to make local Liberal Associations accept trade union or working-class candidates that forced miners' leaders such as Keir Hardie into a reappraisal of the organisational link with Liberalism.[21] The Mid-Lanark by-election campaign has been extensively chronicled and its details need not concern us too much here.[22] What is of more concern is to set Hardie's election effort and the subsequent formation of the SLP within the context of the contemporary debate on the need for a 'labour party'.

II

There were three main constituent parts to the SLP – the Socialists, the Trade Unionists and the Radicals – all of whom had their own views of what a labour party should be. The trade union element of the SLP, originally at least, was largely confined to the miners of central and west Scotland. The argument in favour of the independent representation of miners and for a labour party, as articulated in the pages of *The Miner*, was clearly based upon the weakness of the mining unions in Scotland and the necessity, therefore, of looking to the state to play an interventionist role in the industry.

This view had to confront the 'independent' attitude of the Lib–Lab MPs of North-East England. In the very first issue of *The Miner*, the Northumberland miner MP, Thomas Burt, wrote about the demand for the eight-hour day, 'it seems to me to appeal to Parliament to fix the hours of adults [i.e. adult men] is to weaken the motives for union and self-reliance'.[23] Burt was arguing from a position of strength – his union was strong enough to compel the Liberals to recognise its officials as candidates and both the Northumberland and Durham miners already enjoyed a working day of less than eight hours.[24] The Scottish miners (with the partial exception of Fife which was the only area in Scotland to have won the eight-hour day)[25] were unable to accomplish either and Hardie focused his strategy upon the reality of their position. In reply to Burt, Hardie drew a comparison between the plight of 'the Irish and Highland tenant farmers' and that of the Scottish miners:

> The classes named had the opportunity, as the miner has, of putting things right of themselves; but that which looks well in theory is often found to be very difficult in practice. So it is in this case. The miner finds it next to, if not quite impossible to continue an eight-hour day without some outside help, and he therefore looks with confidence to Parliament to respond to his cry by voting for the Bill.[26]

These words were published in the immediate aftermath of a bitter strike in Lanarkshire which had ended in violence and defeat for the miners. Although Hardie had proposed the tactic of a 'holiday' to restrict output rather than strike action, the use of troops against a mining community set him at odds with the local Liberal establishment.[27] From around this time Hardie can be seen to question the validity of working-class support for the Liberal Party. Increasingly his concern lay not only with securing reforms through Parliament but also in some form of direct labour representation. There was no sudden break in Hardie's thinking, however, and his emphasis could switch from the theoretical end of Liberalism and its ultimate replacement, to the practicality of establishing a labour political presence – a task which might still be integrally related to the Liberal Party.[28]

Hardie was constantly looking for a broader perspective than the merely local or the 'simple' trade union approach.[29] At one stage he came close to arguing that the unions would have to be transformed into political bodies: 'We want a new party – a Labour party pure and simple and the Trade Unions have the power to create this.'[30] However, speaking at the SMNF annual meeting in August 1987 he presented a more modest proposal when he said that: 'The Labour Party will be a distinct organisation from the Trade Unions.'[31] Hardie was consistent in regarding the unions as an essential component but the structure of this intended labour party remained unclear. His decision to contest Mid-Lanark in opposition to the Liberal effectively forced the issue and his campaign made concrete the need for a definite organisation. Hardie was aware of the lack of organisation during the campaign[32] and a month later, on 19 May, the first meeting of the SLP was held in Glasgow.[33] In fact, even before this meeting Hardie claimed that his supporters in Mid-Lanark were busy establishing branches of the SLP.[34]

The formal inauguration of the new party took place at a conference on 25 August, again held in Glasgow,[35] and, increasingly, the centre of gravity of the SLP shifted from the Lanarkshire coalfield into Glasgow. The motivation for Hardie's candidature at Mid-Lanark may have come from the miners and the locality but the significance of his challenge to the Liberals went beyond both. Furthermore, if there was to be a distinct organisation rather than just a series of individual deals with the Liberals[36] it was clear that the mining unions could not sustain this on their own. Hardie's campaign had received widespread comment and support and this was reflected in the inaugural conference.

Hardie's backers could be typefied largely as radicals or left-wing Liberals. They included the Crofters' MP, Dr Clark and the Irish Nationalist leader in Glasgow, John Ferguson, who were elected Honorary Vice-Presidents of the new party.[37] This was no accident. The radical wing of the Liberal Party tended to see the cause of labour representation as their own and Hardie's position appeared that of a radical. In the month before the election Hardie explained his strategy thus: 'Better to split the party now, if there is to be a split, than at a general election, and if the labour party only make their power felt now, then terms will not be wanting when the general election comes.'[38]

This, in fact, was the key to the radical involvement. Among Hardie's supporters was the London-based, land-restorationist journal, The Democrat, edited by the ex-MP William Saunders.[39] The Democrat regarded Hardie as: ' "the Radical candidate", who was being snubbed by an unrepresentative "clique", i.e. the Mid-Lanark Liberal Association'.[40] This identification of labour representation with the radicals' own interest also meant, ultimately, labour's identification with the Liberal Party. Saunders argued: 'If the labour classes are to form a reliable wing of the Liberal Party their just and equitable claims must no longer be either tampered with or evaded.'[41] However, taking an 'independent' line at a by-election was one thing, the pressure for 'unity' against the Tories at a general election was a completely different matter. In 1892 the editor of The Democrat had moved firmly back into the Liberal camp. The SLP was running candidates against Liberals and was forced to expel John Ferguson and Dr Clark for speaking in support of Liberal candidates in seats the SLP was contesting.[42] The basic problem confronting the radicals was what to do when the Liberal Party refused to countenance Labour representation. For some, like James Shaw Maxwell the solution was to move completely towards an 'independent' line and socialism.[43] For most, however, the only course of action was to remain within the Liberal Party where, in Hardie's words he (i.e. the radical) 'has to grin and bear the situation as best he may'.[44] There was also a fundamental difference between the ambitions of the radicals who saw Labour as being a 'reliable wing of the Liberal Party' and the socialist-inclined views of men like Hardie who could, at least theoretically, consider a future beyond the Liberal Party. During the Mid-Lanark campaign Hardie wrote:

> But don't let us be mistaken: sending a 'working man' representative to Parliament is only a beginning, but it is a beginning. . . . We must get rid of this talk of working men having a right to a 'share' in the representation. Why working men and women (using that term to embrace all workers) must have *all* the representation.[45]

25

Sentiments like this had an obvious appeal for socialists as did the SLP's founding programme which, as well as 'constitutional' demands such as adult suffrage, abolition of plural voting, triennial parliaments, payment of election expenses and salaries for MPs, also included social demands for an eight-hour day, nationalisation of the land and minerals, state acquisition of railways, waterways and tramways, and a cumulative income tax.[46] The formation of the SLP occurred at a time when socialists in Scotland were re-considering their existing strategies and the issue of electoral activity.

The socialist movement was in the process of establishing itself in Scotland when it split at the end of 1884, leaving the Social Democratic Federation (SDF) under the leadership of H.M. Hyndman and the breakaway Socialist League (SL) led by William Morris.[47] In Scotland the SL emerged the stronger with Edinburgh (which styled itself the Scottish Land and Labour League (SL&LL)) going over to the SL more or less unanimously and in Glasgow the branch divided in two.[48] Although Edinburgh had been the most active city initially, Glasgow eventually made progress in its propoganda activity and the SL appears to have held an edge over the SDF. As well as establishing itself within Glasgow, the SL sought to take the socialist message into the surrounding districts.

One of the areas where they were relatively successful was Hamilton where William Small established a branch of the SL&LL in late 1884.[49] Thanks to Small, who was a miner's agent and became Secretary of the Lanarkshire Miners' County Federation when it was formed in 1893[50] a high level of activity was maintained amongst the miners with regular speakers from Glasgow. On one such occasion Bruce Glasier, the major activist of the Glasgow SL, addressed a meeting of between two and three thousand miners.[51] During the bitter strike of February 1887 these links were intensified. The SL opened their branch rooms as a temporary strike headquarters and organised a mass demonstration which drew twenty thousand to Glasgow Green.[52]

Activity like this, however, posed uncomfortable problems for the socialists since it begged the question of what to do next. The whole strategy of the SL in particular could be summed up as education for revolution. Its position was stated unequivocally in the founding document: 'our view is that such a body [i.e. a socialist party] has no function but to educate the people in the principles of Socialism'.[53] Although this emphasis was partly due to the desire to clearly disassociate the SL from the perceived opportunism of Hyndman, it did, nonetheless, reflect a genuine belief that partial reforms (the 'dreaded palliatives') could not help the working class but only serve to further reinforce its subordination.[54] However, increasingly, the Glasgow socialists found themselves in the position of getting involved in campaigns which led to the formulation of precisely such demands. As well as their solidarity with the miners, the socialists also took a leading role in the unemployed agitation during the 1880s.

In May 1886 the Glasgow SL organised a mass meeting of the unemployed on the Green to protest at the stopping of outdoor relief and which demanded that the City Council provide work. This demand was not met but, as a direct result of the agitation, the Council decided to keep the soup kitchens open for another week.[55] This partial success cut across the strategy of the SL which had an official policy of 'non-intervention' in the unemployed agitation.[56] The following year, 1887, the Glasgow membership divided over this precise issue. On the one hand there were those who supported the policy of the national executive while, on the other, were those who believed that it was possible to secure a significant amount of relief for the unemployed through the common good fund of the City Council and, more than this, to demand that the Council provide work directly.[57] This section also argued that it would be to the advantage of the SL if it provided leadership – as it had done in the Lanarkshire miners' strike.[58]

At the same time the SL nationally was split over the question of electoral activity. Those who supported parliamentary action were defeated and eventually expelled in 1888.[59] However, there was a crucial debate on the issue at the 1887 Conference which was conducted over a resolution submitted by Hamilton, William Small's branch. This included the demand for the, 'overthrow of the capitalist system' but also called for socialists to be involved in trade unions and co-operative societies, to campaign in local and national elections and, crucially, 'organising the people into a Socialistic labour party'.[60]

Although both the SL and the SDF were national organisations, local branches had a tendency to follow their own lines of development. The differences between the national leaderships were not that clearly drawn in Scotland and, by the end of 1888, there appeared to be a rough consensus among Scottish socialists on the need for a more efficient organisation. This was fuelled partly by a dissatisfaction with

London and resulted in the formation of the Scottish Socialist Federation (SSF).[61] A Conference was organised by the Edinburgh SDF at which most of the socialist forces in Scotland were present and which resolved to form, 'a Delegate Committee to thoroughly organise the propaganda in Scotland'.[62] This Committee was to be based in Edinburgh for the first year and John Leslie was appointed as Secretary.[63] According to Lowe the SSF represented a conscious break from London[64] but, whatever the ambitions behind it, the SSF did not emerge as a separate party. It remained an Edinburgh organisation with the SL and SDF branches linking up and, with the rapid decline of the SL nationally after 1888, it operated, ultimately as the Edinburgh branch of the SDF.

Given this state of flux and debate over tactics, strategy and organisation, it is hardly surprising that socialists began to gravitate towards the SLP. In 1893 Andreas Scheu approached Bruce Glasier about the possibility of a delegate from Glasgow attending the International Congress at Zurich. Glasier informed Scheu that, with the disintegration of the SL there were only the SDF and the Fabians left as socialist organisations and, keen as they would be to send a delegate, it was unlikely they could afford to do so. However, Glasier did suggest that Scheu approach the Labour Party which he was sure would be sympathetic, since many of its members had previously been in the SL.[65] In fact it was Glasgow Trades Council which decided to send a delegate to Zurich and their choice was John Warrington, President of the Council, active in the SLP and who had been an early member of the SL.[66] Around this time the *Labour Leader* commented on the disintegration of the SL that: 'One section of its members drifted more and more towards political action, and identified themselves with the Labour Party programme'.[67]

At the same time the SDF also made an input to the SLP, though its members did not have to leave their own organisation but could maintain membership of both. The SDF contribution was recognised by George Carson who wrote that, 'many of its best members are also active and zealous members of the Labour Party'.[68] In Edinburgh it was the SSF which originally established the SLP in 1892.[69] This action represents a considerable change of opinion amongst the Edinburgh socialists who had not considered the SLP 'worthy of their support' four years earlier.[70] In accepting the need to contest elections and agitate over specific issues the SSF was following the national lead of the SDF which had consistently argued this line. As Hyndman put the 'electoral' case to William Morris: 'we cannot separate ourselves from our epoch in this respect, any more than we can in the matter of dealing with capital and capitalists. . . . You cannot keep an organisation healthy and vigorous without having some immediate work and some immediate aim'.[71] In Scotland the existence of the SLP allowed the SDF to pursue this line in a particular way and its involvement was encouraged by the peculiar structure of the SLP.

III

The SLP had a branch structure like any other party but, at the same time, its 'annual conference' was a much broader affair at which were represented a variety of different organisations: trade union branches, trades councils, co-operative societies, land nationalisation societies, Fabians, SDF, and the branches of the SLP itself. The intention was to make the SLP the instrument for achieving labour representation but to associate with that policy a much wider and more representative body of opinion. After the annual conference was over the annual business meeting of the SLP proper was held. Even here, however, there was little attempt at centralised control. As Hardie made clear, the emphasis was on local autonomy: 'Each branch was a separate practical organisation.'[72]

This approach did not meet everyone's approval since the stress on autonomy could disguise inefficiency at the centre, if not manipulation. James Connolly, who was the secretary of the Edinburgh Central Branch of the SLP, wrote an official letter of complaint to Hardie in 1893 about the 'extremely short notice' give his branch members of the business meeting of the party. His letter also drew a sharp contrast in the significance between this meeting, 'at which the whole policy and programme of the Party is to be declared', and the annual conference, 'a mere Conference of all sections of the working class movement, binding on no-one'.[73] In January 1894 the executive of the SLP stated in its report that, 'the aim of the party is socialism'.[74] However, this begged the question of what was meant by 'socialism'. At the annual conference John Warrington, attending as a delegate from Glasgow Trades Council, moved a resolution, the salient point of which was:

we hereby recommend the workers of Scotland to support energetically the Scottish Labour party, and every similar organisation which has for its object the return to Parliament and to every representative body representatives who will act irrespective of the convenience of any political party in securing justice to labour and the establishment of a just social order.[75]

This was seconded by a delegate from Govan Trades Council who emphasised that, 'the real fundamental principle of the resolution' was labour representation in Parliament.[76] From the SDF, however, an amendment was moved that would delete everything after 'securing' and replace it with:

The socialisation of the means of production, distribution, and exchange, to be owned and controlled by a Democratic State in the interests of the entire community, and the complete emancipation of labour from the domination of landlordism and capitalism.[77]

The mover of the amendment argued that while nationalisation of the land would secure the workers a 'fairer' share of the wealth produced, only full socialisation could provide them with 'the full reward of their labour'. Hardie, acting as chairman, said on behalf of the executive that they were 'aware that there were different parties among the Socialists' and that the resolution had been framed so as to, 'express the idea of socialism without committing the idea of socialism to any one school'.[78] The SDF amendment was lost by 57 votes for to 104 against. Hardie's statement, however, still suggested that the SLP was committed to socialism and this led to an objection from David McLardy, delegate from the Scottish Land Restoration Union, who stated that 'he was not in favour of what was known as Socialism', (which provoked a cry of 'Oh, Dear') and that, 'Unless it was understood that he was not committed to that movement, he must move an amendment.'[79] The radical influence on the SLP, however, was on the wane; no further amendment was moved and the original resolution was then carried unanimously.

This debate was repeated almost verbatim throughout the pre-1914 period. In January 1900 at the conference called by the Scottish Trade Union Congress (STUC) which established the Scottish Workers' Representation Committee (SWRC), the SDF again moved an amendment to include the demand for, 'the socialisation of the means of production, distribution and exchange'.[80] Once again the proposal was defeated. However, after the vote, Robert Smillie who was chairman of the conference and a prominent member of the ILP, argued that the majority were actually in favour of the SDF amendment, only 'there was no special reason for adding it to the resolution'.[81]

The significance of this debate as it occurred within the SLP was that it indicated the development of a particular strategy for socialists. In short, the position of 'independent labour'. When in early 1893 a member of the SLP could claim of Glasgow Trades Council that 'The Council was theirs and they would keep it', he was referring to a vote, 'on the principle of Socialism',[82] and the men behind this success would largely have been members of the SLP – men like Warrington and George Carson. Their position lacked the clarity of the SDF's formulation but their vagueness was deliberate. It was aimed at attracting the widest possible support for the over-riding goal of securing Labour representation while providing a basic 'independent' identity.

At the foundation conference of the ILP George Carson moved, on behalf of the SLP, that the new party's name be the Socialist Labour Pary arguing that: 'In Scotland the Labour Party had come to the conclusion that it was best to call a spade a spade.'[83] Defeated on this issue, the SLP supported the successful motion on the party's object: 'to secure the collective and communal ownership of all the means of production, distribution and exchange'.[84] Howell has described these two decisions by the ILP as, 'a classic compromise – a Labour title and a socialist objective'.[85] It was a solution which fitted the established practice of the SLP.

The formation of the ILP in 1893 did not mark any break with the policies and objectives of the SLP – the pursuit of independent representation remained the purpose of both organisations. However, the eventual assimilation of the Scottish body into the 'National' ILP did mark a subtle change in the nature of the SLP as an organisation. The separate identity of the SLP was lost, to a great extent, since it became simply a 'division' of a larger body where before it had been a party in its own right. The eventual decision to join up with the ILP was only taken almost two years after Bradford, at the final annual conference of the SLP on 26 December 1894. The motion was moved by Hardie and the 53 delegates from 32 Branches voted unanimously in favour.[86]

The SLP also had to forfeit its 'twin-track' approach of annual business meeting and annual conference. The identification of the broader labour movement and other, sympathetic organisations with the 'Labour Party' was lost as the single annual conference of the National ILP became the focal point of organisation and debate. Linked to this the autonomy of the individual branches of the SLP was lost. The ILP, as originally established, took a very similar line to the SLP on branch autonomy but the centre of the party – the National Administrative Council (NAC) – soon began to exert an increasing authority over both organisation and policy.[87] With the formation of the ILP and its identification of itself (despite the choice of name) as a socialist party, this meant that the SDF would eventually have to regard the 'Labour Party' as a rival. This should not be regarded as an absolute division since in certain areas both parties could work harmoniously together.[88] Nevertheless, the nature of the previous relationship that existed between the SDF and SLP was altered.

IV

In the General Election of 1892 3 Glasgow seats were contested: 2 by the SLP and 1 by the Scottish United Trades Council Labour Party (SUTCLP).[89] The SLP candidates stood in Camlachie and Tradeston where they secured 906 votes and 12 per cent and 783 votes and 11 per cent respectively, while the single SUTCLP candidate, for the College constituency, managed only 225 votes and 2 per cent. Disappointing as these results were, some consolation could still be taken from them. Speaking at the SLP conference the following January Hardie pointed out that, 'At the recent General Election the Labour Party was for the first time in evidence as an organised movement.'[90] The 7 labour candidates in Scotland (4 SLP and 3 SUTCLP) had accounted for 14 per cent of the poll. Hardie went on to claim that, 'the same proportion would hold good all over the country, a fact which proves the strength of the labour vote and its power for good if properly directed'.[91] The basis of Hardie's optimism (apart from his own triumph in West Ham) could only have been realistically based upon forcing concessions from the Liberals, since in both Tradeston and Camlachie the SLP intervention was sufficient to deprive the Liberals of victory.

No deals were made with the Liberals in Scotland, however, which was crucial in restricting Labour representation north of the border prior to 1918. At the General Election of 1895 the ILP stood 8 candidates in Scotland, 5 of whom contested Glasgow constituencies.

The Glasgow average poll was 502 votes and 7.5 per cent. Only Bob Smillie, standing for Camlachie, managed to get more than 10 per cent of the votes, and in Hutchesontown, Shaw Maxwell managed to secure only half the number and proportion of votes he received ten years previously.[92] Even the *Labour Leader* had to admit that the Glasgow polls were 'disgracefully small'[93] and after this debacle Labour's parliamentary ambitions became much more circumspect: only one Labour candidate stood in Glasgow at the General Election of 1900 and only two in the Elections of 1906 and 1910.

In 1900 the Glasgow Labour candidate was the only one to stand in the whole of Scotland – this was A.E. Fletcher who stood in Camlachie under the auspices of the SWRC.[94] It was the ILP which was principally behind Fletcher's candidature and they were able to get a significant coalition of forces to support him: the SWRC, the SDF, the Clarion Scouts, the United Irish League, the Trades Council, and most significantly, the local Liberal Association.[95] The key to this coalition was the Boer War which possibly explains the Liberals' failure to promote a candidate of their own, and Fletcher's anti-war stand made him acceptable to the socialists. The 1900 or 'Khaki' election was unique in Glasgow's political history as the first and only time that the city returned to a wholly Unionist (four Conservatives and the three Liberal Unionists) representation to Parliament. Fletcher's performance was certainly creditable, getting over 3,000 votes and 42 per cent of the poll, but the unique circumstances of this election reduces its significance.

Labour eventually made its breakthrough in 1906 when George Barnes, of the Amalgamated Society of Engineers (ASE), won Hutchesontown, defeating both Conservative and Liberal in a three-cornered contest. Both Barnes and Joseph Burgess, the candidate in Camlachie, were members of the ILP, and even if Barnes, 'had no time for Glasgow socialists'[96] the preference for moderate trade unionists as parliamentary candidates was a key feature of the ILP's strategy. Barnes success and the relatively high poll in Camlachie was partly due to Irish support for Labour in preference to the Liberals.[97] Alongside Barnes, Labour also returned Alex Wilkie in the two-member Dundee seat, again in the face of Liberal opposition. Labour's success overall in Britain in returning 30 MPs in 1906, enthused the ILP which, even in Scotland, despite only securing two victories, could share in the general euphoria and even claim a distinctive contribution. Joseph Duncan wrote to his fiancée:

> We have done much better in Scotland than I expected. . . . This is not a big proportion but then it must be remembered that in Scotland we have not a clear fight anywhere. In every constituency we have to fight both Liberal & Tory. Although this makes harder fighting it is much more satisfactory. When we get our men in it means that they go in on our own votes. It declares the open war. . . . It is the clear trumpet call of the revolution.[98]

However, the cause of labour representation in Scotland stubbornly refused to move. In the General Election of December 1910 William Adamson won a further seat in West Fife, giving a grand total of three Scottish Labour MPs. The crucial factor, as regards Labour's performance in Scotland compared with England, was that indicated by Duncan above, the failure of the Lib–Lab pact to operate north of the border. The Liberal acceptance of both Barnes and Wilkie after 1906 was simply the acceptance of a fait accompli, made easier by the 'loyalty' of the Labour Party in Parliament to the Liberal Government. Elsewhere Labour was not strong enough to force the issue and the Liberals in Camlachie were prepared to lose the seat to the Unionists (as happened in all three elections in 1906 and 1910) rather than cede their claim to it to Labour. Even if the non-existence of the Lib–Lab pact in Scotland was partly due to timing – the Scottish Liberals only considered it after Chamberlain's tariff reform campaign had been launched, allowing the Liberal Party to place itself firmly at the head of the Progressive forces[99] – Labour's failure to force concessions reflects both its own weakness and the continuing strength of the Liberal Party in Scotland.[100]

The ILP's first electoral success in Glasgow occurred at the municipal election of 1895 when it ran three candidates and managed to return two of them.[101] This breakthrough, however, was facilitated by the general lack of interest shown in the polls that year due to a complete reorganisation of ward boundaries (necessary after the extension of the city boundaries in 1891) to take place the following year.[102] While most other organisations and individuals were concentrating their energies for the full local 'general' municipal election in 1896 when all seats on the council would have to be re-contested, the ILP took the opportunity of securing at least some sitting councillors. The Trades Council, which had previously 'endorsed' candidates for the municipal elections, took no part in the 1895 contests, but this was because it was planning a much more substantial intervention for 1896. It was clear that this 'general' election would provide a unique opportunity for the proponents of Labour representation and the Trades Council put itself at the front of this movement.[103]

The Council did not intend to act alone, however, but to create an effective 'labour party' which would comprise delegates from the Trades Council, individual union branches, the ILP, the Glasgow Federation of Co-operative Societies and the Irish National League (INL). An inaugural meeting was held with three delegates from each 'central' body at which a programme was drafted. Following on from this a 'large and well-represented' meeting of delegates from branches was held on 12 June at which it was decided to form and run candidates under a Workers Municipal Elections Committee (WEC). This Committee numbered approximately 160 delegates.[104]

Glasgow's 'general' election of 1896 provided a great stimulus to the ILP, much needed after the depressing performance at the parliamentary polls the previous year. In 1894 the SLP had branches in all 7 Glasgow Parliamentary Divisions, plus Govan and the separate women's branch (or Women's Labour Party).[105] In 1895 another 2 branches gave a total of 11 for the Glasgow area. This reflected the national enthusiasm which the General Election campaign provoked but Glasgow seems to have avoided the subsequent 'disappointment and . . . apathy';[106] in 1896 the ILP in the Glasgow area reached a high of 17 branches, a figure which would only be surpassed in 1910.[107]

The 1896 election campaign also fuelled a debate over tactics, not about electoral politics *per se* but whether or not it was correct to ally with non-socialists. One strand of opinion still saw elections as having mainly a propaganda purpose. The educative opportunities of the election far outweighed the value of returning 'two or three Socialists to the Council'.[108] The contributor also sought to distinguish between the co-operators and the trade unionists whom, he claimed, would support socialist candidates anyway and the Irish nationalists who, 'as a party, in and out of the House of Commons, are among the bitterest opponents of Socialism'.[109] This view was supported by another contributor who saw more cons than pros in the coalitions of the 'workers', especially, 'the risk of being obliged to not only vote for, but to run non-Socialist candidates'.[10] However, the very real opportunity which existed for returning a significant number of 'Labour' councillors proved the dominant influence. All ILP branches in Glasgow, save one, were affiliated to the WEC and the following would appear to state the majority view.

> As a Socialist and a Trade Unionist I think the policy now being carried out is the best under the circumstances. Candidates are scarce, money is ditto, and we depend for our votes largely on the non-socialist but fairly sympathetic, yet easily alienated trade union voters. We wish to challenge the personnel of the Council, to do which we must win new seats and keep those we have, and when limited action for a given end is possible, we are justified in seizing the opportunity.[111]

This was a very straightforward exposition of the 'labour alliance' strategy. However, the WEC, or 'workers' party' included more than just the socialists and trade unionists. It also had within its ranks the Irish Nationalists and the Co-operators, and these four distinct groups in total accounted for what we might term the 'forces of the democracy'. Through its own self-organisation the working class was seen as gradually establishing its own agenda in political affairs. Commenting on the Glasgow municipal election of 1894 the *Glasgow Herald* pointed out how 'incongruous' the old, familiar mottoes of 'retrenchment and reform' and 'economy and efficiency' had become:

> especially at this time, when the dew democracy is asking that the Corporation shall become a sort of universal employer of labour, which is to be remunerated at trade union rates and is to go on only for eight hours a day. However this may be, it is the fact that in several of the wards in which there were contests many votes were given on the understanding that the candidates for whom they were recorded were 'sound' on the labour and eight hours question.[112]

Of the four 'democratic forces' that constituted the WEC, the ILP and the trades council involvement need little explanation. The ILP's basic strategy was based upon forming a labour electoral alliance. The trades council had always taken a political role in attempting to secure reforms in the trade union interest and had, since the mid-1880s, accepted the logic of actual labour representation; the increasing dominance of socialists within the council had developed that acceptance into a commitment to 'independent labour'. The Co-operative movement in Scotland generally played a more prominent role in Labour politics than its counterpart in England. Partly this was due to the relative weakness of Scottish trade unionism which gave the

Co-ops a much greater weight within the labour movement in Scotland, but 1896 saw the Co-ops in Glasgow throw their lot in with the WEC largely due to a direct assault upon their own organisation.

This was an attempted boycott by private butchers to prevent Co-op societies buying directly in the meat and cattle market. Essentially the boycott represented an attack by small traders on what they perceived as the unfair competition from the Co-ops which were attracting increasing custom. In 1888 a Scottish Traders' Defence Association had been established in Glasgow which not only attempted boycotts against societies but also sought to victimise individual co-operators at their place of work.[113] When the butchers reactivated this campaign in 1896 they did so in a situation which was very likely to lead the Co-ops into direct political involvement. Not only were the labour forces offering to defend the societies' right to buy in the meat markets, but the whole question of access to the markets could only be decided by the City Corporation since they were publicly owned.

This did not lead, however, to a consistent commitment to work with the 'workers party'. The Co-operative movement was represented at the founding of the SWRC in 1899–1900, but the Glasgow societies had by that time already withdrawn from the WEC. The *Labour Leader* explained the non-involvement of the Co-ops in 1899 as due to the WEC changing its secretary who had been a Co-op nominee.[114] However, the most likely explanation would appear to be that, having secured their position against the private traders, the Co-ops lost interest and reverted to their 'no-politics' stand. Even as early as 1897 the WEC was comprised only of delegates from the trades council, the ILP, and the INL.[115]

The involvement of the Irish in the WEC caused a certain difficulty with the Co-ops who refused to endorse one of the nominated WEC candidates because, 'he was engaged in the wine and spirit business'.[116] At the same time 'municipalisation of the liquor traffic' was one of the items in the WEC programme which all candidates were pledged to. This was a difficult item for the INL since many Irish were employed in the 'trade'. Nevertheless they did accept it and even when an INL proposal to drop this item was defeated in 1898, they did not, on that account, leave the committee.[117]

The identification of the Irish as part of 'the forces of the democracy' is worthy of comment on two counts. One is that the very active role taken by the INL in the pursuit of labour representation through the

WEC qualifies the standard view of the Irish as being an electoral barrier to Labour. Obviously the link at a municipal level was easier to make since the question of Home Rule was not a dominant concern, but this local involvement with Labour does indicate a strong tendency within the Irish community to identify with the interests of the working class. This leads to the second point. The Irish or Catholic-Irish were predominantly working class, in fact mainly of the poorer working class. They were cultivated by proponents of labour representation because of their perceived voting strength and that they were primarily working class. But despite their 'national' identification the branches of the INL provided a voice for members of the largely unskilled, poorer workers who were not, by any means, adequately represented by the 'purely' Labour organisations. As Bruce Glasier admitted of the United Irish League (UIL) – as the INL became – despite all its shortcomings it was, nonetheless, 'a democratic party acting for the poor'.[118]

V

In 1896 the WEC stood under the following 9-point programme.

1 Land values to be the basis of taxation; all to be appropriated.
2 Judicial maximum rents to be fixed for buildings and improvements, based upon cost and condition.
3 Right of Issue and Legal Tender for Corporation Notes, to abolish interest.
4 Acquisition of land by the Corporation for the erection of dwellings, shops, &c.
5 Municipalisation of the liquor traffic.
6 Free libraries.
7 Free ferries.
8 Absorption of unemployed labour, or adequate support for the unemployed by the state or community, as is the case with judges, ministers, police, assessors, army, navy, &c.
9 Minimum wage of public servants to be not less than 30 shillings per week of 44 hours.[119]

In a 'purist' sense this was not a socialist programme since it did not involve the demand for 'socialisation of the means of production, distribution and exchange'. Nevertheless, its precise demands on rents, the unemployed and a minimum wage were local expressions of the type of reform that the majority of socialists supported. The most significant item, however, was the first point, the taxation of land values. This, and the general tenor of the programme as a whole, were largely due to the influence of John Ferguson, Irish Nationalist leader and Glasgow city councillor. Ferguson had been involved, albeit pessimistically, on Hardie's side at Mid-Lanark, and had held an honorary office in the Scottish Labour Party until forced out over his support for Liberal candidates at the General Election of 1892. Ferguson, who was in fact a Protestant from Ulster, owned a successful printing business in Glasgow.[120] As his departure from the SLP shows there was the constraint of Home Rule on his relationship with Labour and Socialist forces. At the local level, however, there was more opportunity for joint co-operation with the Trades Council and the ILP without antagonising the national priorities of the Irish Party, especially given the supposedly non-political character of Scottish municipal politics. Ferguson stood for a political alliance between the 'labouring and trading classes'.[121]

Ferguson's estrangement from the proponents of independent labour representation remained a qualified and temporary breach only, at least at the local level. He was elected to the Glasgow Town Council in 1893 and became the focus of leadership for the small group of 'Labour' members who, after 1896, became known as the 'Stalwarts'. Even before 1896 however, Ferguson had emerged as the de facto leader of the 'social reform' or 'working-class' candidates in Glasgow; his seal of approval seems to have been necessary to give any hope of success. The return of the WEC candidates in 1896 was seen as a means of strengthening Ferguson's position and policy within the council, not least by Ferguson himself. Speaking on the night of the poll, 'He had now at his back, he said, Mr Brown, Mr Shaw Maxwell, Councillor Mitchell, and Mr Cronin, gentlemen who would support him in his programme which he had fought for so vigorously during his past tenure of office'.[122]

Speaking at the same meeting Boyd Brown 'said he would follow in the footsteps of Councillor Ferguson'.[123] Since this meeting was being held in the INL hall and Brown had come third in the same ward as Ferguson had topped the poll in, he may just have been politically tactful, yet there is no indication that the candidates mentioned above, all members of the ILP, had any disagreements with any of Ferguson's policies, or with being identified as his supporters, and on many issues he could even appear in advance of some of his ILP colleagues.

Due to Ferguson, the taxation of land values became a sort of test question at local elections. Ferguson argued that £2 million per annum was paid to the ground landlords for the use of the land on which Glasgow was built. Despite Ferguson not really being qualified to make such a judgement it was, as a later commentator wrote, through it, 'that he managed to draw so much support to his side. The figure of £2,000,000 became as popular as John Ferguson himself'.[124]

In fact there was little that was controversial about much of the WEC programme, so far as campaigning in working-class wards was concerned, so much so that other candidates found no difficulty in presenting similar reform 'manifestoes'. What was distinctive about 1896 and the intervention of the WEC was its organised nature, the electors being asked to support a definite programme rather than only the promises of individual candidates. The Stalwarts did not form a party and the parts eventually reasserted themselves over the sum total, but it did, nevertheless, represent an advance on what had gone before. The existing 'labour' element or 'party' in the town council consisted of John Battersby and A.J. Hunter,[125] both of whom were closely connected with the Trades Council; Battersby had been a previous president in and a member of the parliamentary committee, while Hunter was the Council's secretary, a position he held until 1902.[126] Although they stood as working men and based their appeal on the labour vote they did not seek to disturb the no-party-politics consensus, and were increasingly out of step with the younger socialists on the Council. Even the election of Ferguson and Finlay in 1893 did not mark a crucial turning point, though it and the ILP successes in 1895 gave clear indications of the growing tendency towards organisation of the labour forces.

The year 1896 was seen as a great victory by the Labour forces: of the 11 WEC candidates standing in 8 wards, 5 were returned.[127] This number represents only definite WEC candidates and does not include those given belated recognition on the eve of the poll. In the following year the WEC ran 8 candidates in 7 wards and won 4, a net gain of 3 seats. At the same time Battersby and Hunter were returned unopposed, so the Stalwarts had increased their representation to 11 including 6 ILP-ers. The policy which the Stalwarts stood on and would pursue in the Council Chambers had already been given shape by John

Ferguson. In 1894 he had introduced two (crucial) motions. Firstly, 'That the land values of the city, not being the creation of any individual, but the whole community, should be appropriated to the service of the city.' And secondly, 'That 21s. be the lowest wage for an able-bodied man in the municipal employment for a week of six days.' Out of a total possible vote of 77 Ferguson received 8 votes for the first and 12 for the second. After the 1896 election, both these motions were passed, as well as a proposal to permit a limited corporation fire insurance, and a vote in favour of corporation banking.[128]

In their first two years of activity these were the major successes of the Stalwarts. To take the taxation of land values any further an Act of Parliament was necessary and Ferguson won Corporation assent to pursue such a Bill. While this was Ferguson's major pre-occupation and the means by which to finance other reforms, he did not stand still. Having 'secured' the 21s. with, as he put it, 'the help of my sterling friend and colleague, P.G. Stewart . . . The real living wage will be my next consideration. . . . By this I mean a wage which will afford a proper, moral, intellectual, and physical life'.[129] There was, however, some disagreement among the Stalwarts over this. George Mitchell opposed any further increase 'at present', even though the 21s. represented a retreat from the 30s in the WEC programme, which made no mention of gender, and instead he favoured an eight-hour day, 'which, as every intelligent man knows, must ultimately result in an increase of wages'. This attitude had more than a little of the 'superior' labour aristocrat about it. Mitchell was put out that the tramwaymen still wanted to work Sundays even after having their hours reduced and spread over six days, and having their wages increased by 1/6. In his opinion, of the 12,000 municipal employees, 'there are not more than 3,000 worth fighting for. An even smaller number than that belong to trade unions'.[130]

Other concerns given prominence were free libraries, proposals to establish council workshops, and municipal control of the drink traffic.[131] Housing was covered through attempts, most closely associated with P. G. Stewart, to utilise and extend the terms of the Glasgow City Improvement Acts of 1866 and 1897 to clear the worst slums and provide an amount of council-built housing.[132] However, the advocates of 'social reform' in Glasgow faced a major problem, what was left to municipalise? As P.G. Stewart put it in 1898:

And with regard to the future. Glasgow is in the happy position of having already municipalised everything that even the most advanced among other towns contemplates municipalising. We must therefore look for fresh fields to conquer.[133]

VI

The success of the WEC in getting a significant number of Councillors elected put Glasgow in the forefront of Labour organisation and appeared to set an example which could be followed nationally. In 1901 the *Labour Leader* opened up a debate on electoral strategy under the heading, 'Wanted. A Stalwart Party in Parliament. Can the Forces of Democracy be United.'[134] Ironically, at just this time the 'democratic alliance' which had created the WEC in Glasgow was in the process of decay. The exact structure of this 'Labour Party' in Glasgow had been unclear even in 1896 and, although the Stalwarts became an identifiable grouping on the town council over the next few years, the unity of the alliance gradually dissipated, making it increasingly difficult to identify just who exactly represented Labour in the city chambers. The WEC was not a political party and did not have party discipline. The candidates it adopted had to accept the programme formulated by the WEC but, apart from having to declare the sources of funds beyond WEC contributions, there were no restraints on those standing for office. In 1896–9 this very looseness appeared a positive virtue, especially as it was claimed that the Stalwarts, while retaining, 'fads and influences of old associations . . . never disagree on essentials'.[135]

The loss of the Co-operators seriously depleted the funds of the WEC.[13] The next group to depart was the INL, mainly due to differences with the ILP over the division of seats. The final straw for the Irish came with the death of John Ferguson in 1905 and the ILP claiming his Calton seat as 'Labour', rather than recognising it as 'Irish'.[137] Far from being an example to Labour nationally, Glasgow now appeared to be seriously out of step. After the municipal polls in 1905 and the loss of two 'labour' seats the *Labour Leader* commented acidly, 'Perhaps there are reasons for this which the party in Glasgow will have to take into serious consideration.'[138] With even the Trades Council losing interest in the WEC it had become, more or less, a shell containing only the ILP. Unity of the democratic forces had proven more difficult to maintain than had been thought back in 1896, and the ILP's own ambitions had become a source of antagonism. One later explanation for the break-up stated, 'As the Socialist element grew in strength on the WEC its programme and policy became more exclusively "Socialist". This was not to the liking of the UIL, nor the Co-operators, and as a consequence they seceded.'[139]

As Labour representation on Glasgow Town Council continued to decline throughout the early 1900s, the explanation by activists became more focused upon the need for a more structured organisation. Labour's failure in these years was thrown into sharper relief by the success enjoyed by an individual named Andrew Scott Gibson who, originally identifying himself as a Socialist, fought a number of highly personalised, populist campaigns against the corporation 'establishment' and municipal 'extravagance'. The Glasgow correspondent of the *Labour Leader* regarded the success of Scott Gibson as indicative of the, 'emergence of a type of free-lance candidate which, by claiming affinity with Labour, does nothing but harm to the Labour cause'. What permitted this phenomenon was, 'the absence of a well-organised municipal Labour Party outside the Town Council, with a well-defined municipal policy'.[140] The very loose structure of the WEC, previously regarded as a virtue, was now seen as a hindrance in that it discouraged the development of an organisation with a definite policy and a sense of party discipline.

The successful years of the Stalwarts were quite short-lived. Labour representation did not embark on a constantly increasing trajectory but, in fact, soon went in to a serious decline. The 'democratic' alliance behind the WEC was, more or less, defunct by the mid-1900s. Between 1905 and 1909 Labour only won two elections for the town council, and in 1908 its representation had fallen to a single seat.[141] The break-up of the Stalwarts meant that the WEC took on a more socialist identity – all candidates were members of the ILP and were reliant upon ILP branches for their campaigns. The Labour programme had, in fact, changed little since the original WEC document in 1896 but the loss of the Co-operators, the Irish and the decreasing interest shown by the trades council, left 'Labour' more exposed to the middle-class reaction against the increasing demands being placed upon the rates. The ILP might claim that the Labour vote represented the solid bedrock of out and out socialist support, but this was little comfort for the actual loss of seats it was suffering.[142]

In effect, while Labour's policies had not changed the political climate had. The extension of municipal services and control had been a relatively unproblematic issue in the early 1890s. Municipalisation may have been claimed as an effective local contribution to socialism by the ILP, but it had already been adopted by a majority of the Liberal-dominated town council. Glasgow had achieved a world-wide reputation as the most municipalised city and attracted visitors on that score.[143] From a Liberal viewpoint, which regarded municipal control as a manifestation of 'civic spirit', the Labour councillors could be regarded as simply the most enthusiastic proponents of what was an accepted policy.[144] The last great municipal venture had been the take-over of the tramway network from its American operators. The campaign behind this move had involved socialists and the trades council and its success had allowed Labour to 'swim with the tide' of extending municipal control and win the partial reforms introduced by Ferguson and the Stalwarts.

Part of the problem for Labour was that Glasgow did not appear to have much left to municipalise. Further schemes were suggested, such as coal supplies, milk, banking, housing, but none managed to arouse much enthusiasm and some, e.g. coal and milk, even estranged the Co-operators who already provided these services. Furthermore, at the same time as Labour began to run out of ideas so middle-class (or 'ratepayers') pressure groups began to take the initiative. There had always been an opposition to the growth of public services which, in Glasgow, found its most faithful expression in the leader columns of the *Glasgow Herald*. At the election of John Ferguson in 1893, the *Herald* warned against, 'his overwhelming schemes of municipalisation and confiscation', thereby drawing the connection between public provision and the threat to private property.[145] From around 1900, moreover, the rates issue became much more pronounced and significant. This was due to particularly large increases in Glasgow's rates due to municipal reforms and amenities, and to national reforms and improvements, e.g. in education, which placed more demands upon local authorities. Between 1900 and 1906 the Glasgow Poor Rate more than doubled from 10.25*d* in the £ to over 20*d*.[146]

VII

Back in the 1880s when the first socialist societies were beginning to organise contemporaries were struck by proletarian Glasgow's initial failure to keep pace with middle-class Edinburgh.[147] Gradually, however, Glasgow exerted its leadership on the rest of the country. The concentration of the labour movement in and around the city more or less determined that Glasgow would become the centre of socialist and labour politics in Scotland.

However, the organised labour movement represented only a minority of the working class within its ranks; by 1914 there was still less than 50 per cent of the adult male workforce in trade unions.[148] A political approach that was too centred upon the existing labour movement left unanswered the question of those outwith organisations – women, labourers, the semi-skilled – in fact the majority of the working class. And, moreover, the bulk of the adult population were still without the vote.[149] Examination of the Glasgow electoral areas – parliamentary divisions and municipal wards – shows that the franchise system was heavily biased against the working class and, in particular, the poorer working class. The level of male enfranchisement in the Glasgow parliamentary burgh was around 54 per cent. This was an average figure, however, and varied from over 75 per cent in the Central Division to under 44 per cent in Bridgeton. At the level of the municipal burgh the differences were even more pronounced. In the poorer areas of the city such as Calton and Cowcaddens less than 40 per cent of adult males were on the electoral register, while in the middle-class suburban areas of Langside, Pollokshields and Kelvinside the level of enfranchisement was around 85 per cent. In the 'business' wards of Exchange and Blythswood – where the plural vote was most prevalent – male enfranchisement rates approached 300 per cent.[150]

Despite all this, the ILP and the labour movement generally were strangely silent on the question of the franchise. Writing in the mid-1890s Hardie argued that the franchise was no longer an issue – the previous generation had secured the vote and, 'only the details remain to be adjusted'.[151] One of the 'details' was, of course, the matter of women's lack of the suffrage although Hardie and the ILP did come to support the demand as formulated by the Women's Social and Political Union (WSPU), i.e. of the vote for women on the same terms as it is or may be given to men.[152] The ILP also had in its programme the demand for full adult suffrage but at no time did the ILP or the Labour Party make this a political priority inside or outside the Houses of Parliament. What little thinking there was on the matter tended to be dominated by an ambivalent attitude towards the poor or the 'slum-dweller'.

This attitude involved a mixture of superiority, condescension and fear. Hardie, the 'member for the unemployed' in the 1890s argued the need to discipline the 'loafers' or 'work-shy' who were seen as contaminating the ranks of the genuinely unemployed: 'Treat them as you will and, above all, see that it is made impossible for them to propagate their species.'[153] The slum-dweller was seen as not only an affront to working-class respectability and independence but also as a latent reservoir of support for reaction. Hardie expressed this outlook succinctly enough when he wrote, 'it is the slum vote which the socialist candidate fears most.'[154]

This desire to distinguish the respectable working class from the 'slum-dwellers' was shared by the local ILP leadership in Glasgow. George Carson, who was Secretary of Glasgow Trades Council and one of the most prominent ILP-ers in the city argued for this distinction as strongly as any 'bourgeois' philanthropist. As a representative of the trades council, Carson gave evidence at the corporation's 'Commission on the Housing of the Poor' in 1903. Carson informed the Commission that the trades council was in favour of the proposals of the corporation and had even held a demonstration to that effect but he chose to emphasise that:

> The [Trades] Council is opposed to the suggestion that the Corporation should be restricted to the providing of housing accommodation for the criminal and vicious classes only. If the Corporation are to build houses at all, it must be for the thrifty, industrious and sober working classes for whom such housing accommodation should be provided, the larger portion of these, by reason of their small wages, are compelled to live in houses which are inimical to health, and generally amongst a most undesirable class of people.'[155]

The sentiments expressed by Carson may have been widespread within the labour and socialist movement as regards the 'lumpen-proletariat' but they were by no means universal. Carson's position contrasted sharply with that of Thomas Fraser, a member of the SDF who attended the Municipal Commission as a representative of the stone mason's union. He took a much more class-combative stance and refused to go along with any 'moral' perspective on the working class and poverty. Unlike Carson, who supported the Corporation's idea of housing the 'undesirables' in one-roomed flats built to the cheapest-possible specification, Fraser argued that no one should ever be allowed to live in one-roomed accommodation, and such flats should simply not be built. When asked if the 'drinking habits' of the slum population had anything to do with their shorter life expectancy, Fraser replied in the negative since statistics showed that the 'middle' and 'bourgeois' classes drank more than the working class and, therefore, 'the middle and bourgeois class ought to be in a worse social condition than the workers'.[156]

Fraser's evidence reflects the different political perspective of the SDF which did not regard the franchise as a settled issue. The SDF made the connection between socialist representation and the restricted franchise in Britain. Although it was too weak to lead a suffrage campaign on its own the SDF did treat the franchise as a serious issue and was, at least, consistent in its demand for full adult suffrage.[157] On Clydeside John Maclean argued that 'the larger portion' of electoral support for socialist (as opposed to labour) candidates came from those outwith existing labour organisations, a claim that cut across accepted ILP wisdom on the issue.[158] Its fear of the supposed reactionary tendencies of the 'slum-dwellers' effectively curtailed any possibility of a campaign for franchise reform that went beyond that urged by the women's suffrage movement. Yet, without further development of the franchise Labour's permanent minority position was secured.

The electoral position of Labour in Glasgow in 1906 was confusing and apparently contradictory. At the parliamentary level there was the historic breakthrough in securing the return of the city's first Labour MP in Blackfriars and Hutchesontown, and there had been an encouraging poll in the Camlachie Division.[159] At the municipal level, however, Labour representation, in the organised shape of the WEC, was almost completely wiped out. The promise of 1896 – of a strong and united Labour presence on the corporation had proven impossible to maintain.

Even at the height of its success, however, essentially the WEC had been a pressure-group with 12 councillors at most out of a total of 75. Furthermore, its efforts were restricted to a relatively small number of wards and even had it won every seat it contested the WEC would have remained a minority on the corporation. With the collapse of the 'Stalwart' alliance the ILP had shouldered the responsibility of running

Labour candidates but, without the other 'democratic forces', it had been incapable of sustaining a successful electoral challenge.

However, even if Labour was destined to remain a permanent opposition on Glasgow Corporation, there was still room for improvement in its position. From around 1906 a number of factors emerged which began to shift the political balance more in Labour's favour. In October 1906 the socialist newspaper *Forward* began publishing. Although independent and open to most socialist opinion, *Forward* basically acted as the mouthpiece of the Glasgow ILP. Its influence – as a regular, weekly provider of news and ideas – must have been considerable on the membership. In its very first issue, *Forward* began what was to be series of articles attacking the whole notion of the 'land' or 'single' tax, entitled 'Popular Fallacies – Henry Georgism Exposed'.[160] At the same time a new generation of leaders began to emerge within the Glasgow ILP, men like Thomas Johnston (editor of *Forward*), Patrick Dollan, James Maxton, and John Wheatley who were to gain not only local but national prominence.

The difficulties confronting the ILP in its efforts to re-galvanise Labour as an electoral force in municipal politics were regarded as two-fold: organisation and policy. If the ILP was not simply to contest elections on its own – and experience repeated failures – a new organisation was necessary to replace the WEC. Gradually, opinion began to focus on the need to establish a Labour Party. Achieving this, however, took time and it was not until 1912 that the Glasgow Labour Party was formally constituted. When it was there was a distinct difference between it and the old WEC. The Labour Party was not based upon the 'forces of the democracy' but was limited in membership to the ILP, trades council, Fabians and Women's Labour League. Thus it did not have the 'composite' structure of the WEC but attempted to be a 'controlling body' as regards the selection and running of Labour candidates.[161] Prior to this there had been some movement with the trades council's decision to appoint a new election committee of its own in 1909.[162]

This decision reflected a changing mood in the city. The return of unemployment in 1908 saw the left regain the political initiative. The plight of the unemployed once again made political action and political demands upon the local and national state an issue and the ILP, SDF and trades council all became involved in the campaign.[163] Similarly, the attempt by Glasgow Corporation to exploit the surplus from the tramway as a subsidy for the rates, galvanised the trades council into a successful campaign in defence of the principal that, as the working class were the main users of the trams, they should get the major benefit in the shape of reduced fares.[164]

At the municipal polls in 1909 Labour managed to gain a seat – the first for some years. However, there was no immediate rejoicing on that score; the disappointments of the previous years had gone too deeply to allow that. Despite unemployment and the debate over the tramway surplus, Labour was seen as lacking a major issue on which to base its appeal. As *Forward* commented after the November poll, 'Municipal Socialism is in the lean and dry stage. It stands in need of new ideas and new inspiration.'[165] That much-needed 'inspiration' was housing which, in the immediate pre-War years, under the impact of Wheatley's cottages scheme, became the key issue behind Labour's increasing success.[166] Yet, Labour remained, essentially, a pressure-group.[167] It took the War, the direct action of the rent strike, the growth of Labour's own organisational strength and a further franchise reform before that position could be fundamentally changed.

Notes

1 *Socialist Review*, April 1914.
2 James Kellas, 'The Mid-Lanark By-Election (1888) and the Scottish Labour Party (1888–1894)', *Parliamentary Affairs*, XVIII, 1965, pp. 318–29.
3 If Scotland took the lead other areas were not far behind. See Jack Reynolds and Keith Laybourn, 'The Emergence of the Independent Labour Party in Bradford', *International Review of Social History*, XX, 1975, pp. 313–46.
4 Ian Hutchison, *A Political History of Scotland 1832–1924: Parties, Elections and Issues* (John Donald, Edinburgh, 1986) p. 257.
5 David Howell, *British Workers and the Independent Labour Party 1888–1906* (Manchester University Press, Manchester, 1983), pp. 133–44.
6 W.H. Fraser, 'Trades Councils in the Labour Movement in Nineteenth Century Scotland', in Ian McDougall (ed.), *Essays in Scottish Labour History* (John Donald, Edinburgh, 1978), p. 1.
7 *Ibid.*
8 *Ibid.* The Webbs, writing in 1894, identified 1879 as 'distinctly a low-water mark of the Trade Union Movement', which in Scotland had ruinous consequences due to the failure of the City of Glasgow Bank – 'a blow from which Trade Unionism in Scotland has even yet not recovered;

Sidney and Beatrice Webb, *The History of Trade Unionism* (Longmans, London, 1911), p. 334.
9 Webbs, *ibid.*, pp. 490–91.
10 Roy H. Campbell, *Scotland Since 1707: The Rise of an Industrial Society* (John Donald, Edinburgh, 1985), p. 237.
11 Webbs, *op. cit.*, p. 412.
12 *Ibid.*, p. 411.
13 Fraser, *op. cit.*, pp. 1–2.
14 *Ibid.*
15 G.D.H. Cole, *British Working Class Politics: 1832–1941* (Methuen, London, 1941), pp. 98–9.
16 Roy Gregory, *The Miners in British Politics 1906–14* (Clarendon Press, Oxford, 1968), p. 16.
17 R. Page Arnot, *A History of the Scottish Miners* (Allen & Unwin, London, 1955), pp. 66–70.
18 *The Miner*, January 1887.
19 Arnot, *op cit*, p. 68.
20 *Ibid.*, p. 70.
21 'Assessment of Hardie's relationship with Liberalism must distinguish between organisational and ideological aspects.' Howell, *op. cit.*, p. 144.
22 Kellas, *op. cit.*; K.O. Morgan, *Keir Hardie: Radical and Socialist* (Weidenfeld, London, 1975), pp. 25–33; Fred Reid, *Keir Hardie: The Making of a Socialist* (Croom Helm, London, 1978), pp. 110–115.
23 *The Miner*, January 1887.
24 E.H. Hunt, *British Labour History 1815–1914* (Weidenfeld & Nicolson, London, 1985), pp. 253–4.
25 Arnot, *op. cit.*, p. 51. The Fife coalfield was only on the brink of expansion, however.
26 *The Miner*, March 1887.
27 See Fred Reid, 'Keir Hardie's Conversion to Socialism', in Asa Briggs and John Saville (eds), *Essays in Labour History 1886–1923* (Macmillan, London, 1971).
28 On the end of the Liberal Party see Hardie in *The Miner*, July 1887, and Chisholm Robertson in same, August 1887; see also May 1887 on the end of the capitalist, 'His day is now nearly past.'
29 See Arnot, *op. cit.*, p. 67.
30 *The Miner*, April 1887.
31 *Ibid.*, August 1887.
32 See Howell, *op. cit.*, p. 147.
33 *The Miner*, June 1888.
34 *Ibid.*, May 1888.
35 *Ibid.*, September 1888.

36 See Howell, *op. cit.*, p. 146.
37 David Lowe, *Souvenirs of Scottish Labour* (Holmes, Glasgow, 1919), p. 4.
38 *The Miner*, March 1888.
39 *Ibid.*, January 1888.
40 *The Democrat*, May 1888.
41 *Ibid.*, August 1887.
42 Kellas, *op. cit.*, p. 327; Lowe, *op. cit.*, pp. 112–13.
43 Shaw Maxwell had been a 'land radical' in the early 1880s. He became the first chairman of the SLP in 1888 and the first secretary of the ILP in 1893. Lowe, *op. cit.*, pp. 4, 117.
44 *Labour Leader*, 5 January 1894.
45 *The Miner*, April 1888.
46 Lowe, *op. cit.*, pp. 3–4.
47 The best treatment of socialism in the 1880s remains E.P. Thompson, *William Morris: From Romantic to Revolutionary* (Merlin, London, 1977).
48 *Ibid.*, pp. 350–57. This is also dealt with in James Smyth, 'Labour and Socialism in Glasgow 1880–1914: The Electoral Challenge Prior to Democracy' (unpublished PhD thesis, university of Edinburgh, 1987), ch. 1.
49 Reid (1978), *op. cit.*, pp. 80–2.
50 Arnot, *op. cit.*, pp. 91–2.
51 *Commonweal*, October 1885.
52 Thompson, *op. cit.*, p. 437.
53 *To Socialists*, 1885.
54 Thompson, *op. cit.*, pp. 337–42.
55 *Commonweal*, 22 May 1888.
56 Socialist League, *Report 1888*.
57 J. Bruce Glasier (Glasgow) to Socialist League (London), 24 October 1887, Socialist League Collection, International Institute of Social History, Amsterdam.
58 *Ibid.*
59 Thompson, *op. cit.*, pp. 446–56.
60 *Our Corner*, June 1887.
61 Lowe, *op. cit.*, p. 128.
62 *Justice*, 8 December 1888.
63 *Ibid.*
64 Lowe, *op. cit.*, p. 132.
65 J. Bruce Glasier to Andreas Scheu, 25 May 1893, Socialist League Collection.
66 Lowe, *op. cit.*, p. 122.

67 *Labour Leader*, June 1893.
68 *Ibid.*, March 1893.
69 Paolo Vestri, 'The Rise of Reformism', *Radical Scotland*, April–May 1984.
70 *Ibid.*
71 *Justice*, 31 March 1888.
72 *Labour Leader*, February 1893.
73 James Connolly to J. Keir Hardie, 9 February 1894, Francis Johnston Correspondence.
74 *Labour Leader*, 5 January 1894.
75 *Ibid.*
76 *Ibid.*
77 *Ibid.*
78 *Ibid.*
79 *Ibid.*
80 *Scottish Co-operator*, 12 January 1900.
81 *Ibid.*
82 *Labour Leader*, February 1893.
83 ILP, *Report of the First General Conference 1893*, p. 3. The Proposal was seconded by Smillie.
84 *Ibid.*, p. 4.
85 Howell, *op. cit.*, p. 294.
86 Lowe, *op. cit.*, p. 170. At the same time a motion to form a Scottish 'Council' of the ILP was defeated by 28 votes to 22.
87 See Howell, *op. cit.*, ch. 13.
88 Joan Smith, 'Labour Tradition in Glasgow and Liverpool', *History Workshop Journal*, 17, 1984, p. 38.
89 The SUTCLP was formed in 1891 with the intention of basing a 'labour party' on the trades councils. Its relations with the SLP were soured by personal animosities between Hardie on one hand and H.H. Champion and Chisholm Roberts on the other. The SUTCLP was a very short-lived phenomenon, though its long-term significance lay in its being part of the ad hoc development of independent labour politics. See Howell, *op. cit.*, p. 151.
90 *Labour Leader*, February 1893.
91 *Ibid.*
92 In 1895 Shaw Maxwell was one of five candidates of the Scottish Land Restoration League who stood in the Clydeside area. See Smyth, *op. cit.*, ch. 2.
93 Quoted in Howell, *op. cit.*, p. 161.
94 SWRC, mss notes of meeting of committee, 28 April 1900.
95 Howell *op. cit.*, p. 163.

96 Hutchinson, *op. cit.*, p. 255.
97 Irish support for Labour is discussed in detail in Smyth, *op. cit.*, ch. 4.
98 Joseph Duncan, letter dated 17 January 1906.
99 Hutchinson, *op. cit.*, pp. 259–60.
100 Howell, *op. cit.*, p. 255.
101 *Labour Leader*, 2, 11 November 1895.
102 *Glasgow Herald*, 6 November 1895. Only 5 wards out of 25 were contested.
103 Glasgow Trades Council, *Annual Report* 1895–96.
104 *Ibid.*
105 Lowe, *op. cit.*, pp. 164, 166.
106 Howell, *op. cit.*, p. 329.
107 Information on the branches taken from the published *Branch Directories* and *Annual Reports*.
108 *Glasgow Commonweal*, August 1986.
109 *Ibid.*
110 *Ibid.*, October 1896.
111 *Ibid.*
112 *Glasgow Herald*, 7 November 1894.
113 J.A. Kinloch, The Scottish Co-operative Wholesale Society 1868–1918 (unpublished PhD thesis, University of Strathclyde, 1976), pp. 337–49; W. Maxwell, *The History of Co-operation in Scotland: Its Inception and Leaders* (Co-operative Union, Glasgow, 1910), pp. 329–45; James A. Flanagan, *Wholesale Co-operation in Scotland* (SCWS, Glasgow, 1920), pp. 133–4, 150–55.
114 *Labour Leader*, 7 October 1899.
115 *Ibid.*, 23 October 1897.
116 *Scottish Co-operator*, November 1896.
117 *Labour Leader*, 27 August 1898.
118 Quoted in Howell, *op. cit.*, p. 370.
119 *Glasgow Commonweal*, November 1896.
120 *Labour Annual 1895*, Manchester, 1985; *Labour Leader*, 22 October 1898.
121 John Ferguson to Keir Hardie, 17 May 1888, Francis Johnston correspondence.
122 *Glasgow Observer*, 7 November 1896.
133 *Ibid.*
124 *Forward*, 13 October 1906.
125 *Labour Leader*, 17 September 1898.
126 Fraser, *op. cit.*, p. 5.
127 Glasgow Trades Council, *Annual Report 1895–96*.
128 *Labour Leader*, 22 October 1898, see also 17 September and 1 October.

129 *Ibid.*, 22 October 1898.

130 *Ibid.*, 17 September 1898.

131 *Ibid.*, 24 September and 1 October 1898.

132 *Ibid.*, 1 October 1989.

133 *Ibid.*

134 *Ibid.*, 19 October 1901.

135 J. Connell, *Glasgow Municipal Enterprise* (Labour Leader, Glasgow, 1899), pp. 83–4: 'Indeed the constitution of the Committee is more in the nature of an honourable understanding than a set of hard and fast rules which people are punished for breaking.'

136 Glasgow Trades Council, *Annual Report 1898–99*. The withdrawal of the Co-operators saw the WEC finances drop by £50, about a third of its total funds.

137 Glasgow Trades Council, *Annual Report 1904–05*; *Forward*, 11 November 1911.

138 *Labour Leader*, 10 November 1905.

139 Glasgow Labour Party, *Souvenir of the Thirteenth Annual Conference*, Glasgow, 1914, p. 35.

140 *Labour Leader*, 10 November 1904.

141 *Forward*, 7 November 1908.

142 *Labour Leader*, 7 November 1908.

143 Margaret Sanger, *An Autobiography* (Dover, New York, 1971). Sanger was not overly impressed by this example of 'local socialism'.

144 D.M. Stevenson, *Municipal Glasgow: Its Evolution and Enterprises* (Glasgow, 1914), p. 2. Stevenson had been a sympathiser of the Socialist League in the 1880s.

145 *Glasgow Herald*, 8 November 1893.

146 *Annual Reports of the Local Government Board for Scotland*, PP (Parliamentary Papers) 1901, XXVII, PP 1907, XXXVII.

147 See *Justice*, 31 May 1884. 'So far Edinburgh has far outstripped Glasgow in zeal for the cause.'

148 E.H. Hunt, *British Labour History 1815–1914* (Weidenfeld & Nicolson, London, 1985), p. 296.

149 It has been estimated that, nationally, 60 per cent of adult males had the vote prior to 1918. See N. Blewett, 'The Franchise in the United Kingdom 1885–1918', *Past and Present*, 32, 1965; H.C.G. Matthew, R. McKibbin and J.A. Hay, 'The Franchise Factor in the Rise of the Labour Party', *English Historical Review*, XCI, 1976.

150 These figures are for 1911 and are based on the *Census 1911* (published by Glasgow Corporation) re population and the *Glasgow Post Office Directory* re electorate. The issue is dealt with in detail in Smyth, *op. cit.*, ch. 6.

151 Keir Hardie, 'The Independent Labour Party', in A. Reid (ed.), *The New Party* (London, 1895), quoted in Matthew et al., *op. cit.*, p. 724.

152 *Forward*, 20 October 1906, greeted the women's suffrage campaign as 'another Chartist revival.'

153 *Labour Leader*, 26 January 1895, quoted in Reid, *op. cit.* (1978), p. 168.

154 Keir Hardie, 'From Serfdom to Socialism', quoted in Morgan, *op. cit.*, p. 208.

155 *Glasgow Municipal Commission on the Housing of the Poor*, Glasgow, 1904, evidence of George Carson and James Boyd, p. 550.

156 *Ibid.*, evidence of A. McGillivary and T. Fraser, p. 597.

157 See Smyth, *op. cit.*, for a fuller discussion of the SDF position.

158 *Forward*, 13 August 1910.

159 Joseph Burgess came last in a three-cornered contest but polled 30 per cent of the votes. As in Blackfriars and Hutchesontown, Labour received Irish support.

160 *Forward*, 13 October 1906.

161 Glasgow Labour Party, *op. cit.*

162 Glasgow Trades Council, *Annual Report 1909–10*.

163 Glasgow Trades Council, *Annual Report 1908–09*. 'Unemployment is really the question of the day.'

164 Glasgow Trades Council, *Annual Report 1909–10*.

165 *Forward*, 13 November 1909.

166 J. Melling, *Rent Strikes: Peoples' Struggle for Housing in West Scotland 1890–1916* (Polygon, Edinburgh, 1983), p. 40.

167 By the outbreak of the First World War Labour had 17 councillors or 15 per cent of the total representation. Proportionally this was less than the Stalwarts had enjoyed at the height of their success.

THREE

Taking the leadership of the labour movement: the ILP in Glasgow, 1906–1914

Joan Smith

The central question to be addressed by any historian of the Glasgow ILP between 1906 and 1914 is the cause of its dramatic shift in fortune. As Jim Smyth's essay has demonstrated, the labour movement in Glasgow had lost what municipal base it had prior to 1906 and was also without a unifying programme after Ferguson's single-tax platform had finally been defeated within the Workers' Electoral Committee. Eight years later, however, there was a labour group of fourteen in the city council united around a clear municipal socialist strategy, members of the ILP were leading the industrial struggles of unskilled workers from their positions in the Glasgow Trades Council, *Forward* had become the voice of radical as well as socialist Glasgow under the editorship of Tom Johnston, and the May Day demonstration had grown to thirty thousand. By 1914 the ILP in Glasgow was more than a pressure group, it had become a party and its leaders had been accepted as the leaders of a larger movement, and all this took place *before* the First World War. What happened in those eight years *before* 1914? Can the rise of the ILP in Glasgow be explained by either the traditional view of the ILP, as a party of compromise, or by David Howell's recent thesis that the ILP's rise was always contingent on other forces, or by yet a third explanation of this extraordinary turnaround in political fortunes?

David Howell in his path-breaking work *British Workers and the Independent Labour Party, 1888–1906* has outlined what he believes to be the dominant – but incorrect – image of the ILP in British historiography. This dominant image presents the ILP as a pragmatic, anti-theoretical party, working with the grain of British politics; an effective vehicle for both labour and for socialist politicians as it was prepared to work with Liberals and with trade unionists, unlike the Social Democratic Federation (SDF) and other 'purist' socialist organisations. This image can be viewed both positively, in that socialists achieved entry to parliament, and negatively, in that the price was socialists without socialism. The rise of the ILP is therefore explained by its initial compromises on the question of socialism. But this chapter differs from this view of the ILP for the period 1906–1914; the history of the ILP in Glasgow is not the history of an atheoretical and pragmatic party, nor did its electoralism mean the end of ethical socialism. Nor, however, does this chapter entirely endorse Howell's recent reworking of the national ILP story.

For Howell the rise of the ILP was always contingent. In his argument the mid-Victorian legacy of the ILP – its trade union traditions, optimism about electoralism and about state power, and radical idiom – coupled with the economic difficulties of the period and greater social tensions 'lead us to view ILP development not as the consequence of critical choices, but positioned and moulded by a battery of forces'.[1] Electoralism necessitated the suppression of ethical socialism, while involvement in trade union organisation led to ILP members becoming enmeshed in 'ongoing structures':

> The ILP emerged as a flexible formally socialist party, eventually allying with the unions. This development can be seen as involving the defeat of an alternative project for a United Socialist Party, essentially unity with the SDF in preference to a formal link with trade unionists who might or might not be socialists. Clearly many ILP members considered socialist unity as a significant option to be pursued or avoided. The most prominent evidence comes from the tortuous debate on the question in the late nineties . . . the feeling was strengthened by the restraints involved in the Labour Alliance. When these tensions grew after 1906 it needed only the advent of Grayson to ignite a new controversy.[2]

Howell's primary interest is in the 'suppressed alternatives' of British socialism. Could a different 'progressive' alliance have been formed – one of Liberals, Radicals and Irish Nationalists – in which the ILP could have played a pivotal role? Alternatively, was the SDF so sectarian that of necessity it became the minority party after 1900: was a socialist unity option always impossible? For Howell, the structure of the ILP allowed its leadership to win against the socialist unity option and the partnership between the ILP and the trade unions then made this development less likely. The victory of this partnership led to a labour movement in which the two central socialist understandings of the inevitability of class conflict and the repressive role of the state moved away from the centre of British socialism. Further, the Radical ethos of the ILP led to an emphasis on community organisation, electoralism and progressive evolutionary change within the capitalist system. Accordingly, it is possible to understand the victory of ILP gradualism as an essential precondition to the 'national' settlement of 1931, which was nevertheless, both bitterly and strongly resisted by the ILP.

Howell's work poses this argument superbly showing a depth and range of knowledge of the ILP across many different local communities. Several propositions emerge from Howell's thesis that should be examined against the history of the Glasgow ILP between 1906 and 1914, years in which the ILP came to dominate the city's labour movement. It was Glasgow after all that sent the Clydeside ILP MPs to Parliament in 1922 and who provided the most successful minister of MacDonald's 1924 government, John Wheatley at the Ministry of Housing. Was the ILP in Glasgow atheoretical and pragmatic and going with the grain of popular politics? Indeed, is that what they thought they were doing? What of the suppressed alternatives? How suppressed were they in the west of Scotland? If a Liberal, Radical and Irish Nationalist progressive alliance could have taken root in the nineteenth century it would have done so in Glasgow. Similarly, a united Socialist Party was more possible in Glasgow before the First World War than elsewhere. But Howell's unstated assumptions about the other socialist organisations should not go unchallenged. How *revolutionary* were the alternatives to the ILP in the period before the First World War? Did a verbal commitment to the theory of class struggle or the nature of capitalist production and the state lead to any difference in political practice? In this chapter it will be argued that the Glasgow ILP members' commitment to the Irish and to trade union struggle and to the women's movement was at least as profound as that of members of the avowedly revolutionary SDF or the Socialist Labour Party (SLP). The lack of a clear distinction between 'revolutionary' and 'reformist' before the First World War throughout the British movement meant that the parliamentary socialism of the ILP leadership was not in strong contrast to the marxist tradition of the SDF and the BSP which also accepted a parliamentary road, whereas the anti-electoral approach of the SLP and the syndicalists appeared as one-sided socialism compared with the ILP's involvement in industry and electoralism.[3]

There are two other unstated assumptions in David Howell's work, one general and one particular to Scotland, which would mitigate against a fair assessment of the ILP in Glasgow unless they too were examined. The first assumption, shared by many labour historians, is that trade union struggle was almost the sole basis of the political growth of the labour movement. This assumption ignores the myraid interventions in local politics that grew parallel to, not subsequently from, the growth of trade union membership in the last decade of the nineteenth century. Socialist and labour stalwarts, many of them not from the working class, stood for election to the Parish Council, or the Board of Guardians, to the School Board, and to the municipal council. They stood in order to promote the interest of the working class in welfare and education and in local politics. It was this joint endeavour which led to the original labour alliances.[4]

The corollary of this argument is that industrial struggle is somehow a guarantee of the development of a more socialist or revolutionary politics, than 'community' struggles; in this perspective 'community' struggles are associated with the development of reformism via electoralism. As a comparison of Glasgow and Liverpool demonstrates, 'correct' socialist political traditions cannot be tied to one form of working-class struggle rather than another: the transport workers' strike of 1911 did not lead to a socialist movement in Liverpool because of the city's community structure and the domination of sectarian politics. The privileging of industrial struggle over all other forms of struggle was not John Maclean's perspective when he stood for the Govan School Board; or Pankhurst's; or, after he left the SLP, James Connolly's.[5] All socialists, with the exception of the SLP and the syndicalists, believed in the complementarity of industrial and political action at the local and national level.

The second assumption made by Howell, again shared by many political historians, is that the disputes over Irish Home Rule inevitably led to a shift to the right amongst the Scottish Liberal party and the Scottish electorate. Despite his acknowledgement of the deep-rooted attachment to Gladstonian Liberalism in Scotland, Howell proceeds to argue that it was the challenge from the right over Irish Home Rule which changed the face of Scottish politics. Undoubtedly, the wealthy left the Liberal Party for Liberal Unionism but the issue of

Irish Home Rule did not cause the electorate to shift their support to the Liberal Unionists, or the Conservatives who had always failed in their attempts to play the Orange card.[6]

In Scotland, the majority of Scottish MPs *remained* Home Rule Liberals unlike their English counterparts, a tribute to the strength of Scottish Liberal radicalism. The exception to this was the return of seven Liberal Unionists for Glasgow in the 1900 election, but this was fought in the unique context of the Boer War. In this election, candidates were labelled pro-Boer and anti-Boer, whereas in previous elections they were labelled Home Rule and anti-Home Rule – and seven Liberal Unionists were *never* returned on the anti-Home Rule ticket. The entire position was reversed in 1906 when seven Liberals were returned in an election fought on the issue of free trade.[7] Sectarianism was strong in the ring of coal and iron towns around Glasgow but before 1914 never achieved a significant electoral presence inside the city boundaries.[8]

By subscribing to the received view which overstates the importance of anti-Irish sectarianism Howell's argument about the obstacles to the growth of a successful labour movement in the west coast of Scotland is only partially correct:

> There was a formidable collection of obstacles: the continuing and after 1900, reviving strength of Scottish Liberalism, with its capacity to reflect significant Scottish concerns and qualities; the way in which, particularly in the West, the Home Rule issue provided openings for Unionism; and the normal attachment of the Irish vote to the Liberal Party, with sectarianism providing support for Unionism as well. These barriers were confronted by Labour initiatives which lacked the solid base that strong trade unionism would have provided. Indeed in Scotland, . . . industrial weakness was a spur to political innovation.[9]

In this scenario Labour could only make a significant advance once the Liberal hegemony was broken and the Irish question settled. And as Liberalism retained its hold before 1914 and the Irish question remained alive until 1922, Labour was confined to the margins of popular politics.[10] To the contrary; this chapter will argue that it was *not* the First World War that built the Glasgow labour movement or finally brought an end to Liberal hegemony in the city. Rather, a firmly established labour movement composed of networks of activists in the workshops and the tenements met the challenges of the First World

War. It was these networks which allowed different sections of the Glasgow working class to attempt to construct a mass opposition to government policy on labour in the munitions industry, on conscription, on rents and even to support those socialists who were arrested as anti-war agitators. The Glasgow ILP was replacing the Scottish Liberals as the leading radical force in city politics by 1909 and by 1913 *Forward* was clearly the galvanising hub of the entire Glasgow labour movement presenting a distinctive and cohesive presence in local politics. Moreover, despite the commitment to industrial organisation by the strong Glasgow SLP and John Maclean's support for industrial struggle in the local BSP it would be mistaken to believe that even together these organisations had more members or influence in the shipyards and workshops than the ILP.

The ILP's ascendency was not based on the sublimation of the party's ethical socialism but rather on a constant testing of the limits of both the radical and marxist traditions. In a city in which the Liberals refused to work with Labour and in which there was always a socialist presence, the ILP emerged as a party led by a philosopher of evolutionary socialism, John Wheatley. Moreover, the evolutionary socialist leadership of the ILP did develop a test for their membership: they had to support municipal housing built out of the tramway surplus, that is, they had to be genuine municipal *socialists*, prepared to work to shift the balance of class forces within Glasgow. In Glasgow the ILP represented evolutionary municipal socialism, never simply a shallow electoralism. On the Glasgow left the dominant model of socialist advance was the hugely successful German Social Democratic Party. In this context, the ILP were not considered opportunists, nor did they give up their distinctive form of socialism.

I

At the height of the revival of Liberal enthusiasm in 1906 labour municipal candidates suffered a demoralising defeat.[11] However, after 1906, the radical revival could be used by Glasgow socialists to challenge the acts of the Liberal government itself and to carve out a different form of radicalism for the city. Despite the municipal election results there were two events in 1906 that heralded the replacement of Liberal radicalism by a broad-based socialist movement: the election of John Barnes as Glasgow's first Labour MP and the foundation of *Forward*.

Barnes victory as a Labour candidate against a Liberal in the Hutchestown and Blackfriars constituency was not due to a revolt of the local branch of the United Irish League (UIL) against national policy in order to vote the Labour ticket. On the contrary, the decision to support Barnes was taken by the UIL executive in accordance with their policy to support pro-Irish Home Rule candidates and in general to work for the return of a Liberal Government. Usually the UIL only supported Labour candidates when they were endorsed through the electoral pact with the Liberals, but Scottish Liberals were firmly opposed to pacts with Labour candidates and in this case the Liberal candidate refused to support Home Rule. Barnes himself predicted that if he had the Irish vote he would win by 300 and he did in fact win by 310.[12] The 1906 victory for Labour in this constituency was, there-fore, caused by the failure of Scottish Liberalism both to adapt to Labour's presence and to maintain its commitment to Irish Home Rule, and it was this which created the space for the Labour movement in Glasgow.

The foundation of *Forward* demonstrates exactly the same failure of Liberal radicalism. While *Forward* was edited and partly owned by the ILP-er Tom Johnston it was, from its first edition in October 1906, regarded as a forum for all progressive opinion in Glasgow. *Forward* began its life as a paper committed to the reorganisation of progressive thought among ILP and Labour supporters and radical Liberals in a city where radical Liberalism and Gladstonianism remained strong. Indeed, the Young Scots Society, a group which included individuals heavily involved in establishing *Forward*, had been founded during the Boer War as an attempt to revive Gladstonian Liberalism in Glasgow. The fact that *Forward* did not remain a paper of all progressive thinkers but rapidly became the paper of labour and socialist thinkers after the unemployment crisis of 1908 suggests an inherent failure within Liberalism and progressivism *prior* to the First World War.[13]

This attempt to bring together all the elements of progressive politics around a new radical paper began well. Initially, *Forward* concentrated on settling accounts with current Liberalism. The case for Irish Home Rule was articulated through the Young Scots slogan of 'Home Rule all Round' and the demand for a new constitution while a policy of land nationalisation succeeded the single-tax position.

Forward also opened its pages to a lengthy debate about enfranchising women which finally settled on a policy of universal franchise. This demand for mass citizenship irrespective of gender or class was another vital break with a radicalism which envisaged that women should have the vote on the same terms as men, debarring the majority of the working class through the property-holding qualification.[14] At the same time *Forward* repudiated the single-tax philosophy of Henry George (and, therefore, the legacy of John Ferguson in Glasgow) during a debate over a Liberal Bill of 1907 which proposed social reforms through the creation of small-holdings. Other articles countered the liberal temperance argument that poverty was caused by the intemperance of working men. Through constant engagement with Liberalism *Forward* was vital both in the development of the Glasgow ILP's evolutionary municipal socialism and in building a bridge between radical and socialist opinion.

The reviving radicalism had no truck with the ideas of 'New Liberalism' so crucial in areas such as Lancashire. The philosophy expressed by Winston Churchill in the *The People's Rights* was alien to Glasgow socialists and their radical tradition. *Forward* rejected the concept of the 'people' as one that included landlords and armament manufacturers, crofters and workers. Conflict was still seen in the old Liberal, Gladstonian vision of the 'classes versus the masses', although the concept of class began to carry more socialist meaning within it. Hatred of the traditional enemy, the Dukes and the land owners, was expressed and surpassed in Johnston's diatribe against the Scottish landlords, *Our Noble Families*, serialised in *Forward*.

The concept of the 'nation' was subject to the same radical scrutiny and any proposals for social reform were always subject to the tests of which class paid and which class benefited; labour exchanges were seen as a fraud but old age pensions were accepted because they come out of taxes. In Glasgow it was not New Liberalism that elected Liberal MPs but old Liberalism: in 1906 it was the threat to free trade that secured the return of seven MPs and in 1910 it was the Peoples' Budget and the traditional hatred for the House of Lords.

But despite the strength of this old liberal sentiment among the labour movement, a strength that the young movement was able to build on, there could be no 'progressive' alliance. In Glasgow, Scottish Liberalism clearly separated itself from a rising Labour movement; in October 1906 the Scottish Council of the Liberal Party dissociated itself from 'a party the avowed object of which is the complete destruction of those principles of individual liberty for which Liberalism has always contended'.[15] By 1908 this anti-Labour current displayed their concern for individual liberty by ousting John Battersby from the Hutchestown and Blackfriars Liberal Association for his 'socialist sympathies'. Since the 1880s John Battersby had been the leading Liberal working man in Glasgow, and early leader of the Glasgow Trades Council. His summary dismissal by the young turks of Glasgow Liberalism showed how far from a 'progressive' alliance Scottish Liberalism was and strengthened those who believed that the way forward for progressivism was through Labour.

Battersby's easy dismissal in the midst of the 1908 unemployment crisis casts doubts on Howell's argument that one alternative might have been the development of a 'progressive' alliance in the 1890s. This incident took place after a *revival* of Gladstonian Liberalism during the Boer War led by the Young Scots Society. Ultimately the employment crisis of 1908 under a Liberal government would have raised questions in any progressive alliance over where its constituents' first loyalties lay: with the working-class movement or the Liberal government? It also casts doubts about what the revival of Scottish Liberalism actually meant by this period. If there was to be no support for working-class demands during the unemployment crisis of 1908 from any radical liberal quarter then the death of Liberalism comes *before* 1910–1914, where Dangerfield's thesis in *The Strange Death of Liberal England* places it.[16]

The doubts cast on Howell's 'alternative' are even greater if one considers the emergence of a group of Catholic Socialists in this period. John Wheatley was originally a member of the United Irish League. His transition from Irish nationalist and radical Liberal to the leading philosopher of evolutionary socialism in Glasgow occurred publicly through debating whether a Catholic could be a socialist, rather than merely supporting Labour, in the pages of the *Glasgow Observer*. In the summer of 1907 he debated with the Belgian Priest Father Puissant on the possibility of a Catholic being a socialist and clearly won.[17] In this debate Wheatley was addressing a nascent labour consciousness among the Irish electors. Many UIL members had canvassed enthusiastically for Barnes precisely *because* he was a Labour candidate. Although the leadership of the local UIL branch had been split before voting to support Barnes, the membership of the branch and of the more radical Wolfe Tone and Home Government branches turned out enthusiastically, despite Catholic Church support for the Liberal candidate.[18]

The Catholic Socialist Society was founded in October 1906 and within a year had 100 members. It was effectively a Catholic version of the ILP and had its own column, *Catholic Socialist Notes* in *Forward*, and a post office worker, William Reagan became its secretary.[19] The anti-landlord ideology of Johnston's *Forward*, an inheritance from nineteenth-century radical Liberalism, also fitted the beliefs of the Irish movement. One letter, replying to Father Puissant in support of Wheatley, asked:

> Does Father Puissant ever think of the thousands of Irish people that have been driven from Ireland by a privileged class i.e. the landlords. . . . When the Rev. Father proves to us that the Almighty God created this country for the dukes or landlords then we will cease being socialists.[20]

Any 'progressive' alliance formed in this or an earlier period would have faced major political splits, some along class lines within the Irish movement, some within the radical movement, and, with the economic crises of 1904 and 1908, among trade unionists and socialists. Instead of the development of 'progressivism', labour and socialist policies became an increasingly independent and established strand among working-class thought in Glasgow. In 1908 *Forward* reviewed the activities of Campbell-Bannerman's administration against the precepts of good Liberalism. It argued that the Liberals had created more peers per year than the Tories, that old age pensions had not yet been brought in, that France and Britain had floated a loan to save the Russian Duma and that John Morley had outlawed political movements in Indian universities. The same issue denounced British imperialism's role in Egypt.[21] At the same moment the *Glasgow Observer* was denouncing the Irish Council Bill of 1907 and the sixty-one Liberal MPs who voted for the Tory-introduced Convent Inspection Bill.[22] The most visible sign of this growing disillusionment with the Liberal Government was the huge May Day demonstration in 1908.[23]

The real turning point for the growth of the labour movement in Glasgow came with the slump of 1908 in which large sections of skilled workers were laid off. Of the 18,200 unemployed men in the census taken by the Glasgow Distress Committee, 38.4 per cent were skilled workers of which more than two thirds were from engineering and metal work.[24] The great shipbuilding centres of Govan and Patrick suffered as much if not more.[25] The unemployment of 1908 was significantly different from earlier recessions, notably that of 1904. In 1904 the skilled unions had raised and distributed money to support 'their' labourers. But in 1908 it was the skilled men themselves who required assistance. Craft union coffers were drained by the demand for 'idle' benefit whose very availability testified to the craftsman's expectation of high levels of job security. Thirty local craft trade unions paid benefit to 16.7 per cent of their combined membership of almost 25,000 men at a cost of £56,827. By contrast, the twelve general unions who did not pay idle benefit in 1908 had an unemployment rate of 30.8 per cent.[26] It was skilled working men and 'respectable' handymen who were going to the labour exchange, to the Charity Organisation Society and to the Lord Provost's Fund; half of the applicants to the fund were applying for the first time.[27] Alongside dockers, three-quarters of whom were out of work in Govan, the other unskilled workers who had suffered unemployment before, were new groups of workers being put on relief work or advised to emigrate. And this was happening under a *Liberal* government.

The first unemployment demonstration was actually organised for 25 January 1908, Burns night, by the SDF and sympathisers, with the exhortation 'Do honour to your national bard by demanding the right to work on his anniversary.' Left socialists continued to lead the unemployed agitation until the Glasgow Trades Council and the ILP established their Unemployed Committee. After that they took the role of leading the actual unemployed on day-time demonstrations and protests while the Unemployed Committee called out trade unions and socialist groups on city-wide demonstrations. The Unemployed Committee was therefore created and used to lead the more official side of the movement by the two organisations, the ILP and the Glasgow Trades Council, that would ultimately create the Glasgow Labour Party.[28] The 'Right to Work' demonstration organised by the ILP Unemployed Committee for 27 June 1908 brought thirty-five thousand protesters drawn from forty-three trades and unskilled workers on to the streets. The joiners carried the banner that they had carried on the 1832, 1866 and 1884 reform demonstrations led by Liberals with the slogans:

They are unworthy of freedom, who hope for it from hands other than their own.

We'll never swerve. We'll stand apart. We'll have our rights. We will be free.

But the speakers on the demonstration were not from a wider radical movement but from the Unemployed Committee, the trade unions, the trades council, the SDF and the ILP.

After 27 June an 'Agitation Committee' was formed among the unemployed themselves to organise weekly demonstrations. This was led by a former SDF member, John McAteer. In September 1908 1,000 rushed the city chambers arguing that the official labour movement had utterly failed. The following Wednesday the Agitation Committee led a demonstration to the Lord Provost's house that was broken up by the police. This led to the Unemployed Committee and the Agitation Committee holding a joint Glasgow Green demonstration on the following Sunday which Samuel Boal, the Protestant lecturer, attempted to break up, followed by a seven thousand strong demonstration in George Square and a week of local meetings.[30] But with McAteer arrested and demonstrations in the city square banned, the impetus was lost and the Unemployed Committee and the Agitation Committee amalgamated and assumed additional responsibilities for preparing for the 1908 municipal elections.

Here lies the problem that confronts Howell's other 'suppressed alternative' for socialist politics in Britain: would it have been possible for a more radical socialist tradition to have been maintained on the left of the Labour Party through the maintenance of an alliance between the SDF and the ILP? In Glasgow, the city that was to become the most theoretically sophisticated and well organised socialist industrial city in Britain, that possibility had already been lost before 1908, which was the first time that socialist politics took root widely among different groups of the working class in Glasgow. The labour movement in Glasgow had a place for the SDF, but it was a minor one and that was decided by character of the SDF itself.

Nationally, the British SDF was not only committed to a gradualist marxism that in its political electoral practice left little to choose between it and the ILP, it was also deeply sectarian and effectively 'owned' by a leadership that was incapable of incorporating more creative socialist talents or, indeed, any systematic orientation towards industrial work. This had led, first, to the creation of a Glasgow branch of William Morris's Socialist League and second to the creation, in 1903, of a British version of the American De Leon movement, the Socialist Labour Party, whose sole orientation was on industrial unionism and socialist education. In Glasgow the 1903 split decimated the SDF and led to the building of the SLP at the very point at which the labour representation tradition in Glasgow was convulsed by John Ferguson's single-tax philosophy. The SDF involvement in the unemployed agitation in 1908 signalled its re-emergence as a force in Glasgow politics; although led by an ex-SDF member it was in this agitation that John Maclean emerged as a leading SDF figure. However, this re-emergence of the SDF occurred too late to challenge the central leadership of the revitalised ILP in 'official' labour politics.

Further, the generally accepted argument that it was necessary to 'settle' the Irish question before labour politics could take off in the west of Scotland, can also be seen to be untrue. During the 1908 unemployment agitation Samuel Boal, having switched from anti-Catholic agitation to anti-Socialist, went on to organise Orangemen to break up socialist open-air meetings at their usual pitches. But this attempt was fought off by the combined efforts of all socialists, including the SLP. Samuel Boal was successful in organising in the east end of the city and in Whiteinch, and could mobilise a few thousand in these two areas but outside of these areas he was weak and even in those areas his meetings could be countered by several thousand socialists.[31] Moreover the existence of the Catholic Socialist Society, the growing importance of John Wheatley in the ILP, the sympathy for the Irish case in *Forward* all suggest that a Labour consciousness was developing among the city's Irish, and that socialists sympathetic to the Irish Nationalist cause were vital to this process.

By 1909 the Glasgow labour movement had attained the size it was to maintain until the First World War. In May 1909 thirty thousand turned out on the May Day demonstration, the same numbers that were reported in 1912 and 1913. It was these thirty thousand marchers, drawn from the four corners of the city, who carried the socialist vision in Glasgow. This vision was not one which abandoned ethical socialism for electoralism. In the *Forward* report of the 1909 May Day demonstration pride of place was given, not to the trade unionists and the ILP branches that marched, but to the Socialist Sunday Schools and to the international platform.

> Conspicuous in Sunday's procession appeared the large contingent from the Socialist Sunday Schools with banners and gaily decorated lorries. Bridgeton School deserves special mention. The finely decked maypole, with streamers flying attracted general attention. Hundreds of children marching all together must have stirred strange thoughts in the minds of otherwise smug spectators. At Platform No 5, a large concourse gathered. We commenced by singing that hopeful song 'Forward, the Day is Breaking', after which the clear voices of a boy and a girl were heard repeating the Text (Socialist Tenth Commandment) the words being taken up by all present.[32]

The report added that there were now eighteen Socialist Sunday schools in Glasgow teaching the meaning of socialism and the precepts of socialist service. The International platform had Lithuanians and Lettish comrades 'mainly from the mining districts' and speeches were made in Lithuanian, Lettish, German and Yiddish while the absence of 'Comrade "Petroff", the Russian propagandist', was regretted.

Significantly, Tom Johnston's participation in the Highland Land League as vice-president during the same year established labour's radical credentials. At the 'Budget' demonstration of 1909 forty thousand marched and one hundred thousand met on Glasgow Green including 'Liberals and socialist, Home Rulers, Irish and Scottish, co-operators and temperance reformers'.[33] The slogans were direct: 'Pass the Budget.' 'End the House of Lords.' 'Home Rule All Round.' This was the last great demonstration in the Liberal reform tradition of 1832, 1867 and 1884. Once again the joiners' 1832 banner was paraded. Three of the platforms were occupied by the labour movement and platform 11 was 'The Ladies Platform'.

P.F. Clarke's thesis that the revival of Liberalism in Lancashire was due to the 'New Liberalism' of Lloyd George's social reform programme, and that the Liberal Party could have become the party of progress, simply does not reflect what happened in Glasgow.[34] It was the appeal to the old Liberalism of free trade that won the 1906 election in Glasgow, and it was the appeal against the House of Lords and for the crofters that won the elections of 1910. But this old Liberalism could not tackle unemployment, poverty and industrial unrest as the 'workers' party.' It could create administrative solutions such as labour exchanges and national insurance systems that were *opposed* by Glasgow labour leaders in the Trades Council; it could not lead a progressive movement against unemployment and poverty.

The ILP that developed in Glasgow in the years 1906–10 was a party whose spirit and history does not fit the 'traditionalist' view; it was not atheoretical. In this period the ILP was busy defining itself against Liberalism and also against right-wing Catholicism, just as in the next four years its position would be defined against syndicalism and against labour representation as an end in itself. It was a principled pragmatic movement: pragmatic enough to work through every available labour movement institution, and sufficiently principled to try and infuse those institutions with ethical socialism.

If the 'contingent' growth thesis fails to explain developments between 1886 and 1906 then it also does not explain the history of the ILP in Glasgow after 1906. The 'suppressed' alternatives were clearly found wanting in the unemployment crisis of 1908. In many ways it was because the ILP in Glasgow was the heir to radicalism and ethical socialism that *it* grew rather than the sectarian socialist organisations. Electoral activity was the ILP route to the socialist land; and in a period where international socialism was dominated by the German Social Democratic Party only the SLP thought there was an *alternative* route to electoralism and their commitment to industrial unionism and socialist propaganda meant that they did not even participate in the unemployed agitation.

More than this, the ILP was also very active in all spheres of industrial work. Part of the Liberal tradition was a commitment to the 'separation of powers', especially the separation of the economy from the state. After 1906 there was a parallel division of labour operating in the Glasgow labour movement: the ILP began to run political intervention while the Glasgow Trades Council ran industrial intervention. Individual ILP-ers were very active in all elections, in their workplaces, in their trade unions and in the Glasgow Trades Council. When industrial unrest did erupt it was the ILP that was best positioned to grow through that eruption.

II

The predominance of skilled labour in Glasgow's shipbuilding and metal-working industries meant that the industrial unrest which swept across Britain between 1910 and 1914 did not radically restructure the city's labour movement. Those unskilled and semi-skilled workers who did strike were supported by other sections of the Glasgow labour movement and were loaned organisers by the Glasgow Trades Council, and those organisers were often ILP members. Strikes by dockers, seamen and mill women roused the sympathy and organising talents of the already well-organised socialists of Glasgow. But while this industrial unrest created an initial sympathy for syndicalist strategy the major political question in Glasgow remained the failings of the Labour Alliance in Parliament. Locally the main issue was how to consolidate the now thirty thousand strong socialist labour movement into a city-wide political force both at the municipal and parliamentary level. There were no parliamentary gains in the 1910 elections in Glasgow and Scottish Liberalism remained as hostile as ever to a pact with Labour. Gains were made in Scotland as a whole in the municipal elections in November 1910 including the election of John Wheatley for Shettleston by a margin of two votes. In the years before the First World War the Glasgow ILP began to develop minimum demands that all socialists who wished to stand as labour candidates had to accept. It was these minimum demands which formed the basis of a municipal socialist platform.

Many of these issues first emerged after the triennial elections to the Scottish School Boards in 1909 when over sixty labour and socialist representatives were elected. W. Martin Haddow had then convened a meeting of all the Labour and Socialist School Board members to discuss their core demand for the medical inspection and feeding of necessitous school children at which only fifteen of the elected representatives attended.[35] This low attendance was partly ascribed to the fact that some Labour candidates to the school boards had the support of the United Free Church in their candidature and were therefore not prepared to adopt a full socialist attitude to the school board. The shortcomings revealed by Haddow's post-election meeting provided the stimulus for the organisational changes in Glasgow's Labour politics which brought Wheatley, Maxton and Dollan, the central figures in city politics for the next two decades and more, to the fore.

Over the next three and a half years a central question for the Glasgow ILP was the construction and imposition of a united policy on all Labour and socialist candidates in local elections. In Glasgow the argument that the election of ILP candidates represented the election of socialists without socialism was inaccurate by 1913–14 when the policy was finally complete. Certainly the ILP did not place class struggle and the ownership of the means of production at the top of the agenda; theirs was an *evolutionary* socialism focused on the municipality.

Attempting to seize the initiative in March 1910 the old Workers' Election Committee began a series of conferences on joint action on all local public authorities. The Workers' Election Committee, after this initial conference attended by two hundred and fifty delegates, asked all interested parties to affiliate, a proposition opposed by the Glasgow Trades Council.[36] Instead, in January 1911 three delegates from the ILP met with three delegates from the trades council to formulate *their* centralised election policy.

In November 1911 the Labour group rose to ten on the city council, adding four new seats. This was followed in March 1912 by the formation of the Glasgow Central Labour Party to replace the earlier Worker' Election Committee. This meant that instead of a loose alliance of socialists, ILP-ers and trade unionists there was now a party machine with representation from the Women's Labour League, the Fabian Society, the Co-operative Defence Association, the Registration Committee, and the Govan, Partick, Hutchesontown, Central and Camlachie Labour Representation Committees. The central purpose of this machine was to increase the Labour group's power on the city council and to formulate and impose a more coherent united socialist policy beyond that of mere Labour representation.

In 1912 the Labour group lost three representatives in Glasgow but because the city boundaries were redrawn to include, Govan, Patrick and Shettleston it now numbered twelve, including John Wheatley.[37] These elections were notable as the first fought on clear party lines: the old 'independents' now stood as anti-socialist candidates. Deep divisions remained among the twelve Labour councillors with a bare majority following Wheatley's lead over municipal housing. In 1913 the Labour group spent the entire year working out its policies.

From February to July 1913 the Central Labour Party and the Labour group devised a full municipal socialist programme on local income tax, liquor, rates, corporation works, municipal banking, laundries, milk, coal distribution and bread.[38] Finally, the group turned to the question of housing. On 30 September Wheatley's contentious proposal to use the Tramway surplus to build municipal cottages to rent at £8 a year was endorsed and made the test of membership of the Labour group. Wheatley's leadership was confirmed by the 1913 municipal elections with 6 gains; by July 1914 the Labour group had 18 members.

By the beginning of the First World War, the Labour group on the city council had surpassed all the previous achievements of the old Workers' Electoral Committee. They had built their own Central Labour Party without the organised involvement of the SDF or the Irish movement. They had established a centralised municipal socialist strategy with the question of municipal housing being built on the tramway surplus as a test of candidature for the group: this test effectively excluded the old right-wing labour representation tradition. They had formed themselves as the political arm of the official labour movement alongside the trades council and in both ILP members took central leadership roles. *Forward*, under Tom Johnston, was the acknowledged paper of the entire Glasgow labour and socialist movement and through that paper their vision of municipal socialism took root within the Glasgow working class.

Further, the Labour group in Glasgow, led by Tom Johnston in *Forward* and John Wheatley in the Town Council, effectively surmounted the 1911–14 challenge from the left. That challenge was not only mounted from the SLP, SDF and the newly-formed BSP but also from its own members. For two years before 1910 Glasgow ILP members had been concerned with the poor political performance of the Labour Party. Debate on the viability of the 'Labour Alliance' as a road to socialism had surfaced in the ILP during 1908, following Victor Grayson's election as an independent socialist MP in 1907 and the poor showing of the Parliamentary Labour Party, but on three other issues the Glasgow ILP sided with the left: they wanted ILP candidates to describe themselves as 'socialist and labour', they were unhappy with the previous year's work of the Labour Party and they supported Victor Grayson's right to keep his salary.[39]

In 1910 Tom Johnston and John Maclean debated the continuation of the 'Labour Alliance' in *Forward*.[40] Johnston argued that because the Labour Party was the 'wage earners' party' it was the heir to the British marxist tradition and that the Labour alliance of ILP, trade unions, and Labour Party should continue. Against this Maclean argued for a united *Socialist* party. The foundation of the BSP was the final outcome of the 'Labour Alliance' debate; Grayson's call for a new socialist party was made in August 1911 and 219 delegates attended the Manchester Socialist Unity Conference. The conference was attended by 41 delegates from the ILP, 31 from Clarion Scouts, 48 from local socialist and representation committees, 12 from branches of the BSP that had already been formed and 86 from the SDP.[41]

The Glasgow ILP, with its municipal socialist policies and toleration of open disillusionment with the national Labour Party suffered only a handful of individual defectors to the BSP, including Harry McShane, but no loss of branches. Without any ILP branch defections, the BSP in Glasgow was based on the old SDP branches. By 1911 Glasgow was the strongest centre of the SDP outside London with six branches in the city and one in Govan and John Maclean's classes in marxist economics were attended by socialists from all organisations making him one of the best-known Marxists in the region. It was these old SDP branches that became the core of the BSP in Glasgow. Nationally, the BSP also came to be dominated by the old SDP leadership and the chance of a 'Socialist Alliance' alternative to the 'Labour Alliance' was lost.

Part of the original impetus towards a new 'Socialist Alliance' was given by the national strike wave of 1910–11. In Glasgow John Maclean attempted to construct a new policy of both industrial and political intervention for the BSP by opposing both the Labour Party's 'all politics' activities and the syndicalists' 'all industrial' activities. He used his column in *Justice* to put forward a combined socialist strategy; agitating on behalf of all strikers and advocating a municipal policy that was an amalgamation of John Wheatley's policy of subsidised municipal housing out of the Tramway Surplus and demand for higher wages for council employees.

But for rank-and-file Glasgow ILP members John Maclean's 'socialist' strategy must have sounded very similar to the municipal demands of left ILP leaders combined with the exhaustive activity of the ILP trade unionists in the Trades Council. Before the First World War even marxist socialists like John Maclean could not put forward a radically different socialist alternative because they still saw political struggle in similar terms to the evolutionary socialists: the workers would take power through parliament and the trade unions. The only alternative perspective in Glasgow was that of the SLP with their emphasis on industrial organisation at the work place.

In Glasgow it was the trades council that advised and established support committees and loaned organisers to groups of unskilled workers during their disputes. In the 1910 docks dispute when men were leaving the union because of executive indifference it was Trades Council organisers who re-enlisted the disaffected dockers.[42] Similarly, in 1911 Emmanuel Shinwell was seconded from the Trades Council to the Seamen's Union during their dispute. During the strike wave that involved women textile workers across Glasgow, Miss Dicks and Kate Maclean of the National Federation of Women Workers constantly reported back to the Trades Council, who organised demonstrations in their support.[43]

In this period the Trades Council became more than merely a 'parliament' for Glasgow trade unionists. While not interfering in the work of the skilled unions it supported the growth of unions among unskilled, semi-skilled and women workers. Through their work on the trades council some ILP-ers became prominent trade union organisers. However, those ILP men who were tradesmen in the engineering and shipyard works primarily worked through their own trade union organisation; skilled engineers were not among the council's leadership and many engineering union branches remained unaffiliated. The trades council, therefore, found difficulty in organising the semi-skilled men in engineering and it was this situation that the SLP exploited.

Outside the city, SLP members had attempted to organise semi-skilled engineering workers at Singers, Clydebank, from 1906 and used their factory base to attack 'political' labour organisations in the town for neglecting workers outside the craft societies. The Singers dispute of March 1910 became a test of 'industrial unionism' its defeat was a severe reverse for the SLP which reverted to being an almost exclusively propagandist party.

The foundations of non-skilled unionism in Glasgow were laid not by the dramas of the far left but by George Kerr, an ILP-er, who directed the Workers' Union's steady drive to organise semi-skilled engineering operatives. The Workers' Union grew from 5 Scottish branches with 250 members in 1911 to 40 branches with 9,000 members in 1914, the majority of whom were in Glasgow. It was the semi-skilled engineering workers in Weir's of Cathcart who led the way; a factory with the most organised factory committee before the First World War, led by the ILP-er James Messer.[44]

The only successful attempt at organising on an industry-wide basis before the First World War also began from the work of other ILP members on the Govan Trades Council under Harry Hopkins. Working under this traditional umbrella of local trade unionism they formed an industrial forum for workers in the shipyards and engineering works of Govan and Partick. The unofficial strike on 1 May 1913 in three Govan and three Partick shipyards for new piece rates indicated the strength of local organisation.[45] The 1915 rent strike centred in these two areas under the leadership of men and women who had been politically organised through the ILP housing committee and industrially through the Govan Trades Council.

In Glasgow it was also possible for left ILP-ers like Tom Johnston to win the political debate against syndicalism. Initially Johnston was sympathetic to Tom Mann's stress on industrial 'direct action'. But Mann's opposition to any political action after the 1911 Liverpool Transport Strike led to both right and left ILP-ers condemning syndicalism in the pages of *Forward*. Tom Johnston argued that the more municipal and state employees there were the more socialist voters there would be and pointed to the example of Germany where:[46] 'One man in every four is a state servant, and one man in every three (and the proportion steadily increasing) a voting socialist.'

The ILP in Glasgow had their own theory of working-class democracy. For the ILP socialist municipalities would provide local democracy in a socialist state. The idea that socialists only organised at the workplace simply did not fit the inherited democratic traditions and practices of Glasgow working men. The yearly May Day demonstrations, the organisation of children into Socialist Sunday Schools, the work of women ILP members in the Housing Committee which backed up the central tenet of municipal socialist strategy, the demand for £8 cottages, all point to the breadth of ILP involvement in all aspects of popular politics. Their commitment to democracy also led to their support for the women's suffrage campaign, which was also admired by John Maclean and the miners. Helen Crawfurd recalled that it was Tom Johnston who organised the defence at Mrs Parkhurst's meeting in Glasgow; he got dockers and navvies to throw out the students who were attempting to disrupt her meeting.[47]

Moreover, it was possible for Johnston, Wheatley *and* John Maclean to take an evolutionary view of municipal socialism. The labour movement in Glasgow did not face a hostile protestant working class. In Liverpool protestant sectarianism more or less dictated a syndicalist approach to organisation; socialist trade unionists pinned their hopes on the idea that one big strike wave would sweep aside both religious sectarianism and the political basis for Tory Democracy and Catholic Nationalism. This happened briefly during the 1911 Transport Strike but a year later all the old organisations were back in command.

Sir Edward Carson's visit to Glasgow during his Covenant campaign to save Ulster from Irish Home Rule illustrates how contained Orangeism was in Glasgow. In Glasgow the Orange Order never dominated the imagination of the leading sectors of the working class, the skilled working men of engineering and shipbuilding. The strength of the Orange Order in the west of Scotland lay in the coal and iron and steel towns around Glasgow. Forty thousand marched in the July 1912 Orange Walk in Coatbridge with special trains from Glasgow and from the neighbouring iron and steel towns.[48] The choice of Coatbridge, with its large Catholic population, was provocative, as was the meeting of the world Triennial Conference of the Imperial Grand Order in Glasgow eleven days later.

Yet when Sir Edward Carson arrived from Glasgow after his great Covenant meeting in Belfast and Liverpool, there were only 7,000 at his Glasgow meeting compared with the claimed 80,000 and 100,000 in Belfast and Liverpool.[44] The United Free Presbytery of Glasgow refused to discuss a resolution expressing opposition to the 'supremacy of the Papacy in any part of the Kingdom'.[50] The Friendly Societies of Glasgow's skilled men regularly marched alongside Hibernians, the Catholic Friendly Society, during annual celebrations. Indeed, a Labour baillie defended the corporation's toleration of the Council of the Imperial Grand Order because of 'the Friendly Society part of the Council's organisation'.[51] The churches, community bodies and unions of Glasgow's skilled working men remained aloof from Orange extremism, a phenomenon they associated with a lower class of workers.[52] It was precisely the weakness of religious sectarianism that allowed the ILP to build its broad-based support and conceive of political change as a gradual process.

In *Forward* Johnston advocated Home Rule by contrasting Ulster and Donegal where 'there is no exclusiveness, no boycotting, no sectarian strife of any kind'.[53] Indeed, Johnston's defence of the priests as 'sons of the peasantry' brought a protest from another Home Ruler who pointed out the anti-socialist role played by the priests and the Ancient Order of Hibernians.[54] There was considerable personal contact between Glasgow socialists and their counterparts in Belfast and Dublin. Johnston and Harry Hopkins were regular visitors to Ireland and James Connolly's *Forward* column from Belfast supported Larkin in his fight to unionise Dublin. Larkin never abandoned political action for direct action, both he and Connolly were municipal socialists as well as Home Rulers and proponents of unionisation. *Forward* was a natural ally for them during the Dublin lockout of 1913.

From September 1913 to January 1914 the Glasgow labour movement devoted its energy to organising the largest city collection for the Dublin lock-out outside of Dublin. *Forward* was the centre for the collection raising £3,000 in a period when unskilled men earned 21 shillings a week, and skilled men 35–42 shillings a week. Collections were taken at socialist branches, workshops, cinemas, football gates and in the street, quite apart from trade union branches. It was the ILP who organised demonstrations on behalf of the Dublin strikers, putting up speakers from the trades council, and had Larkin speak at their large Sunday night meetings.

The response of the Glasgow labour movement to the Dublin strike illustrates the breadth and depth of the activist network that was to sustain the movement during the war. The weekly Irish Subscription List which appeared in *Forward* for the duration of the lock-out contained several thousand individual names drawn from across the city and donors of workplaces from every industrial sector. Unorganised groups such as 'sorting clerks at the GPO' or 'a few clerks' or 'from a tailor's workshop' regularly sent donations. *Forward* also received over one thousand individual donations from people who were not active members of any Labour or socialist group. Above all, these collections demonstrate the vital coordinative role played by *Forward* and the centrality of the ILP to the Glasgow labour movement as a whole.

The Dublin subscription list also reveals a significant difference between the Glasgow and the Govan trades councils in their relationship to their constituent communities, workshops and union branches. While the Glasgow Trades Council encouraged its affiliates to organise donations, the Govan Trades Council, under Harry Hopkins of the ILP, organised collections directly. The Govan Trades Council's efforts soon included collections inside virtually every local shipyard and factory, and in the area's tenements, the United Free Church and at Ibrox, home of Rangers, the protestant football club.

The Govan workforce were thus led by a Trades Council with sophisticated leaders coordinating experienced activists with deep roots in the community.

In Glasgow before the First World War there was no clear demarcation between 'revolutionary' and 'reformist'. The demarcation was between the tiny group of industrial syndicalists and the rest. The majority shared similar policies and held joint demonstrations. Differences were beginning to emerge over electoralism versus direct action, but probably only Wheatley and Maclean understood how fundamental their differences were. By the end of 1913 Wheatley was the pre-eminent philosopher of evolutionary socialism while the marxist Maclean sought ways of reconciling industrial and political action. But in this search the ILP held all the cards. The unskilled workers of Glasgow were not organised by right-wing trade union leaders or by syndicalists but by ILP members.

The revolutionary socialists of Glasgow entered the war with a practice at variance with their theory alongside the ILP, an organisation whose practice was often identical to that of the BSP, only better executed. SLP propaganda could not make them an effective political force in a city where the political reformists were also strong trade unionists. The ILP *membership* was much more than merely the 'municipal' socialists of Glasgow; ILP-ers were firmly established in every nook and cranny of the labour movement. It was this quality which made it possible for Wheatley to have more influence on the leadership of the Clyde Workers' Committee than John Maclean during the First World War.

III

This chapter has placed the establishment of labour politics in Glasgow firmly before the First World War. It was not the war itself which created the Glasgow labour movement but the contradictions within liberalism prior to the war, demonstrated during the 1908 unemployment agitation. From 1908 to 1914 a new political confidence developed among the young labour movement which provided the basis for the shop stewards' movement, the development of rent strikes and the building of a peace movement on Clydeside during the war. The ILP in Glasgow was a 'left' ILP committed to the virtues of municipal socialism and trade unionism. They were 'ethical socialists' building Socialist Sunday Schools for young people and women's organisations for housing as vehicles to a better future for working people. There was no contradiction between their ethical socialism and electoralism. They also had a vision of the future socialist commonwealth composed of self-governing communities. It was a strong, deeply rooted labour and socialist movement that entered the Great War and the strongest and most deeply rooted organisation in the Glasgow working class was the Independent Labour Party.

Notes

1 David Howell, *British Workers and the Independent Labour Party 1888–1906* (Manchester University Press, Manchester, 1983), p. 391.
2 *Ibid.*, p. 393.
3 The SDF might pose the electoral exercise as an educational one, and the ILP as a reformist one but it was difficult to distinguish reformist and revolutionary before 1914, before the divisions created by the different responses to the First World War and the Bolshevik revolution led to lines being drawn between reformists and revolutionaries. See Harry McShane and Joan Smith, *No Mean Fighter* (Pluto, London, 1978), pp. 53–5.
4 *Ibid.*, pp. 26–7.
5 After the defeat of the 1913 Dublin strike both Larkin and Connolly mounted a municipal election campaign in Dublin in 1914, in order to confront the bosses of Dublin in another forum. It was the weakness of syndicalism that it did not mount such political confrontations; in Liverpool Tom Mann avoided the political confrontation with protestant conservatism. See Joan Smith, 'Labour Tradition in Glasgow and Liverpool', *History Workshop*, 17, 1984; and Joan Smith, 'Class, Social Structure and Sectarianism in Glasgow and Liverpool 1880–1914', in R.J. Morris (ed.), *Social Structure in Nineteenth Century British Cities* (Leicester University Press, Leicester, 1986).
6 Ian Hutchison, *A Political History of Scotland 1832–1924* (John Donald, Edinburgh, 1986), p. 192.
7 *Ibid.* and Smith, 'Class, Social Structure and Sectarianism', pp. 184–97.
8 I have argued elsewhere that the strength of radicalism in Glasgow actually contained the political consequences of sectarianism, see Smith, 'Labour Tradition' and 'Class, Social Structure and Sectarianism.'
9 Howell, *op. cit.*, pp. 171–2.
10 *Ibid.*
11 *Forward*, 10 November 1906.
12 *Glasgow Observer*, 31 March 1906.
13 P.F. Clarke, *Lancashire and the New Liberalism* (Cambridge University

Press, Cambridge, 1971) argues that Liberalism did not decline before the First World War because of the rise of New Liberalism.

14 *Forward*, October 1906–February 1907.

15 *Forward*, 27 October 1906.

16 George Dangerfield, *The Strange Death of Liberal England* (Constable, London, 1936).

17 The Catholic *Glasgow Observer* was the Catholic paper owned by Diamond which took a radical Liberal and Labour stance. He owned about twenty-two local papers and his editorial policy brought him into trouble in Liverpool which was more right-wing Catholic than he was.

18 *Glasgow Observer*, 13, 20 January, 31 March, 14 April 1906.

19 This was not because the Glasgow ILP was Protestant, rather because it was secularist: when the *Glasgow Observer* described *Forward* as 'our excellent little friend', it made it clear that it was opposed to Catholics being socialists while the socialists were working for secular education.

20 *Glasgow Observer*, 27 July 1907.

21 *Forward*, 18 April 1908, a reprint of an article which had already appeared in the Glasgow University Socialist Student magazine, *Socialist Torch*, 20 June 1908.

22 *Glasgow Observer*, 23 May 1907.

23 *Forward*, 18 April, 20 June, 9 May 1908.

24 *Glasgow Herald*, 1 September 1909.

25 *The Times*, September 1909, one of a series of articles on unemployment in major towns.

26 Glasgow Trades Council, Annual Report 1908–1909.

27 *Glasgow Herald*, 19 October 1908.

28 *Forward*, January 1908.

29 *Ibid.*, 4 July 1908.

30 *Forward*, September 1908 passim.

31 In response to the activities of the Agitation Committee the Unemployed Committee had begun to describe themselves as the committee of the 'genuine unemployed'. McAteer's committee was clearly as disillusioned with the SDF as the ILP and the trades council; *Forward*, September 1908 passim.

32 *Forward*, 8 May 1909.

33 *Glasgow Herald*, 20 September 1909.

34 See Clarke, *op. cit.*

35 *Forward*, 9 October 1909.

36 Glasgow Trades Council, Minutes, March 1910.

37 *Forward*, 9 November 1912, attributed the losses in the city to a united attack by the Catholic *Glasgow Observer*, the temperance groups and the 'anti-socialists'. Wheatley's election was bitterly opposed by the Irish

Nationalists. He was denounced in his own parish church and a Catholic mob burnt an effigy of him outside his own home in June; *ibid.*, 6 July 1912.

38 The programme also included the proposal for a municipal bank because the working class were only getting 2.5 per cent interest but the city was paying 5 per cent. The most debated item was municipal control of drink because of the strong temperance tradition. See Keith Middlemas, *The Clydesiders: A Left Wing Struggle for Parliamentary Power* (Hutchinson, London, 1965).

39 *Forward*, 17 April 1909.

40 *Ibid.*, August–September 1910.

41 *Justice*, 7 October 1911.

42 Glasgow Trades Council, Minutes, 9 November 1910.

43 *Ibid.*, see June, August 1910 for reports on the Neilston Mill girls' strike which initiated the strike wave and which had the Glasgow labour and socialist movement, under the banner of the Glasgow Trades Council, marching in their support.

44 For Weirs Works Committee before 1914, see McShane and Smith, *op. cit.*, p. 59, and Alan McKinlay, 'Employers and Skilled Workers in the Inter-War Depression: Engineering and Shipbuilding on Clydeside 1919–1939' (unpublished DPhil thesis, Oxford University, 1986), ch. 2.

45 *Justice*, 10 May 1913.

46 *Forward*, 8 June 1912.

47 Helen Crawfurd, Memoirs, unpublished mss, Marx Memorial Library; more generally, see Eleanor Gordon, *Women and the Labour Movement: Scotland 1850–1914* (Oxford University Press, Oxford, 1990), ch. 7.

48 *Glasgow Herald*, 8 July 1912.

49 *Ibid.*, 2 October 1912.

50 *Ibid.*, 2 October 1912. Similarly the Catholic Church in Glasgow had attempted to ban UIL branches using Church property for the Home Rule meetings. The churches in Glasgow were committed to retaining public order in the city and restraining sectarianism.

51 *Ibid.*, 17, 18 July 1912.

52 Callum Brown, *The Social History of Religion in Scotland since 1730* (Methuen, London, 1987).

53 *Forward*, 31 August 1912.

54 *Ibid.*, 21 September 1912.

FOUR

Work, culture and politics on 'Red Clydeside': the ILP during the First World War

Joseph Melling

The Independent Labour Party rarely figures in studies of the 'Red Clydeside' era in Scottish politics. Only in recent years have historians realised the critical role played by the party in the rise of socialist politics in Britain.[1] Much of this research has focused on the early years of the ILP and its contribution to the formation of the Labour Party, rather than its part in the transformation of popular politics during the decade 1914–24, when Labour surpassed the Liberals as a radical force in national politics.[2] In Glasgow and west Scotland the shift in popular support was particularly dramatic, culminating in the election of the famous 'Clydesider' MPs during 1922–4. The origins and character of political movements during these years is the subject of continuing debate, as is the significance of the war itself in the rise of socialist politics. Some of the most influential contributions to the debate have presented these years as a vital period of class struggle when marxist politics gave the Clyde workers a prospect of socialist revolution.[3] In contrast a number of recent studies of workers' campaigns have stressed the defensive conservatism of industrial labour and the extremely limited support enjoyed by such marxists as John Maclean. It is now almost conventional to dismiss the claims for class struggle on the Clyde and document the poverty of marxist politics.

This new orthodoxy on the myth of Red Clydeside leaves a number of unresolved questions about the evolution of popular politics in west Scotland. There remains the problem, for example, of Glasgow's rapid advance from its position as a bastion of Scottish Liberalism in 1914 to a city dominated by Labour politics in the 1920s. Other areas of Britain shared in Labour's forward march but few could claim comparison with the parliamentary and municipal successes recorded in west Scotland during the inter-war years.[4] Further questions can be posed about the contribution of the different socialist parties to the making of

Clydeside politics and the content of Scottish socialism. This requires some review of the changing relationship between constitutional and revolutionary politics. The wartime conflicts have been variously seen as a stage in the evolution of the Labour Party, and as a vital transition from the immature politics of syndicalism to the rise of a modern Communist Party. Writers who stress the role of direct action in class struggle have often dismissed the progress of Labour as the expression of a passive 'Labourism'. This has obscured the importance of the war in the changing composition of the Labour coalition and the dynamic role of the ILP. Yet it was the ILP which responded to the opportunities provided in the First World War and in doing so provided a major impetus towards socialism in Scotland. To explain the success of the party and its relative neglect in the major studies of the period, we can briefly review the state of the debate on the Clydeside politics in the early twentieth century.

<h1 style="text-align:center">I</h1>

The conflicts which swept industrial Clydeside in the early years of the twentieth century have been seen as the most vivid expression of renewed class struggle throughout British society. In a formidable collection of studies, marxist historians detailed the transition from a stable Liberal order in the mid-Victorian decades to the sharp class politics of the 1914–18 war.[6] Many historians locate the origins of this new class politics to changes in the world of capitalist production. The pressure on profits and the progress of new technologies threatened the position of the skilled worker, pushing artisans to adopt radical policies. Secondly, the growth of new forms of trade unionism and the internal reform of the older craft societies served to weaken sectional divisions within the working class and permit collective consciousness. Thirdly, the growing conflicts in industry and society weakened the hold of Liberal and Labourist values, whilst socialist and syndicalist ideas spread rapidly before 1914.[7] The emphasis on workplace skill was confirmed by the subsequent generation of research on the labour process during the 1970s which restored the workplace to a central place in class politics.[8]

This emphasis on industrial production and workplace skills can be also found in James Hinton's seminal study of class conflict on the Clyde during these years.[9] Hinton portrays the industrial struggles of the war years as a confrontation between organised workers and the forces of capitalism. In the process the skilled engineering trades moved from a narrow craft sectionalism to the threshold of class leadership as they fought the capitalist state from their powerful position on the shopfloor of the munitions workshops. The militant workers were led by a brilliant group of radical shop stewards, who received their political education from the small syndicalist and socialist parties that flourished in pre-War Glasgow. This enabled them to analyse the nature of the technical changes that were transforming the workplace before 1914 and to oppose the collaborationist policies of the older union leaders. From their origins as syndicalists and revolutionaries, the stewards formed the Clyde Workers' Committee (CWC) to lead the rank-and-file revolt against the British state and went on to help found the Communist Party after the war.[10]

The strength of Hinton's work is his explanation of the 'Red Clydeside' years as important episodes in the remaking of class politics in Britain. The resistance to wartime dilution in Glasgow and the internal conflicts within the workforce and unions are presented as part of the natural politics of class struggle. Hinton's account also stresses the critical role of the revolutionary party in class leadership. Both the syndicalist Socialist Labour Party and the marxist British Socialist Party influenced the engineering shop stewards at vital moments in their campaigns against new technologies and scientific management. The crushing of the workers' challenge to capitalism followed the confrontation between a ruthless state and a workforce weakened by internal divisions and a lack of political vision. Hinton suggests that the defeat of the militant rank and file was also due, in part, to the opportunistic tactics of ILP-ers such as David Kirkwood under the shadow of John Wheatley. In the longer term, the triumph of the Labour Party and the restoration of a pragmatic 'Labourism' in the 1920s marked the decline of revolutionary class politics.[11]

This study of class war on the Clyde has become the focus of vigorous debate in recent years, as liberal historians have challenged marxist interpretations of popular politics. These historians reject the explanation of political choice in terms of economic determination and argue for the autonomy of state institutions from class power.[12] Hinton's account of Clydeside socialism has been criticised in these terms by writers such as McLean and Reid.[13] McLean argues that workplace resistance to the government's production policies was

85

sustained by the profound conservatism amongst the craftsmen in the engineering plants. The craft unions had to manage the reactionary prejudices of their members whilst containing the challenge from small groups of political activists. They lost control when the CWC militants exploited the defensive instincts of the Scottish engineers to damage the government's dilution programme, but as soon as the Ministry of Munitions isolated the radicals in early 1916 the movement collapsed.[14]

McLean argues that the legacy of workplace unrest was a narrow sectionalism that weakened the political development of the labour movement and inhibited the Labour Party in the post-war period. McLean's evidence shows that the British state, far from acting as a repressive arm of industrial capitalism, was a complex ensemble of liberal institutions that responded in a pragmatic way to competing interests and immediate problems.[15] The analysis offered by contemporary marxists was based on a complete misunderstanding – or misrepresentation – of the political responses of the liberal state. More immediately the impact of workplace sectionalism was to divide the workforce and destroy Labour's prospects. It was only after the decline of industrial conflict and religious sectarianism in the 1920s that Labour found a secure constituency of support in Glasgow.[16] The success of the Labour Party's housing and rents crusade during the war years gave it a far stronger base of support than the bitter disputes over industrial skills and wages. The clear intention of McLean's work is to reveal a sharp break between wartime producers' struggles and the rise of Labour as a modern political party.

This attack on Hinton's account succeeded in damaging the marxist interpretation of 'Red Clydeside' but not in destroying it. McLean confirms Hinton's analysis of craft sectionalism in the engineering shops but argues that such conservative attitudes were dominant amongst skilled workers throughout the war years. The recent work of Reid is designed to complete the destruction of the marxist interpretation of Clydeside by showing that Hinton misunderstood the basic nature of workplace change and trade union politics.[17] Much of Reid's case is based not on a critical review of the engineering trades but on an argument that Clydeside's massive shipbuilding yards saw a very different pattern of innovation and unrest at this time. The shipyard trades were not diluted by the introduction of female labour and proved very successful in defending job controls as well as extracting concessions from the government.[18] One reason for the triumph of craft regulation on the waterfront was the strength of the shipyards' campaign against the unpopular 'leaving certificates' imposed under the 1915 Munitions Act. So effective were the conservative craft societies in their opposition to the employers and the state that the government was persuaded to radically amend the controversial legislation and respond seriously to union complaints.

Reid supports McLean's argument that Clydeside unionists were primarily concerned with wages and working conditions, which gave the shop stewards their key function in the workplace. Frictions did arise between permanent officials and shopfloor activists in engineering, concedes Reid, though the experience of the shipyards shows that this experience was not shared by the shipbuilding trades. There was no general revolt of the rank and file against the leadership.[19] The very success of official unionism in its dealings with the wartime government demonstrated that sympathetic reforms could be secured within the existing system of government. Ministers and civil servants resisted the demands of leading employers for industrial conscription and favoured the union side from the outset.[20] The government was encouraged in its pro-labour policies by public and legal opinion, as became apparent during the deportation controversy of 1916.[21]

From recent accounts of war on the Clyde there emerges a radically different view of the working-class unrest. These historians argue for a dismantling of the popular and political mythologies of the Red Clyde. Central to the whole analysis is a positive view of the British state. Rather than viewing the state as an agency of capitalist repression, these writers argue that a class definition of political institutions is untenable and that the popular experience of benign government was one of the most important influences in the support for Labour socialism after 1918. Wartime collectivism laid the foundations of post-war Labour socialism.[22]

The value of this debate lies in the recognition now given to the significance of radical reformist, rather than revolutionary, politics in the rise of Scottish socialism. In response to these criticisms, historians such as Joan Smith have sophisticated the marxist interpretation of class politics in Glasgow and explained the success of Labour in terms of the specific occupational and political cultures of west Scotland rather than workplace conflicts.[23] Other writers have stressed the limitations of explanations which regard political action as the outcome of workplace struggle. Trade unions are now more commonly depicted as fortresses of craft and gender sectionalism, retaining an economistic or 'Labourist' strategy for defending their members against innovations.[24] Such narrow sectionalism served to obstruct the progress of Labour politics, which depended on non-work struggles by women and the unskilled to advance its cause.[25] These local struggles helped the Labour Party to break away from the ideology of Labourism in the early twentieth century, though the rebuilding of union defences in the inter-war years restricted this advance.

The debate has also contributed to a broader discussion of class politics in the nineteenth and twentieth centuries. The issues raised by Joan Smith in her study of Scottish workers correspond to the debate on Chartism and the continuities between a rationalist and libertarian tradition amongst handicraft artisans and the discourse of class in Victorian Britain.[26] In Joan Smith's Glasgow the decisive influence in the rise of Labour was the pre-existence of a radical libertarian culture that attracted artisan support. The transition from Liberal to Labour politics is explained in terms of a gradual evolution as Liberalism steadily declined from the 1880s. It was not until the 1920s that the disintegration was complete and Labour assumed its dominant position.[27] This trajectory carried a large section of the skilled workforce towards Labour, but at a critical moment during the war a space opened for a revolutionary socialist challenge to the employers and the state. With the defeat of the revolutionary shop stewards the space closed and Labourism ruled supreme.

(This view of Labour's progress echoed McLean's argument that it was only in the 1920s that industrial and religious divisions were finally overcome and the party's future secured) There also remain some basic conflicts of interpretation in these studies. The debates turn on three key areas of Clydeside politics: firstly, the politics of production in the industrial workplace; secondly, the part played by non-work campaigns and cultures in the making of Labour politics; and thirdly, the role of the British state in the handling of wartime unrest. The attitudes of skilled workers to new technologies and other sections of the labour force remains a matter of debate. Similarly, the trade unions are variously depicted as conservative bureaucracies which upheld Labourism, and as powerful defenders of craft privileges whose leaders were able to colonise the British state.[28] The significance of campaigns outside industry in the building of a Labour constituency is widely acknowledged, but the emphasis placed on different movements and their political content is in dispute. Historians agree, for example, that the great rent struggles of 1915 were completely distinct from the shopfloor protest over dilution, though McLean sees the housing unrest as a step towards constitutional reform whilst Foster implies it was part of the class conflict inspired by workplace issues.[29] Views of the state similarly range from a marxist analysis of capitalist hegemony and a reconstitution of the 'power bloc' in the early twentieth century, to liberal portraits of the impartial state which sought to balance interests and protect its own integrity.[30]

This essay will argue that the existing debate on the wartime unrest does not provide a satisfactory explanation of the rise of socialist politics in west Scotland. The terms of that debate actually serve to obscure some of the more salient features of these struggles, including the critical role of the ILP in orchestrating the various campaigns of protest. The efforts of historians to establish a primacy for a particular kind of activity in the making of workers' politics has focused attention on the industrial workplace and the formal institutions of the state. In the course of this discussion a vital distinction between social power and formal politics has been lost. It is essential to examine work, culture and politics in terms of the social relations of British capitalism rather than to focus exclusively on the formal institutions of society. The distribution of resources and power provides the basis for political engagement. The following section outlines an alternative analysis of Scottish society on the outbreak of war in 1914 and the sources of power and authority in urban Clydeside.

II

Industrial capitalism dominated west Scotland in the years before the First World War. Clydeside employers had taken advantage of the low wages and poor organisation of local ironworkers to establish a comparative advantage over other shipbuilding rivers in the mid-nineteenth century. By 1914 this situation had changed as union organisation and wage demands forced up the price of labour along the river. Within the space of a few decades the shipyard and engineering trades had built up powerful craft fraternities and customary controls over production. In these particular conditions the contract of employment and the formal control of labour could not secure effective levels of output. Although the owner's possession of the plant and his legal right to control production were undisputed, neither gave the employer a sufficient power to manage labour.[31] British industry relied on three further policies to enforce its command of the workforce: firstly, the assertion of basic management prerogatives as the foundation of all efficient production; secondly, the defence of a clear hierarchy of authority which entailed the work supervisor acting as the defender of the employers' interests; and thirdly, organised action to enforce these rights against intransigent workers. At moments of serious unrest, from the 1850s to the 1920s, industrial capitalism rallied around the doctrine of the 'right to manage'.

Clydeside employers combined to impose their authority on the Amalgamated Society of Engineers (ASE) as the major opponent of their policies in the great lockout of 1897–8, inflicting a serious defeat on the craftsmen. At these critical moments the employers' leaders mobilised the different firms against the workforce by presenting the struggle as one of defending their authority over production. This appeal had a powerful ideological force as well as providing an issue of principle on which to attack the unions. It also enabled the local firms to argue that their inability to withstand market competition was the result of union restrictions. In fact, there were a range of issues on which employers and labour were in conflict before 1914, as leading firms tried to renovate their technologies and achieve more flexibility in the use of labour. These disputes affected shipbuilding as well as engineering plants and culminated in a number of bitter disputes over the control of the labour market and the physical supervision of output by trade foremen. The masters had asserted their right to manage in 1898 but the practical challenges to the authority of the employer remained a prominent feature of Clydeside industry before 1914. The political implications of capitalist authority were usually submerged beneath the practical issues at dispute, but they had not been resolved by the victory of 1898.

A consequence of the continued struggle over the control of labour was the development of fresh strategies by the institutions of capital and labour. Unions such as the ASE were forced to accept centralised bargaining and to respond to the changing environment of the pre-war years. The growth of procedures restricted the autonomy of the district membership and encouraged the appointment of shop stewards to deal with shopfloor complaints and liaise with local officials. These reforms were introduced by the engineering unions at a time of intense debate amongst the active membership on the question of internal democracy.[32] The 'forward' section of such unions included ILP socialists as well as Scottish syndicalists.

It was the practical experience of increased workloads and the threat of deskilling technologies that gave these union progressives a strong base of support on Clydeside. The late, rapid unionisation of the region had profound consequences for the region's labour organisations. Local employers remained bitter opponents of the unions down to the war, often insisting on their personal understanding of the workforce and resenting the intrusion of officials. The local workers looked to the district officials rather than the national executive as the real leaders of the Clyde trades. The late arrival of strong unionism also explains the influence of the distinct trades councils which co-ordinated the policy of the various societies in different parts of west Scotland.[33]

In the years before the outbreak of war, employers and unions fought a series of battles over the control of work as the engineering and shipbuilding firms pressed forward with policies to increase output. Although the engineering lockout gave the federated firms a strategic advantage after 1898 the craft trades were able to defend local customs and practices against management policies, especially in the shipyards where the skilled workers clung tenaciously to their areas of work. The imposition of central agreements did not prevent the persistence of conflicts over district autonomy and working practices. This was particularly true of the shipyards where the unions joined the engineers in a bitter campaign of resistance to the introduction of discharge notes before the war. The failure of the employers to impose these certificates on the workforce and the difficulties they faced when trying to tighten the supervision of work is clear evidence of the resilience of craft autonomy.[34] In the aftermath of the fiasco over the leaving certificates, the local shipyard firms reached an informal agreement with the unions to monitor the shipyard workers and weed out acknowledged 'bad workmen' and the firms in return virtually conceded a closed shop for the craftsmen.[35] This form of institutional policing by the unions did not mean the end of workplace autonomy. In fact, the societies were so influential because they could claim to

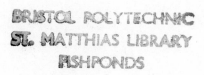

restrain the frictions on the shopfloor, whilst ensuring that autonomy was protected through union membership. This was particularly true of the shipyards, with their primitive conditions of work and strong district identities, rather than the more routinised and disciplined pattern of work and bargaining in the engineering trades.

In the struggles of the pre-war years the introduction of new technology and 'American' techniques were fiercely contested on the Clyde. Amongst the ASE members activists such as Frank Rose, another ILP-er, warned of the dangers of the 'machine monster' and the destruction of the craftsman. A celebrated strike at the Singer works in Clydebank gave local syndicalists in the Socialist Labour Party an opportunity to denounce 'American' management and win support for shopfloor confrontation. In the engineering trades the older generation of Labour activists, such as George Barnes, found themselves forced on the defensive by craft unrest and political activists who included ILP-ers as well as the SLP. The new radicals were prominent in the official district committees of the unions as well as in the 'unofficial' capacity of shop stewards and they could only hope for support in devising practical policies for the Clyde workers. The nature of workplace politics was not determined simply by the conditions of production or by the internal debates of the unions, but by the practical experience of workers who retained personal convictions about the ways in which their rights could be defended. Their acceptance of employer authority was conditional on some reciprocal recognition of these values. Before 1914 the bitter contest between the rights of management and the customs of labour focused attention on the basic principle of authority and persuaded some firms that a reassertion of capitalist prerogatives was needed.

The conflict over these basic principles shows the importance of cultural values in industrial society. For culture not only consisted of a mass of retained values which people used to understand their world, but was a resource that formed part of the economic and social relations of urban Scotland. Working people had access to fewer cultural as well as material resources in pre-war Glasgow, with a lifestyle dominated by the laborious working day. The physical structure of the tenement city enclosed working-class families within a social division of labour and formed the main space for female labour. The wives of skilled workers were seldom employed outside the home after childbirth and spent their lives struggling to maintain the living standards of the family. The practical divisions of labour formed the basis of popular culture on the Clyde: the nature of work and the reliance on hand techniques to construct massive producer goods in the shipyards and engine shops gave the Scottish industries their craft pride and primitive masculinity. Practical judgement and personal knowledge were vital to the working of the craft fraternity: individual foremen had to rely on trade rules and their own experience in hiring or firing the tradesman. Women were almost totally excluded from this world and the public bars where workmen swapped their stories and their experiences. Large numbers of Glasgow women did find paid work in a variety of occupations before 1914, but the bulk of married mothers found their own collective experience in the tenement, the communal washing house and the purchase of goods and services for the family.

These practical relationships not only fixed the access to the labour market for Glasgow people but largely determined the kind of cultural resources which they could enjoy. The institutions of Scottish society, including the religious, legal and political agencies, confirmed this unequal access. Local tradesmen could expect to take an active part in the various bodies they joined. Women were usually deprived of the recognition that would reward their contribution. Some historians have argued that this resulted in the narrow economism of the male unions and the radical character of women's campaigns at this period. In her illuminating study of working-class culture in Glasgow, Joan Smith has emphasised the intellectual and political loyalties of the skilled artisans in the decline of religious sectarianism and the rise of Labour.[36] The difficulty with such arguments is that they explain political developments in terms of the logic of the labour market and the institutions of the skilled workers. The experience of Glasgow suggests that the source of popular politics were extremely wide before 1914, and that the growth of a socialist constituency resulted from a series of campaigns that involved practical issues of production and consumption as well as moral challenges to existing authority.

These campaigns included the range of local struggles on the provision of services to school children and the attempts to restrict the influence of victuallers and spirit dealers in the city. Activists within the local Co-operatives pushed for improved standards of service and public criticism of the private dealers who adulterated food or sold spirits with groceries. The ILP engaged in the debates over health and mortality amongst children, as well as pressing for better standards of inspection and school meals in such burghs as Govan. Labour made its dramatic intervention before 1914 on the housing front by proposing the scheme of basic cottages at cheap rents financed by the surpluses from municipal services, attacking their opponents as the landlords' friends. It was John Wheatley who realised that Glasgow socialists were making a serious bid for moral authority in the working-class neighbourhoods and moved quickly to reassure the Catholic Church that its position was not threatened by the spread of socialism. In fact, the ILP's moral crusade on issues such as spirit dealing and its appeal for temperance amongst its supporters did present a code of personal and political values distinct from those of the churches.

On the eve of the war the ILP could not claim a decisive influence in producers' or consumers' associations in west Scotland. Its numerical and political strength was slight compared to that of the Liberals and it found it difficult to break through in municipal elections.[37] Yet its achievement could clearly be seen in the presence of a network of activists who led a number of key organisations in the Clyde area. But the ILP's open structure and its recognition of distinct interests gave the party an influence well beyond its numbers on the outbreak of war. The war itself gave the ILP an opportunity to extend this influence when the institutions of Liberalism were drawn into a profound crisis of authority by conflicts at the workplace and in Scottish society. It was the capacity of the ILP to adapt to this situation and to translate its doctrines into practical demands that explains its remarkable success during the war.

III

The events which placed Clydeside at the centre of national politics had their origins in the massive demand for wartime munitions. The Clyde valley soon became a vital source of military supplies for the British government and within a year of the outbreak of war, unrest on the Clyde forced the Liberal Government to reconsider its whole strategy for the war economy. It was this vital role in the manufacture of munitions that explains the extraordinary bargaining power of the Scottish workers throughout the war years. The engineering and shipbuilding trades discovered this as early as February 1915, when they demanded serious treatment of the engineers' wage claim. Faced with the threat to essential supplies, the military departments and the civilian Cabinet agreed that the employers could not be left to conduct industrial warfare outside the control of the state. It was also clear that the demand for skilled workers was such that their position in the labour market was so formidable that the subordination of craftsmen to the employers' discipline could not be guaranteed.

This was the context for the negotiation of new labour market controls between government and organised labour in the spring and summer of 1915. The problems of maintaining employers' prerogatives at the workplace whilst manufacturing consent for government policy within the unions, explains the complicated series of struggles that took place during 1915 and the early months of 1916. Beneath the turmoil of unrest it is possible to trace the growth of a political consciousness amongst industrial workers on the Clyde. The expression of this consciousness was shaped by the established pattern of industrial activism, including the tensions between rival stewards and officials in the Clyde district. More important than these frictions, however, was the move towards broad campaigns between separate unions in the autumn of 1915. The ILP-ers were to play a critical role in orchestrating this movement.

The outbreak of a major strike in support of the engineering unions' wage demand in early 1915 was the first real sign that the Scottish metalworkers were a force to be reckoned with. Most historians have treated these incidents as a dress rehearsal for the more serious confrontation over dilution. The Clyde Labour Witholding Committee was formed amongst the workers in the radical general engineering shops of Glasgow – later to surface as the celebrated CWC. The tensions between ASE officials and rank-and-file workers, already apparent in the February unrest, have also been stressed as a key to the leadership of the militant workers by 'unofficial' shop stewards.[38] The model of workplace unrest outlined in such studies is open to criticism, particularly as west Scotland possessed a complex regional economy with a number of distinct industrial centres and an enormous range of occupational skills. It is apparent that the geography and the chronology of the 1915 struggles are more complex than earlier historians appreciated. The internal politics of the leading trade unions are also more complicated than a simple dichotomy of officials and shop stewards, or even craft conservatives and radicals.

In the February struggle the ASE was only the leader amongst a host of unions which organised tradesmen in the metalworking plants on the Clyde. Frustration with the wage freeze which had been in force since 1912 was aggravated by the rising cost of living and the loss of craftsmen to the armed forces in the early months of war. Within the ASE there continued a fierce debate on the best strategies for defending the union, which had formed the background to the rise and fall of George Barnes as union secretary before the war.[40] Struggles between 'forward' and moderate factions were apparent amongst the officials as well as in the district committee of the union, complicated in west Scotland by the prominence of the ASE on the various trades councils and the jealousies which existed between the rival unions. These influences can be seen in the demands of the February strike. The ASE demanded a wage advance of 2d an hour on three grounds: there was an erosion of pay since the 1912 settlement which meant a substantial increase was needed; the engineers faced rising prices and living costs as a result of the war; and the firms themselves were enjoying 'a rich harvest' from lucrative war contracts. These demands were dismissed by the engineering and shipbuilding firms – both sectors employed large numbers of engineers – who suggested that the workers should take advantage of piecework payments and unlimited overtime to increase their earnings.[41]

After a wave of strikes affected some of the major industrial plants the government intervened and forced the employers to seek a compromise settlement with the tradesmen. The partial victory of the workers was secured by the participation of a wide range of trades and occupations besides those engaged in general engineering, including brassmoulders such as William Gallacher, and the chronology of the strike does not reveal a clear divide between 'radical' engineering plants and the more 'craft conservative' specialist workshops. If anything, there was a cumulative strike movement which involved a wide range of specialist and general engineering works, ancillary workers as well as the recognised artisans of the engineering trades.[42] The February conflict did expose important divisions between some union officials and the more forward sections of the membership. Local ASE officials such as Bunton and Brodie were extremely apologetic about the aggressive actions of the men, suggesting to the employers that they had 'exhausted every means in their power' to get the men to continue working overtime, and later to persuade them to return to work.[43] Bunton suggested that the District Committee of the ASE 'entirely disapproved of the action of men' and ordered them to return to their benches in February 1915, supported by the national executive of the union.[44]

These comments suggest that there were a number of tensions within the ranks of unions such as the ASE. Firstly, there were conflicts between moderate officials and stewards on one side and the progressives who included members of the ILP, SLP and BSP. Secondly, there were the different trades and the separate centres, which had their own views. Thirdly, the national executive of the unions was trying to hold the membership behind a single line of policy, whilst manipulating the unrest to push the government into concessions. The outcome of the February unrest seems to have been direct action by the radicals and a challenge to moderate officials on the District Committee of the ASE. Faced with this situation the government came to rely increasingly on private information supplied by moderate officials, whilst the employers were angry to find that the government was more interested in solving strikes by arbitration rather than crushing the unions.

Given the frictions within the unions, the most remarkable feature of the February strikes was the capacity of the different trades to co-operate in a general wages campaign against their employers. The celebrated Labour Witholding Committee seems to have functioned mainly as a co-ordinating group for active shop stewards, striving to hold the strike campaign together in the face of employer hostility. With the settlement of the dispute by Askwith the Committee faded out of existence.[45] In presenting their case the unions also condemned the profiteering activities of the employers, denying to the firms the moral high ground in the controversy over shortages of shells. This attack on excessive profits was to be a recurring theme in the arguments of the unions and marked the first step in the move against war capitalism.

An immediate result of the unrest was the efforts of the government, and more particularly Lloyd George, to devise a more rigorous munitions policy. The creation of a new Ministry of Munitions was part of a process in which the state itself was reconstituted through a series of reforms which transformed the peacetime institutions into agencies capable of directing a massive military effort. The extent to which industrial interests influenced the creation and conduct of the new ministries is open to debate, but the new powers of the state were undeniable.[46] Against this background of conflict on the floor of industry, there was a bigger struggle for the control of munitions production within government itself during the first half of 1915, as the military departments sought to retain their influence over munitions contracts. The War Office and Admiralty retained a close connection with the major arms suppliers in 1914–15, whilst adding new business advisers such as Booth to their staff of consultants. The military personnel lacked the expertise in industrial relations that had been accumulated at the Board of Trade in the Edwardian years, and to meet the deficiency the War Office introduced a network of Armaments Committees where the employers, unions and local officials could resolve production problems in the key munitions areas.[47]

The failure of this policy can be traced to the serious frictions between employers and unions over the question of production prerogatives. Both sides feared the intrusion of the state into industry and the opportunities which it gave their opponents to extend control of the workplace. Since the military departments had little practical understanding of the existing rules of the game in collective bargaining, they found the February strikes bewildering. This confusion allowed Lloyd George a clear advantage as negotiations were opened up with the unions for a new agreement on output.[48] The real importance of the new Munitions Ministry lay in the civilian control of military production. With the defeat of the armed services departments it was clear that there would be no early moves to industrial or military conscription. Industrialists soon discovered that they had gambled on the wrong side in backing the War Office and the Admiralty, whilst also failing to meet the delivery dates for lucrative military contracts.[49] Their access to the Munitions Ministry was by invitation only. Aggressive Clydeside masters such as W.D. Weir gained influence by brutal determination but the new ministry was never merely a pliant tool of business interests.[50]

The key to Lloyd George's political strategy was his belief in business methods and political bargaining. The minister was convinced that he could recruit business talents to run the war machine, whilst relying on his own political skills and the experience of his officials to 'square the interests' with the unions.[51] Throughout the negotiations of 1915–16 the Liberals equated the prerogatives of business with the pursuit of efficiency in producing munitions, whilst conceding to the unions a recognised role as the representatives of labour interests. By drawing union leaders into a complex web of undertakings, the Munitions Ministry succeeded in frustrating the employers and increasing suspicion of national agreements amongst the branch membership of the unions. The majority of firms relied on their provincial associations to deal with government and the limits of their political skills in the new conditions of war production were severely exposed in the negotiations for the introduction of new Munitions legislation. Their frustrations were apparent at Whitehall but Lloyd George believed he could meet their demand for discipline without involving them in the bargaining over the legislation. The result was the introduction of serious restrictions on the movement of labour approved by union leaders in July 1915, which gave the local industrialists legal sanctions against intransigent workers. The scene was set for a crisis in Clydeside industry.[52]

The Clyde shipbuilders seized on the new Act not only to destroy the wartime bargaining power of labour but also to infringe the pre-war customs of the shipyard trades. These attacks on the Clyde craftsmen had a more dramatic impact in the yards, where the autonomy of the workers had been secured by a delicate balance of practical freedoms and union discipline before the war. The engineering industry was more familiar with centralised procedures and management control of technology, with the result that the unions were anxious to reach a detailed agreement with government than to allow local struggles to challenge management prerogatives.[53] These differences in structure and practice help to explain the prominence of the shipyards in the bitter disputes over the Munitions Act. The origins of the struggles were frequently petty acts of intolerance by a trade foreman, though behind the trivial incident lay the basic principle of trade rights as employers tried to use the local munitions tribunals to reinforce management power. Lloyd George and the Federated shipbuilders completely underestimated the shipyard workers, believing that the courts could 'make a real example' of a few tradesmen and break the resistance.[54]

The imposition of labour controls under the Munitions Act provoked massive resistance during the summer and autumn of 1915. The significance of the movement lay not in demonstrating the dominant role of the shipbuilding sector in wartime unrest, but rather in creating the conditions for co-operation between shipyard and engineering unions in opposing the government.[55] The local trades councils played a critical role in forging this unfamiliar alliance of unions, particularly the Govan Trades Council under Harry Hopkins. It was the threat issued by the Govan activists that forced the government to take the protest against the imprisonment of strikers seriously and to appoint an urgent commission of enquiry under Balfour and Macassey.[56] Arguably, this campaign posed no real threat to the state because of the absence of political activists such as those who dominated the CWC. After all, the struggle was held together not by the 'backbone of craft militancy' in the general engineering workshops and the CWC, but by shipbuilding tradesmen.[57] In fact the movement was not confined to the shipyards and neither were the shipyard stewards entirely divorced from local politics. The shipbuilding districts had already seen the creation of 'vigilance committees' to monitor events within industry and possibly also reporting on problems of price rises in the shipyard committees.[58] Hopkins used the anti-Munitions campaign to mobilise a general campaign of resistance in Govan, ably assisted by John S. Taylor of the ASE.[59]

Rather than seeing the Munitions resistance as the preserve of the shipyards, and the subsequent dilution struggle as the concern of engineering activists under the CWC, it is possible to interpret the movement against the legislation of 1915 as one of the conditions which led to the rebirth of the CWC in the autumn of that year. Certainly, the Munitions Act had a greater impact on the sensibilities of the shipbuilding craftsmen, with their frequent movements between and within yards. It is also clear that the dilution of skilled labour by the introduction of untrained male and female workers proved to be far more practicable in the machine shops of the engineering plants than in the complex and physically demanding world of the shipyards. But in principle and in practice the two questions were related. The Munitions Ministry assumed, and the craftsmen certainly believed, that the powers given under the 1915 legislation could and would be used to overcome any resistance to the introduction of state policies. In the critical autumn and winter months of 1915–16, engineering and shipbuilding workers faced the shared threat of enforced dilution. It is this common perception which explains the bitter reception given to Lloyd George when he visited Parkhead Forge, one of the largest engineering plants in west

Scotland, during Christmas 1915, and was greeted as the architect of the repressive measures that engineers as well as shipbuilders had fought in the autumn.[60]

The leader of the Parkhead shop stewards, David Kirkwood, was to become the most celebrated and controversial personality in the story of the CWC. It is around the CWC and its role in the dilution struggle that the conflicting views of workplace politics on the Clyde have turned. The details of how the government pushed forward the dilution of vital munitions work in the winter and spring of 1915–16, including its suppression of the Labour newspaper *Forward* and the deportation of leading CWC stewards, have been discussed at length elsewhere.[61] Most of the debate on the dilution struggle has turned on the role of the state in handling the Clydeside crisis. Radical historians have argued that the state was intent on crushing any political challenge by the shop stewards whilst revisionist writers insist that wartime legislation should be seen as a major concession to the claims of organised labour.[62]

The difficulty with such interpretations is that they view government policy almost wholly in terms of the balance of power between industrial capital and labour. It is true that the strategic value of wartime manufacturing gave these producer groups a real leverage in political circles, but the progress of state policy was determined by the structures of government and the intellectual practices of civil servants as well as conflicts in society and the state. In the process of policy making the key institutions were attempting to reconstitute themselves to meet the exigencies of wartime production. Not only the central ministries but various producer and consumer groups responded to the demands of war by strengthening their organisation and strategic decision making. Each move towards a realignment of the institution became the subject of political debate. Since these bodies normally defined the boundaries of interest which an institution claimed for its members, each initiative involved a recalculation of interests and preferences for those engaged. This can be seen in the creation of the Munitions Ministry itself, when the state reformed itself to encompass the control of munitions production and also sought to realign the unions to central agreements on output. The results included serious friction within the unions as radical changes were decided at national level, and a radical reappraisal of their own policies by employer leaders such as Allan Smith.[63]

Such reforms were simply responses to the objective needs of the state to sustain a massive war effort. The existing structures of government and working practices of the law-makers provided the filter through which national priorities were received. Perhaps most fundamental of all was the principle of legitimate and lawful authority, which was as axiomatic to the British civil service as the notion of the 'public interest' served by the state. These notions are the common threads in the internal and external discourse of state servants during the war years. The discourse ranged from discussions of national efficiency and scientific management to debates on conscription and union democracy, but throughout there was the assumption that there could be no efficient war production unless there was a clear line of authority in public and private management.

During the conflicts of 1915–16 the government was still uncertain as to the precise nature of the challenge it faced on Clydeside and the most effective means of dealing with embattled workers. Since institutions and organisations were in flux it was extremely difficult to predict the outcome of specific shop steward initiatives. It is the turbulence and uncertainties of workplace conflicts that explains the Munitions Ministry's hesitant progress in the winter of 1915–16, rather than any Machiavellian scheme in Whitehall. Internal dissension within the unions seemed to offer scope for local rather than national agreements as the way forward in Glasgow. Once it became clear that the shop stewards claimed an active and concerted role in the management of the workplace, and were ready to resist the legal authority of the state to defend this claim, the response of the government was swift and uncompromising. There could be no division of the fundamental authority of the state and no dilution of the rights of management to control output. Union officials had a place in the recognised order of things. They were to represent their members' interests using agreed procedures. Any disruption of such agreements could not be tolerated.

Reaching this conclusion absorbed most of the winter of 1915–16, as the employers pressed for various forms of industrial conscription amidst continuing unrest and the unions fought to prevent dilution being used as a basis for massive new controls over labour which might continue after the war.[64] The ASE emerged as the strongest union involved in the discussions and was divided over the concessions made under the original Munitions Act and the best means of safeguarding the trade during dilution. These problems caused serious frictions between the Clyde District and the national executive, prompting further struggles between radicals and moderates within the union's District Committee whilst helping the unofficial CWC to extend its influence over the area. Given the past failures of the executive to protect the members against hostile legislation and a widespread suspicion of centralised procedures to deal with dilution, the activists of the CWC captured the middle ground in the local debate over dilution.

It is often assumed that in this period the dominant influence over the shopfloor activists was that of the Socialist Labour Party and the marxist classes organised by John Maclean of the BSP. Yet the most powerful socialist party in Glasgow was the ILP, which had influential members in almost every working-class organisation in the city. Its influence can be seen in the dilution contest. John Wheatley's own power base was in Shettleston, scene of the great Parkhead works and a centre of ASE influence under David Kirkwood. According to *Forward*'s report of the Lloyd George visit to the Beardmore plant, the shop stewards presented a clear proposal to the minister for a radical dilution scheme, explaining that: 'Joint Management is what is wanted – the State, the Employer or Organiser, and the Workers' Committee.'[65] Such a clear expression of goals betrays the hand of Wheatley rather than the vocabulary of Kirkwood, and set the agenda for subsequent discussion of dilution in the socialist press.[66]

Similar conclusions can be drawn from the reports of negotiations between the ASE District Committee, where ILP-ers were prominent, and local officials of the ministry during January 1916.[67] At this point the government faced intense criticisms from the Clyde employers, as well as pressure from the ASE executive to reach a national agreement on dilution underwritten by the state. The Ministry warned local unionists that:

> no further conditions could be agreed to locally precedent to the introduction of dilution and . . . the Government could not agree to hand over the arrangements for labour dilution to any Committee. It was the intention of the Government to introduce the dilution scheme in each shop.[68]

Behind this determination was the realisation that if any general principle of joint-determination was conceded then there was a real danger that the authority of the employers, the union leaders and the state itself could be seriously damaged. The legitimate authorities had to be protected.[69]

Progress was dependent upon the Clyde workers' acceptance of some form of dilution. At this point Kirkwood broke the deadlock by proposing a single-plant agreement for Parkhead. Although marxist historians have often denounced Kirkwood as a political opportunist, to suggest that his plant agreement broke a common political front is surely to misread the situation in early 1916.[70] The Parkhead scheme was only one of at least sixteen dilution programmes in place by the end of February, including those negotiated by CWC hard-liners Gallacher and Muir.[71] It seems that it was the ILP, rather than the revolutionary parties, which provided the main inspiration for the CWC at this period and it was Messer – another ILP-er – who presented the general plan for dilution on the Clyde to the Dilution Commissioners, outlining a co-ordinated plan of joint control over dilution. Such activists were alternatively seen as flexible negotiators and as a 'disloyal socialist minority' by local Ministry officials.[72]

In this respect, the ILP made the running in coming forward with practical arrangements for dilution at district and plant levels. It is true that John Maclean warned the CWC against such compromises and demanded an open political strike to end the war and defend working-class living standards.[73] It is also true that a conflict over Kirkwood's freedom of movement at Parkhead led to the crisis that ended in the deportation of activists and the crushing of the CWC. What is open to question is whether the collapse of the CWC was an inevitable consequence of the ILP proposals on dilution, and also if Maclean's strategy for class politics offered a viable alternative for the Clyde workforce. The incident which provoked the crisis at Parkhead appeared trivial but actually involved a basic principle of workplace control: whether the management could assert their right to restrict the leading shop steward to his own place of work. The claim by the ASE to supervise the working conditions of the female dilutees forced the employers to consider their basic prerogatives and it was on this principle that the Clyde industrialists found common cause.

These firms were soon claiming that the CWC had laid plans for 'dynamiting the machinery', as well as opposing military service. Faced with this frenzied atmosphere and the claim that the Clyde socialists were in revolt against their own executive officers, the government acted swiftly to deport key figures in the CWC and crush any sympathetic strikes.[74] Within a few weeks the Munitions Tribunal had imposed sentences on strikers and dismissed the shop stewards' claims as preposterous demands against property, 'not to be countenanced in any Court of Law'.[75] The principle which united employers, Ministry officials, lawyers and even union officers was the threat posed by the shop stewards to the lawful authority of management. Although the ILP-ers had a practical grasp of the procedures for overseeing dilution, they had assumed that the employers would accept a significant degree of workers' control – enforced by the shop stewards and underwritten by the continued bargaining power of the workforce as well as an agreement in the plant. It soon became clear that the employers would tolerate no intrusion on their right to manage and that the state would support the established institutions of authority in any crisis.

The immediate result of the deportations was a collapse of confidence within the ASE District Committee and the resurgence of moderate influence within the unions. The ILP-ers had failed to anticipate the defeat of the stewards and had to fall back on emphasising the 'responsible' attitude of local workers in the face of management attacks. It was with these lessons in mind that the shipbuilding unions manoeuvred during the rest of 1916 and 1917 to defend their control of shipyard work. Despite the confident predictions of dilution officials, the Clyde basins were much less amenable to rapid deskilling and the use of female labour.[76] The employers themselves were less than certain of the gains to be made from such policies and the dangers of provoking continued unrest on the waterfront.[77] As the war progressed it was on the government's initiative, rather than that of the employers, that scientific and welfare management policies were promoted in industry. Similarly, it was the leading figures in the national business confederations, such as Allan Smith of the Engineering Employers' Federation, rather than the strong provincial bodies of industrialists, who developed a more sophisticated approach to the central state. The executive officers of the confederations and the unions became more relaxed in their mutual dealings with government, but relations on the Clyde remained largely unchanged.[78]

The political legacy of these industrial struggles was a complex one. Local activists were intimidated by the deportation of prominent shop stewards and the sentences handed down by the courts, though the dilution agreements remained and the government was anxious to limit the use of force against the trade unions. The Munitions Ministry's policy was to promote the recognition of responsible trade unionism and to invite moderate Labour figures to take part in policy making.[79] The Labour Party executive in London reciprocated by giving tacit support to the war effort and refusing to support pacifists in their opposition to recruitment campaigns. Party leaders expected local trade unions to reflect this political realism and contain the influence of socialists in the party.[80] Unfortunately for the moderate members of the party executive, west Scotland refused to follow the expected pattern and by 1917–18 the Scottish situation was causing serious concern in London.

The advanced socialism of the Scottish party was partly due to a resurgence of activities in unions such as the ASE and the trades councils, where ILP-ers held influence. As the threat of industrial conscription returned during 1916–17, they were able to recapture influence on the shopfloor. More important than the role of socialists within the unions, however, was the determined campaigning of the ILP on conditions outside the workplace. The collective experience of struggle within industry over basic principles of freedom and reward in their dealings with the state explains the support given to trade unionism in these years, but it was their contacts with the struggles over consumption that changed workers' sensibilities and gave producers a new awareness of the need for political reconstruction. In this transition urban movements for better housing, led by the Glasgow ILP, were to prove critical.

IV

The scale of the wartime rent strikes on the Clyde has been recognised by commentators on 'Red Clydeside', though their political significance is a matter of debate. Historians have usually seen the campaign as a broad social struggle, largely confined to the shipyard districts and quite distinct from the rise of the Clyde Workers' Committee and the building of a class politics. Even those writers who emphasise the importance of the housing question in Labour's electoral platform, contrast the spread of support for better housing with the immature sectionalism of Scottish industry.[81] Such arguments obscure the impact of the rents campaign on the workers' families in west Scotland, and the way both women and men were drawn into the struggle against the landlords. Adapting their practical skills to the conduct of struggle, the urban workforce was able to utilise its own cultural resources and moral claims in the battle with the houseowners.

In this respect, the salient feature of the Clyde rent strikes was not their distance from workplace unrest, but precisely the way in which the industrial and housing protests combined to challenge the authority of landlords and the state. By the autumn of 1915 the government believed it was facing a major crisis of authority, which threatened war production on the Clyde and elsewhere and that a restriction of rents on working-class housing was a political necessity to safeguard munitions production. The government was determined to restrict the political impact of the rent strike victory and to suppress the implication that radical reform could be secured by a determined campaign of direct action. To understand the success of the rents struggle and the relative failure of direct action in the dilution conflict, we have to examine the role of the ILP in the stand against Glasgow's landlords.

The origins of Glasgow's peculiar role in the making of housing policy can be traced to the structure of its urban economy. The dominance of the heavy metalworking trades in the occupations of the Clyde is well known, with a clear division of social roles between male craftsmen and their wives and daughters.[82] Men continued to control the public institutions of the city and to confirm their relations with the craft fraternity in the drinking bars, which served as houses of call for those seeking work and contacts with fellow tradesmen. The physical boundaries of the social division of labour were also marked by the structure of the tenements which characterised Clydeside housing throughout these nineteenth and early twentieth centuries. The price of land and the burden of feu rents paid to the landowner, reinforced the cultural style of the Victorian tenement and led to an extraordinary concentration of people in the three- and four-storey blocks which surrounded the factories and shipyards. Women found that they had to work within a confined space that dictated the sharing of basic amenities, such as toilets and laundries in the common ground of the tenements, whilst struggling to raise a family in two or three rooms.

The ILP adapted its urban campaigns to these conditions, with women activists using the washing house roof as a platform to address the tenement housewives. Recognising the reluctance of many women to become involved in political life, the ILP relied on such bodies as the

Co-operative Women's Guild to prepare the ground and make the case for a consumers' politics in the neighbourhood. A similar strategy was pursued on the housing question, with the ILP devising a 'dual politics' that gave Labour spokeswomen a leading role in the housing movement whilst retaining the non-party principles of local associations. The Glasgow leadership of the ILP realised that flexible tactics were essential if local housewives were to be brought into Labour's crusade for better housing. This policy of colonising autonomous groups and building a network of activists throughout the city, was already in place at the outbreak of war and was to prove invaluable in the conduct of the rent strikes.

It was the extraordinary shortages of housing in wartime Clydeside that transformed a limited, if promising, ILP initiative into a major platform of Labour politics on the Clyde. Sharp increases in rents were confined to fairly well defined areas around the shipyards and engineering shops, particularly in the hard-pressed burghs of Govan and Partick. These areas enjoyed a clear identity as separate burghs of the Glasgow area until 1912 and were characterised by large concentrations of skilled metalworkers, though each also possessed significant numbers of low-paid labourers and aged pensioners. The firms of factors who collected the rents were equally well known and as migrant workers flooded into the key munitions districts in search of high wages, the landlords gave notice of rent rises in many districts during the spring and summer of 1915.

The ILP seized the opportunity to appropriate and direct the wide range of distinctive campaigns which arose in the first year of the war. At the first sign of protest, ILP speakers were despatched to organise street corner and hall meetings and offer resistance to the factors. Local women devised such effective tactics of direct action as the bombardment of rent collectors with flour and peasemeal. With the ILP orchestrating the protests and presenting the tenants' case in the press, the courtroom and before the official enquiry into rent rises, the campaign was so effective that by autumn 1915 the government conceded defeat and introduced legislation to restrict the rents of all working-class houses for the duration of the war.[83] The numbers on strike were deliberately exaggerated by ILP-ers such as Andrew McBride and Agnes Dollan as they sought to extend the strike wave across the Clyde, but it would be wrong to understate the actual extent of support which the rents struggle enjoyed in the city during 1915.

To suggest that the rents unrest was wholly confined to 'shipyard areas' ignores the presence of major engineering works in these districts and the existence of parallel strikes in other centres of engineering production. The most frequent reference to the occupations of the strikers appearing before small debts courts in 1915 was that of 'munitions worker'. The munitions industries covered every trade defined by the state as essential to wartime production. Engineering as well as shipbuilding workers were classed as munitions labour. In an important sense the statutory controls of the labour market under the 1915 Act and the absence of such restrictions in the housing market created the conditions for generalised conflict on the Clyde.

Local activists were critical in bridging sectional and gender divisions at this period. Not only did Harry Hopkins of the ASE lead the campaign against the Munitions Act but he played a prominent role in the rents strikes of autumn 1915.[84] As a progressive on the ASE District Committee, Hopkins formed one of the vital links in the network of industrial and political connections that gave the ILP such a presence in the struggles of these months. Nor were the CWC activists completely absent from the rents protest. John Wheatley had spent years agitating in the Shettleston area on social conditions. After persuading David Kirkwood to join the ILP on the outbreak of war. Wheatley served as political adviser to the Parkhead stewards and undoubtedly encouraged their letter of protest at the rent rises in the autumn of 1915.[85] Whilst it is true that the CWC as such did not take a leading role in the housing unrest, neither did any shipyard vigilance committee, but each played a significant part in persuading the government that legal actions against the tenants would provoke resistance in the munitions plants.

The relationship established between the practical intellectuals of the ILP and industrial and community activists produced a fresh political leadership on the Clyde which had the ability and confidence to challenge the government. This challenge unfolded during the rents campaign and took three distinct forms. The most immediate problem for the landlords was getting the courts to convict tenants and enforce eviction orders against defaulting families. This legal challenge raised basic questions about the rights of property during war and the parallel conduct of the Munitions Tribunals in dealing with violations under the 1915 Munitions Act. The second kind of opposition was the articulation of a moral resistance to the factors and the state on the question of 'patriotic rents', as the rent strikers turned the discourse of patriotism against the 'Profit Huns' among the landlords who were evicting the families of servicemen and munitions workers. John Wheatley showed himself a master of such moral denunciation in leading the defence of the McHugh family in Shettleston at a vital moment in the unrest. A direct attack on the politics of Liberalism formed the third type of challenge posed by the ILP to the government in the autumn of 1915. Local activists were able to exploit the bitter hostility to the Munitions Act to attack Lloyd George and demonstrate that the free market was damaging the war effort.[86]

It was the skill and self-confidence of the ILP-ers which also startled Lloyd George and his entourage when they visited Glasgow at the end of 1915. Politicians who had managed the national officials extremely well arrived on the Clyde to discover they could expect no deference from workers like Kirkwood, who had detailed proposals of their own to present to the government.[87] The reaction of Whitehall to the report of the fiasco at the mass meeting addressed by Lloyd George was to suppress the ILP *Forward* and other socialist newspapers. In trying to find some legal pretext for their action, civil servants like William Beveridge laboured to demonstrate that the ILP paper had supported the rent strikes and inspired the industrial workers to a similar campaign on the shopfloor.[88] However clouded was the view from Whitehall, such memoranda indicate that government took the challenge of the ILP seriously and found it very difficult to counter without resorting to repression of free speech.

The strength and flexibility of active ILP-ers in industry persuaded the Dilution Commissioners of the need to reach some understanding with the Clyde workers on munitions output.[89] When the local agreements resulted in deadlock at Parkhead the government was reluctant to intervene until the ILP and SLP stewards threatened to mobilise general resistance. At this point the politicians and civil servants had to gamble on direct repression of the unrest in support of the principle of the legitimate authority of the employer. In the aftermath of the March 1916 deportations, the government sought to sustain its own authority by continued consultation with the national union officials and the accredited leaders of the Labour Party. A formal system of political bargaining was created as the state extended its network of committees, without a radical change in the distribution of decision-making.[90] Such moves dealt with the immediate crisis of authority in spring 1916, but they compounded the longer-term difficulties facing the Liberal Government. Criticisms of the official leaders of the unions and the Labour Party were sharpened as the state advanced towards military and industrial conscription in 1917–18.

Critics of the official spokesmen of the labour movement were particularly prominent in Scotland, where the ILP was able to build on its successes of 1914–16 and extend its support within the Labour Party and the unions. The Scottish Housing Association was dominated by Clydeside activists and seems to have established a close relationship with Smillie of the Miners' Union, who was to denounce housing conditions in his campaign for the nationalisation of the coalmines after the war. On the industrial front, David Kirkwood was celebrated by the Labour Party as the original hero of Red Clydeside when it enquired into the deportations in 1917–18.[91] Harry Hopkins and his allies led the progressives on the ASE's Glasgow Committee from 1917 until their defeat during the famous Forty Hours Strike of 1919. In such ways the ILP-ers were able to sustain their demand for socialist policies within the Labour Party and resist London's efforts to marginalise the socialists on the Scottish Advisory Council in 1916–18.[92] The growth of ILP membership during the war and the prominence of such outstanding women activists as Helen Crawfurd and Agnes Dollan also prevented the male unionists from dictating the agenda of Scottish Labour.[93]

It is significant that so many of the Scottish ILP campaigns should have emphasised not narrow work questions but general principles of libertarian rights during the war. In this respect, the campaigns shared some ground with the pre-war Radicals who occupied the left of the Liberal Party, but the concern for popular liberties was a distinct strand of the ILP itself as it fought to defend the right to moral conviction in a society at war.[94] When insisting on the rights of tenants, workers and pacifists the ILP not only challenged the Liberals to qualify the state's claims on society, but also made a case for Labour as the defender of working people against irresponsible authority. The organisations created by the ILP enabled different groups on the Clyde to engage in effective struggles that appropriated the discourse of civil liberties whilst expressing a class agenda in politics.

V

This chapter has argued that the existing studies of wartime Clydeside neglect the central role of the ILP in the remaking of Scottish politics. Marxist interpretations have usually focused on the shopfloor workers, mobilised behind local cadres of revolutionary parties in a direct challenge to the capitalist state. Liberal historians have seen the industrial struggles as conservative and sectionalist in character, as craft workers defended their customary autonomy against the reforms proposed by employers and government. The British state portrayed by Hinton is almost unrecognisable in recent studies, which document the conciliatory and collectivist quality of wartime policies. Socialism gained ground, according to a recent view, not by the direct action of organised labour but as government initiatives provided a practical model of state socialism.[95] The debate on wartime legislation has shed some light on the dynamics of state intervention in these years but provides only a partial view of the ensemble of forces which transformed popular politics in the early twentieth century.

A more persuasive explanation of the ascendancy of socialism on the Clyde is based on an examination of the social relations of production and power in society, and the ways in which the forces of resistance came to challenge the state itself in the war years. As the state became engaged in a massive war effort that demanded enormous supplies of munitions, the production of arms acquired a strategic importance that dominated the political agenda. In the pre-war years a delicate balance had been maintained between the prerogatives of capitalism and the autonomy of the workforce. Unions had accepted responsibility and influence in return for policing the agreements reached. If the boundaries of legitimate behaviour were demarcated by practice and procedure then the authority of the employer was upheld by a strict hierarchy of command and the prospect of dismissal.

It was this basic relationship which the war disrupted. The extraordinary bargaining power of workers removed the usual sanctions of the employer. This power was demonstrated in the strikes of February–March 1915 and persuaded Lloyd George of the need for a new framework of voluntary and legal restrictions. Industrialists found their control over production eroded as the workforce challenged the authority of the foreman and the employer's right to large profits. The right to manage was itself being questioned. The logic of the situation gave workers the power to challenge the state as well as the employers. When the Munitions Act of 1915 provided legal sanctions to restrain munitions workers, an open revolt against the legislation was always possible. The debate on whether the Clyde craftsmen were essentially radical or conservative in their resistance to state policies overlooks the basic point that all craft workers were seeking to defend themselves against fresh exploitation. Trade union officials as well as shop stewards were trying to develop an institutional and legislative response to the problems of increased output. For the Clyde activists, local autonomy and direct control was the only means by which the progress of dilution could be properly controlled. This implied a direct challenge to the employers' sole rights to manage.

The ILP's major contribution was to recognise the importance of the existing institutions of civil society in west Scotland and to use these bodies to orchestrate a general campaign of resistance during the autumn of 1915. The Clyde was always going to be a major centre of munitions production but not necessarily the scene of the greatest resistance to government policies. It was the ILP-ers in the Govan Trades Council, on the ASE District Committee and in the Clyde Workers' Committee itself, that co-ordinated the dramatic campaigns of 1915–16. Faced with the practical difficulties of monitoring the dilution programme and securing shopfloor control, it was Kirkwood and Wheatley that framed a scheme of shop committees on the Clyde. It is true that the safeguards did not protect the activists when the employers and government crushed the shop stewards' challenge to management authority at Parkhead and were criticised by John Maclean and others for their naivety. The problem with the revolutionaries' analysis, however, was that only a decisive confrontation with the massed employers and the state could have secured the kind of political breakthrough they demanded, and if the Parkhead crisis did not produce a massive response it is difficult to see a direct attack on capitalism providing the basis for a mass movement.

These producers' struggles forced the state to reconstitute important parts of government and elaborate its own procedures for dealing with capital and labour. Government could not merely respond to prevailing market power and overlook the historical constructions of laws and institutions within capitalist society. The legal sanctions imposed in 1915–16 proved crude instruments for handling labour policy and the munitions courts fell into obscurity during the later part of the war. It was during the great consumers' campaigns of 1915 that the new law courts were in danger of becoming a public theatre for political debate on the Clyde. The social division of labour in industrial society gave women the main responsibility for organising working-class consumption. Their influence within the structure of tenement society was considerable but the scope for formal or collective action against the suppliers of housing, goods and services was obviously limited. The cultural practices of working people were dominated by the masculine skills of tool-using within the craft fraternities, whilst the pub and the theatre provided the space for self-expression outside working hours.

It is remarkable that Glasgow women should have felt able to react so aggressively to the rent and price rises of 1915. The personal and legal authority of the housefactor had to be confronted during the day when the men were at work. In this situation the neighbourhood women had to assemble their own cultural resources to resist the landlord and the threat of eviction. Here the ILP made its greatest contribution to the wartime unrest by organising the rent strikers in local groups, under the umbrella of a general committee but encouraging autonomy in each district. In conducting the rent strikes, activists drew on the practical experience of workplace struggle as a resource for challenging the authority of the houseowner. As a result of its strike successes the ILP was able to form a vital network of activists and influence across the city that underpinned the party's post-war election campaigns.

The various challenges to the authority of property and the state during the war also weakened the moral claims of Scottish Liberalism. It is possible to see the war as a juncture in which traditional Liberalism gave way to constitutional Labourism as the skilled workers switched their allegiance to a radical reforming party and the franchise was extended to the lesser skilled.[96] In this light, rent strikes gave Labour a strong constituency of support for housing reform. This reading of the wartime unrest understates the degree to which popular politics were thrown into flux as the familiar landmarks of Liberalism were destroyed by state expansion. Amidst the decay of political identities, socialism itself became the subject of intense debate in 1917–20. Economic and political sectarianism faded as socialists within the Labour and other parties reappraised the scope for social reconstruction. Within this extended forum of political debate, labour organisations continued to criticise the repressive actions of the state as it extended military and industrial conscription during 1917–18. The insistence on libertarian principles was not merely a residue of declining Liberalism but an authentic theme in socialist discourse.

In this transformation of political values the ILP's role was critical. Its strength was to recognise the importance of existing institutions and personal connections in the construction of a socialist alternative, rather than to impose a doctrinal strategy and discipline on the complex situation that prevailed in wartime Glasgow. The ILP captured the leadership of different campaigns because it practised a form of dual politics, simultaneously rooted in everyday life and conventional political arenas, which ignored party boundaries and was based only on the discipline of the specific project, not the party card. This meant that a broad coalition of social groups could be assembled in support of various speakers at Glasgow Green. The emphasis on 'making socialists' allowed the ILP to avoid some of the more bitter sectarian squabbles over political doctrine during the war and appeal for a moral stand on the war. Even more important was the ILP's firm grasp of organisational strategy and the presence of high-calibre activists like Harry Hopkins and Andrew McBride. By their leadership of popular struggles in the war these people associated the ILP with a clear alternative to the Liberals who dominated pre-war Glasgow politics.

The flaws in ILP politics also became apparent in the critical years of war. In the conflicts of 1915–16 the Clydeside activists assumed that their bargaining power and local influence was an adequate base from which to confront the British state. The victory of movement politics in the rent strikes seemed to confirm this. Hostility to the London government was widespread. It only became clear in the dilution struggle that the specific conditions of the Clyde were not reproduced elsewhere and that the sabotage of production did not deliver political power. The ILP learned the lesson by building up its influence within the unions, the housing movement and within the Labour Party in Scotland. The peculiarities of the Scottish remained an important element in the fostering of a distinct identity for socialists beyond the border, and nowhere more visibly than in the making of the 'Red Clydeside' mythologies. It was the theatre of the Red Clyde that sustained the Glasgow celebrities in their election to power in 1922–4. By this time the sectarian divisions on the left had already signalled a change in the quality of popular politics and the end of the ILP's most significant period of development.

Notes

In writing this essay I owe a special debt to colleagues who discussed the ideas with me over a period of years. In particular I wish to thank Keith Burgess, Bob Lewis, Alan McKinlay, Jeff Porter, Alastair Reid and Steven Tolliday.

1 A.J.B. Marwick, 'The Independent Labour Party in the Nineteen-Twenties', *Bulletin of Historical Research*, XXXV, 1962, pp. 62–74; Robert Dowse, *Left in the Centre: The Independent Labour Party 1893–1940* (Longmans, London, 1966); David Howell, *British Workers and the Independent Labour Party 1888–1906* (Manchester University Press, Manchester, 1983); William Knox, *Scottish Labour Leaders 1918–1939* (Mainstream, Edinburgh, 1984).

2 Howell, *op. cit.*; Stephen Yeo, 'A New Life: The Religion of Socialism in Britain, 1883–1896' *History Workshop Journal*, 4, 1977, pp. 5–56.

3 William Gallacher, *Revolt on the Clyde* (Lawrence and Wishart, London, 1936); Walter Kendall, *The Revolutionary Movement in Britain 1900–1921* (Weidenfield and Nicolson, London, 1969); James Hinton and Richard Hyman, *Trade Unions and Revolution: The Industrial Politics of the Early British Communist Party* (Pluto, London, 1975); Raymond Challinor, *The Origins of British Bolshevism* (Croom Helm, London, 1977); Joseph Melling, 'Clydeside Industry and the Building of Class Politics, 1750–1971', *Bulletin of Society for the Study of Labour History*, 52, 1987, pp. 54–8, reviews the field.

4 Joan Smith, 'Labour Tradition in Glasgow and Liverpool' *History Workshop Journal*, 17, 1984, pp. 32–56.

5 Henry Pelling, *The Origins of the Labour Party, 1880–1900* (Oxford University Press, Oxford, 1965), p. 218. 'The fact was that the British working class as a whole had no use for the conception of violent revolution'. Ross McKibbin, *The Evolution of the Labour Party, 1910–1924* (Clarendon Press, Oxford, 1974), and 'Why was there no Marxism in Great Britain?' *English Historical Review*, XCIX, 1984, pp. 295–331. Recent radical surveys include Keith Burgess, *The Challenge of Labour* (Croom Helm, London, 1980) and Richard Price, *Labour in British Society* (Croom Helm, London, 1985), particularly ch. 6.

6 John Saville, 'The Ideology of Labourism' in R. Benewick, et al. (eds), *Knowledge and Belief in Politics* (Allen & Unwin, London, 1973) and Saville's *The Labour Movement in Britain* (Faber, London, 1988), pp.

2–22, outlines his influential argument that a 'labourist' outlook paralysed working-class politics before 1900.

7 Bob Holton, *British Syndicalism, 1900–1914* (Pluto, London, 1976); Richard Price, *Masters, Unions and Men* (Cambridge University Press, Cambridge, 1980), pp. 236–67.

8 Jonathan Zeitlin, 'From Labour History to the History of Industrial Relations', *Economic History Review*, XL, 2, 1987, pp. 159–84, provides a critical survey of recent work.

9 James Hinton, *The First Shop Stewards' Movement* (Allen & Unwin, London, 1973). Alastair Reid, 'Glasgow Socialism' *Social History*, 11, 1, 1986, pp. 89–97, for one response.

10 Hinton, *op. cit.*, pp. 83–5; James Hinton, 'The Clyde Workers' Committee and the Dilution Struggle' in Asa Briggs and John Saville (eds), *Essays in Labour History 1886–1923* (Macmillan, London 1971), pp. 156–8.

11 Stuart Hall and Bill Schwarz, 'State and Society, 1880–1930' in M. Langan and Bill Schwarz (eds), *Crises in the British State 1880–1930* (Hutchinson, London, 1985), pp. 25–9 and Bill Schwarz and Martin Durham, ' "A Safe and Sane Labourism": Socialism and the State 1910–1924', in *ibid.*, p. 144.

12 Henry Pelling, *Popular Politics and Society in late Victorian Britain* (Macmillan, London, 1968); Iain McLean, *The Legend of Red Clydeside* (John Donald, Edinburgh, 1983).

13 McLean, *ibid.*, pp. 100–10; Alastair Reid, 'Dilution Trade Unionism and the State in Britain during the First World War' in Steven Tolliday and Jonathan Zeitlin (eds), *Shop Floor Bargaining and the State* (Cambridge University Press, Cambridge, 1985), p. 49.

14 McLean, *ibid.*, pp. 129–38, 240–1.

15 *Ibid*; also Rodger Davidson, 'War-Time Labour Policy 1914–1916: A Re-Appraisal', *Scottish Labour History Society Journal*, VIII, 1974, pp. 4–5, and 'The Myth of the Servile State', *Bulletin of the Society for the Study of Labour History*, XXIX, 1974, p. 64, for a critique of Hinton's approach; Jose Harris, *William Beveridge* (Oxford University Press, Oxford, 1977), pp. 210–11.

16 McLean, *op. cit.*, pp. 49–67, 85.

17 Reid, *loc. cit.*

18 *Ibid.*, pp. 60–5.

19 *Ibid.*, p. 65.

20 Reid, *ibid.*, pp. 63–4.

21 *Ibid.*, pp. 60–1, 69–70.

22 *Ibid.*; Gerry Rubin, *War, Law and Labour: The Munitions Acts, State, Regulation and the Unions, 1915–1921* (Clarendon Press, Oxford, 1987), pp. 204–9.

23 Joan Smith, 'Commonsense thought and Working-class Consciousness:

Some Aspects of the Glasgow and Liverpool Labour Movements in the Early Years of the Twentieth Century, (unpublished PhD thesis, Edinburgh University, 1980).

24 Zeitlin, *loc. cit.* (1987), endorses some of these views.

25 Michael Savage, *The Dynamics of Working-Class Politics: The Labour Movement in Preston 1880–1940* (Cambridge University Press, Cambridge, 1987), pp. 168–9, 187. Joseph Melling, 'Industry, Labour and Politics', *Business History*, XXXI, 2, 1989, pp. 114–19.

26 Saville, *op. cit.* (1988); G. Phillips, 'The British Labour Movement before 1914' in Dick Geary (ed.), *Labour and Socialist Movements in Europe before 1914* (Berg, Oxford, 1989), pp. 11–47.

27 Smith, *thesis*, pp. 187–8, 322–33.

28 Hinton, *op. cit* and Price, *op. cit.*, are influential representatives of these views. See also John Holford, *Reshaping Labour* (Croom Helm, London, 1988).

29 McLean, *op. cit.*, pp. 154–73; John Foster, 'Strike Action and Working Class Politics on Clydeside, 1914–1919', Paisley College, 1989. I am grateful to Professor Foster for permission to cite his unpublished paper.

30 Hall and Schwarz, *op. cit.*, 'outcomes were determined in the first instance by political struggle'; McLean, *op. cit.*, pp. 176–8, 200–1; Reid, *op. cit.* (1986), pp. 94–7; Davidson, *op. cit.* (1974), p. 64, but see Davidson's later *Whitehall and the Labour Problem in Late-Victorian and Edwardian Britain* (Croom Helm, London, 1985), for a more subtle discussion.

31 G.A. Cohen, *History, Labour and Freedom: Themes from Marx* (Oxford University Press, Oxford, 1988), pp. 5–13, argues that legal rights only confirmed 'real economic power.'

32 *Engineering* 28 May 1911; 'The Labour Unrest', *Athenaeum*, 1917, p. 269; Jonathan Zeitlin, 'The Labour Strategies of British Engineering Employers, 1890–1922' in Howard Gospel and Craig Littler (eds), *Managerial Strategies and Industrial Relations* (Heinemann, London, 1983), for a contrasting interpretation. ,

33 Joseph Melling, 'Scottish Industrialists and the Changing Character of Class Relations in the Clyde Region' in Tony Dickson (ed.), *Capital and Class in Scotland* (John Donald, Edinburgh, 1982); Callum Campbell, *The Making of a Clydeside Working Class: Shipbuilding and Working Class Organisation in Govan* (Our History, 78, London, 1986), pp. 5–16, for Govan.

34 Joseph Melling, ' "Non-Commissioned Officers": British Employers and their Supervisory Workers, 1880–1920' *Social History*, V, 2, 1980, pp. 183–221; Keith McClelland and Alastair Reid, 'Wood, Iron and Steel: Technology, Labour and Trade Union Organisation in the Shipbuilding Industry, 1840–1914' in Royden Harrison and Jonathan Zeitlin (eds),

Divisions of Labour: Skilled Workers and Technological Change in Nineteenth-Century England (Harvester Press, Brighton, 1984).

35 Joseph Melling, 'The Servile State Revisited: Law and Industrial Capitalism in the Early Twentieth Century', *Scottish Labour History Society Journal*, 24, 1989.

36 Smith, 'Common Sense and Working-class Consciousness', pp. 332–3, for Glasgow artisans and the ILP.

37 Ian Hutchison, *A Political History of Scotland, 1832–1924* (John Donald, Edinburgh, 1986), pp. 256–65; Smith, *'Common Sense and Working-class Consciousness'*, pp. 427–8 for a discussion of 1913 elections.

38 Hinton, *op. cit.*

39 Smith, *'Common Sense and Working-Class Consciousness'*, pp. 490–91 for criticism of Hinton's description.

40 Brian Weekes, 'The Amalgamated Society of Engineers 1880–1914: A Study of Trade Union Government and Industrial Policy (unpublished PhD thesis, Warwick University, 1970) ch. 8.

41 Minutes of the North West Engineering Trades Employers' Association (hereafter NWETEA), Glasgow, 19–29 January 1915, 10–18 February 1915; Minutes of Clyde Shipbuilders' Association (hereafter CSA), Glasgow, 18 February 1915. Although the engineering and shipbuilding firms acted together, the structure of their industries differed in many respects.

42 W.R. Scott and R. Cunnison, *The Industries of the Clyde Valley during the War* (Oxford University Press, Oxford, 1924), pp. 74–5, 114–117; Hinton, *op. cit.*, 1973, p. 109.

43 NWETEA, 25 January, 17–18, 22 February, 2, pp. 23–30 March 1915; Hinton, *op. cit.* (1971), pp. 159–60, and *op. cit.* (1973), pp. 106–7.

44 NWETEA, 10–18 February 1915; Gallacher, *op. cit.*, p. 37.

45 *Ibid.*, pp. 41–3 for Gallacher's account of Committee; Hinton, *op. cit.*, pp. 113–15.

46 Lynden Macassey, *Labour Policy – False and True* (Thornton Butterworth, London, 1922), pp. 137–9, claimed that the state even relieved employers of their management responsibilities.

47 For the context see Clive Trebilock, 'War and the Failure of Industrial Mobilisation, 1899 and 1914' in Jay Winter (ed.), *War and Economic Development* (Cambridge University Press, Cambridge 1975), p. 149; R.J. Irving, 'New Industries for Old? Some Investment Decisions of Sir W.G. Armstrong, Whitworth & Co. Ltd., 1900–1914', *Business History*, XVII, 1975, pp. 162–9; D. Crow, *A Man of Push and Go: The Life of George Macaulay Booth*, Rupert Hart-Davis London, 1965), p. 87; R.J.Q. Adams, *Arms and the Wizard: Lloyd George and the Ministry of Munitions* (Harvard University Press, Cambridge Mass., 1978), pp. 22–3.

48 Lloyd George's *War Memoirs* quoted in F. Owen, *Tempestuous Journey: Lloyd George His Life and Times* (Hutchinson, London, 1954), p. 293; C. Addison, *Four and a Half Years: A Personal Diary from June 1914 to January 1919* (Hutchinson, London, 1934), 28 May 1915; Chris Wrigley, *David Lloyd George and the British Labour Movement* (Harvester, Brighton, 1976), p. 132.

49 NWETEA and CSA, 7 April 1915, joint meeting of the associations. Crow, *op. cit.*, pp. 107–11; Trebilock *op. cit.*, p. 155; Wrigley, *op. cit.*, p. 132, for the speech of Allan Smith to Birmingham employers at the Armaments Output Committee on 20 April 1915.

50 P. Kline, 'Lloyd George and the Experiment with Businessmen in Government' in K.D. Brown, (ed.), *Essays in Anti-Labour History* (MacMillan, London, 1974); Hinton, *op. cit.*, pp. 27–36.

51 Lord Balfour of Burleigh and Lynden Macassey, *Report of the Commission of Enquiry into Industrial Unrest in the Clyde District* Cmd 8136, p. 2 para. 2; *The Official History of the Ministry of Munitions* (HMSO, London 1920) (hereafter *HMM*), I iv, p. 41, and IV ii, p. 58; Scott and Cunnison, *op. cit.*, p. 76.

52 *HMM* IV ii, pp. 58–50; David Kirkwood, *My Life of Revolt* (Harrap, London, 1935), pp. 102–9; Harris, *op. cit.*, pp. 213–14.

53 Wrigley, *op. cit.*, p. 82; Reid, *op. cit.* (1985).

54 'Minutes of Conference between the Ministry of Munitions and the Shipbuilding Employers' Federation: the Application of the Munitions Act to the Shipbuilding Trades', 12 August 1915, pp. 5–6, 13: PRO MUN5 48/300/9.

55 Reid, *op. cit.* (1985), pp. 93–6.

56 *Balfour–Macassey Report*, Cmd 8136, p. 2; *HMM* iv II, p. 58.

57 Hinton, *op. cit.* pp. 161–2.

58 Joseph Melling, *Rent Strikes!: Peoples' Struggle for Housing in West Scotland 1890–1916* (Polygon, Edinburgh, 1983); Smith, *'Commonsense and Working-Class Consciousness'*, p. 470 notes the ILP involvement in local bodies which acted for the War Emergency Workers' National Committee.

59 Melling, *Ibid.*, McLean, *op. cit.* also discusses the rent strikes.

60 Kirkwood, *op. cit.*, pp. 102–9.

61 James Hinton, *op. cit.* (1971), pp. 156–8, 167–70; Terry Brotherstone, 'The Suppression of *Forward*' *Scottish Labour History Society Journal*, I, 1969, pp. 5–23; James Hinton, 'The suppression of the *Forward*: A Note', *Scottish Labour History Society Journal*, VII, 1973, pp. 24–8; McLean, *op. cit.*, pp. 49–77; Harris, *op. cit.*, pp. 220–2.

62 *Ibid.*; Reid, *op. cit.* (1985).

63 Addison, *op. cit.*, 7 July 1915; Adams, *op. cit.*, pp. 82–5; Keith Middlemas,

Politics in Industrial Society (Deutsch, London, 1979), pp. 76–7; Harris, *op. cit.*, pp. 213–14, all give some insight into political bargaining with the trade unions and employers.

64 Ministry of Munitions files (MUN 5), 5/73/324/15/9, provide details of progress of dilution to the end of February 1916, with Weirs playing a prominent part; *HMM*, IV, iv, pp. 98–9.

65 *Forward*, 1 January 1916.

66 *The Worker*, 8 January 1916, for Gallacher's attack on Kirkwood and the insistence that the Clyde Workers' Committee scheme was 'the *only* scheme before the country'.

67 Hinton, *op. cit.* (1971), pp. 167–8; Harris, *op. cit.* p. 221; Middlemas, *op. cit.*, p. 79.

68 NWETEA, 21 January 1916.

69 The Clyde engineering employers had demanded, directly and via William Weir (Scottish Director of Munitions) strong action. Iain McLean, 'Labour in Clydeside Politics 1914–1922' (unpublished D. Phil thesis, Oxford University, 1971), p. 54, gives the full text of Paterson's letter.

70 Gallacher, *op. cit.*, pp. 102–7; Hinton, *op. cit.* pp. 156–159.

71 NWETEA, 29 February 1916, lists the firms involved. Significantly, the location of the plants does not fit Hinton's geographical model of Clydeside militancy.

72 Hinton, *op. cit.*, p. 156; Wrigley, *op. cit.*, p. 162; McLean, *op. cit.*, pp. 74–5.

73 Smith, *'Common Sense and Working-Class Consciousness'*, pp. 498–502 suggests that MacLean possessed the means to connect the workplace struggles to the crusade against the war itself.

74 NWETEA, 23 March 1916.

75 NWETEA, 23–29 March 1916.

76 CSA, 21 March 1916, for Macassey's declaration that all customs which restricted the advance of shipyard dilution would be abrogated and 'nothing would be left undone to increase production'.

77 CSA, 15 October 1915, 3 July–30 August 1916; *HMM*, IV, iv, p. 135; Reid, *op. cit.* (1985), p. 66 acknowledges that the Clyde employers were uncertain about dilution.

78 'Minutes of Conference between the Ministry of Munitions and the ASE', 24 February 1916: MUN5 70/324/6.

79 CSA, 10 March–3 July 1916, for the government's attempts to involve Henderson of the Labour Party in the new Labour Advisory Department.

80 Labour Party, National Executive Committee Minutes (hereafter NEC Minutes), 18 April, 28 November–13 December 1917.

81 McLean, *op. cit.* pp. 154–79; see also Gallacher's caustic remarks on

ILP-er George Kerr's efforts to rouse the February strikers of 1915 on the housing question, *op. cit.*, pp. 40–1.

82 R.A. Cage (ed.), *The Working Class in Glasgow, 1750–1914* (Croom Helm, London, 1987), pp. 38–43, 66–75; T.C. Smout, *A Century of the Scottish People 1830–1950* (Fontana, 1987), pp. 42–57.

83 Melling, *op. cit.* (1983).

84 *Ibid.*; Smith, *thesis*, p. 464 quote's *Forward's* profile of Hopkins including his early interest in social reform questions.

85 Melling, *op. cit*; McLean, *op. cit.*

86 Joseph Melling, 'Clydeside Rent Struggles and the Making of Labour Politics in Scotland, 1900–1939', in Richard Rodger (ed.), *Scottish Housing in the Twentieth Century* (Leicester University Press, Leicester, 1989), pp. 54–88.

87 Kirkwood, *op. cit.*, pp. 109–14.

88 'The Suppression of the Glasgow *Forward*', Notes of Lt. Col. Levita, 5 January 1916, '[Ben] Shaw, the socialist, states, that the men think that as they got the better of the Government over rents by intimidation, they will be able to do the same over the Munitions Act': MUN 5 70/324/18.

89 *HMM*, IV, iv, p. 135.

90 Rodney Lowe, *Adjusting to Democracy: The Role of the Ministry of Labour in British Politics, 1916–1939* (Oxford University Press, Oxford, 1986), pp. 90–5.

91 Gallacher, *op. cit.*, pp. 126–31.

92 NEC Minutes, 16 October 1917.

93 For leading women, see Helen Corr's essay in Knox, *op. cit.* The ILP's membership in west Scotland doubled between 1915 and early 1917 and then trebled again to 10,000 members by spring 1918, according to *Forward*, as cited by Smith, *thesis*, p. 499.

94 NEC Minutes, 16 October 1917.

95 Reid, *op. cit.* (1986), pp. 95–6.

96 C. Cook, 'Labour's Electoral Base', in C. Cook and T. Taylor (eds), *The Labour Party* (Longmans, London, 1981), pp. 84–99; McLean, *op. cit.*, pp. 176–84.

FIVE

'Doubtful wisdom and uncertain promise': strategy, ideology and organisation, 1918–1922[1]

Alan McKinlay

The Glasgow ILP drew its vitality from the personal involvement of its membership in a broad range of long-term radical projects and short-term protest movements: housing and rents, municipal politics, anti-war and no-conscription, organising non-skilled workers and the shop stewards' movement. Before 1914 the ILP had become the organisational intersection of a series of progressive social networks, the hub of radical activity from the shopfloor, the teeming tenements of the Glasgow communities, to the council chambers. The ILP's integrative role within the Clydeside left was massively enhanced during the war years. The inevitable result of this extraordinary range of activities was an ever-increasing ideological eclecticism; between 1914–18 the party became host to every shade of radical thinking, from advanced liberalism to doctrinaire marxism. The openness of the ILP and the commonalities of thought evident among Clydeside's socialist community make the mutually exclusive categories of 'revisionist' and 'revolutionary' inappropriate to capture the fluidity of left-wing opinion during this period. The Glasgow ILP of the Great War is best understood not as a conventional political party but as a loosely organised democratic movement whose primary political terrain was the factory floor and the street corner. Post war changes in Labour Party organisation and the return to conventional politics made it impossible for the ILP to sustain its historic tolerance of diversity, a transition made even more difficult by a membership explosion based on recruits accustomed only to protest politics. The immediate post-war years witnessed profound realignment at all levels of the labour movement. Interpretations of this crucial period have been refracted through a pervasive preoccupation with the fate of the shopfloor militants who led the wartime shop stewards' movement and the labyrinthian politics of the tiny marxist sects which congealed to form the Communist Party of Great Britain in 1920.[2] This obsession with the conversion of a handful of revolutionary socialists from syndicalism to bolshevism has obscured the seminal role of the ILP in the realignment of the British left in the immediate post-war period.

If the first major theme of this chapter is the qualitative shift in the nature of the ILP's organisation after 1918 then the second is the uncertainties of this transition period in popular politics. Uncertainty was generated not only by the untried possibilities of the first truly mass electorate but also by the realignment of the left initiated by the reorganisation of the Labour Party, the formation of the CPGB and the inspirational example of the 1917 revolution. It is against this backdrop that we must set the slow disintegration of the networks of activists which linked wartime industrial and community protests. The wartime unrest had compelled co-operation within the Clydeside socialist movement drawing previously opposed political groups into temporary, ad hoc coalitions around particular issues. These were overlapping conflicts, their leaderships drawn from a common pool of political activists, particularly in the case of the rent strike and the shop stewards' movement.[3] Above all, it was ILP-ers whose long links with industrial and community movements placed the party at the centre of Glasgow's left leadership. Crucially, the bonds between the city's wartime political leadership remained profoundly personal rather than organisational.[4] It was precisely this personal dimension which became envenomed during the process of realignment on the left which began after the Armistice and which has distracted attention from the more important structural and strategic shifts in popular politics.[5] The question is, could the ILP have acted as an organisational broker to prevent the disintegration of these activist networks in the immediate post-war period?

I

The reconstruction of the Labour Party through the adoption of the 1918 constitution fundamentally altered the shape of British socialist and labour politics. Organisationally, the Labour Party shifted from a loose, regionally based federalism towards a more unitary national structure. The 1918 constitution altered the terms of the uneasy coalition of committed socialists and trade unionists for whom Labour was little more than a convenient vehicle for limited legislative reforms.

The ILP was no longer guaranteed representation on the Labour Party executive but was now formally subordinated to the wider party both at annual conference and in candidate selection at constituency level.[6] Not only did the 1918 constitution threaten the ILP's power-base it also brought the party's very existence into question. At a stroke, by adopting a socialist programme and constituency organisation the Labour Party challenged the ILP's ideological and organisational raison d'être. Between 1918 and 1922, however, the tension implicit in the ILP's changed relationship with the Labour Party remained latent.

Despite their awareness of the threat the 1918 constitutional changes posed for their party, ILP activists were openly dismissive of the Labour Party's new powers to enrol individual members: 'the shilling a year Labour Party'.[7] Similarly, in its statement to the 1918 conference the ILP National Administrative Council referred to what it termed the 'nominal membership' which the new Labour Party constitution encouraged: low subscriptions

> may be an inducement to large numbers of people to affiliate who do not feel inclined to join the Independent Labour Party because of the larger calls it makes, both financially and upon their active work and co-operation. But a large membership is not necessarily a source of strength. The strength of a Party depends upon the character and enthusiasm of its individual members, and we have no doubt that the ILP, with its unceasing activities, its persistent propaganda, and the inspiring idealism of its Socialism and Internationalism, will continue to attract all the men and women into the membership who are really of value to the effectiveness of a political party.[8]

Indeed, the ILP's national leadership somewhat optimistically anticipated that the new local Labour Parties would stimulate rather than injure the ILP by providing a recruiting ground or half-way house for the nominally committed. The assumption that worthwhile recruits would naturally gravitate to the ILP was a sentiment which struck a chord with Clydeside activists deeply suspicious of the influx to the ILP nationally of anti-war liberals 'who had not been proved in the principles of Socialism'.[9] For ILP activists anxious that the party remain socialist a further uncontrolled membership expansion was a danger to be avoided rather than an opportunity to be exploited.

While the ILP's national leadership urged that no local ILP should

openly oppose the formation of constituency Labour parties or provoke the hostility of the host body, platform calls for continued, even
accelerated, recruitment put the ILP in an anomalous position. Such
was the potential overlap of organisation and ideology that James
Maxton, now advised individual ILP-ers to think and act 'with a dual
personality' mindful of their long-term vision of socialism, pursued
through the ILP, and the short-term reforms which required the
maintenance of the alliance with the Labour Party.[10] As Sidney Webb
and Arthur Henderson, the architects of the 1918 constitution,
expected, the very imprecision of Clause iv, the socialist commitment,
permitted it to serve a unifying purpose in a party which had
experienced, and anticipated the continuation of severe ideological
conflict, almost to the point of disintegration.[11] Clause iv gave the
Labour Party an emotive and intellectual appeal not only to the
electorate but also to constituency activists. Clause iv was the
touchstone of a still fragile party unity. For the trade union leaders, the
adoption of a vague socialist commitment was a convenient method of
satisfying the growing body of socialist opinion in the unions, constituencies and factories without committing the party to a specific
legislative programme.[12] Whatever the organisational tensions
implicit in the 1918 constitution, the promise of Clause iv was that it
made the Labour Party the potential vehicle for radical social transformation, a possibility dependent upon the ILP's presence at all levels
of the wider party.

If the 1918 constitution presented serious problems for the ILP then
it also offered significant opportunities. At the very least, socialists
could no longer be marginalised ideologically: Clause iv legitimised
the place of active socialists in the labour alliance. More than this,
Clause iv was an open challenge to the ILP to transform socialism from
a distant, utopian doctrine to the basis of party policy. It was precisely
this new-found legitimacy which the Glasgow ILP leadership used as
its main argument to counter voices within the party that it should
disaffiliate from the Labour Party and to rebuff external critics. During
a public debate with the marxist Socialist Labour Party, James Maxton
maintained that the energies of the socialist community should not be
dissipated by the formation of a new communist party or the maintenance of an impotent ideological purity. Rather, 'revolutionary
socialists' should use the socialist commitment of Clause iv to bring,

themselves into organic connection with the rest of the workers of the country. The big majority of workers . . . were in the Labour Party and, although he knew that many of them did not accept [Clause iv] it was therefore the function of Socialist organisations to get the non-Socialists to understand the principle, and so give the average view among the workers a full Socialist consciousness.[13]

For Maxton, maintaining the Labour alliance of trade unions and socialists was a strategic rather than an ideological imperative which did not take precedence over socialist beliefs. Crucially for future developments, Maxton's acceptance of Labour Party discipline was vitally qualified: tolerable 'as long as they were not asked to turn their backs on the principles of Socialism. . . . But the experience of the ILP had shown that it could be within the Labour Party without losing anything', a point borne out by the ILP's opposition to the war. The organic metaphor deployed by Maxton also suggests strong continuities with the language of the pre-war socialist community whose first purpose, irrespective of ideological allegiance, was to accelerate the evolution of progressive opinion through education.[14] To be sure, there were considerable differences in emphasis and focus between the mainstream of the ILP and the syndicalists and marxists for whom the workplace was the cradle, and bitter industrial experience the midwife, of political consciousness. Beneath this ideological and organisational heterogeneity, however, the ubiquity of evolutionary imagery ensured that the ILP's strategic arguments for remaining within the Labour Party had enormous resonance within Clydeside socialism.

Despite the clear position adopted by the Glasgow leadership there was considerable – and sustained – opposition from the party's rank and file. At the 1920 Scottish Divisional Conference six Clydeside branches advocated severing the ILP's connection with the Labour Party. If the ILP remained within the Labour Party it would not only be tainted with Labour's past and future compromises but be outflanked by more radical parties on the left. The main constituency for disaffiliation was from young delegates attracted to the ILP during the wartime industrial unrest who maintained 'the complete independence of politics . . . was now generally accepted by those who took an active part in the organisation of the workshop, and the bulk of the rank and file of the ILP accepted the same position today'.[15] In this scenario the role of the ILP was purely agitational, abstaining from all conventional political channels. John Wheatley's reply to this 'singularly unfortunate' motion is significant not only for his reaffirmation of the strategic necessity of continued adherence to the Labour Party and parliamentarism because of the changed opportunities of a mass electorate but also for his conciliatory attempt to woo left-wing opinion.

> The propaganda of the ILP, and its co-operation with the Labour Party had brought them to the threshold of a great national triumph. The principle involved going to get their emancipation by class solidarity or by division into groups. He wanted the Marxians to realise that the latter meant, Workers of the World Divide! and not, Workers of the World Unite![16]

Equally significant, Wheatley's position was to confirm the ILP's independent – and distinctive – role within the labour alliance, a role, moreover, which was of increased importance given the proximity of political power. Wheatley's intervention was not only important within the Scottish ILP, now the most numerous region within the party, but also a powerful counterweight against the important voices on the national leadership arguing that with the adoption of Clause iv it was time for the ILP to subsume itself completely within the Labour Party. The motion for continued affiliation to Labour was comfortably carried by 147 to 53. While it would appear that there was still a significant minority advocating more explicit links with non-parliamentary movements and a complete break with Labour this was virtually the death throes of such sentiments within the Clydeside ILP. By the close of 1920 the formation of the British Communist Party, the ILP's decisive rejection of affiliation to the Moscow-led Third International and the downturn in ILP membership effectively marginalised any lingering residues of the wartime shop stewards' movement.[17]

How then did the ILP pursue its strategy of maximising its influence within the Labour Party? The ILP could not realistically hope to decisively shape Labour Party policy through an annual conference dominated by trade union block votes. The alternative was to maintain and increase its influence at all levels of the Labour Party, particularly local and national executives and through the parliamentary party. There were good reasons for ILP optimism; not only was the party in a period of unparalleled growth consolidating its premier position in British socialism, it also enjoyed considerable leverage within the structure of the newly constituted Labour Party. Almost half of the

1918 Labour Party National Executive Committee were ILP-ers, including Jowett, Maxton, Snowden and MacDonald as treasurer.[18] In Scotland in general and Clydeside in particular the position of the ILP within the Labour Party was even stronger. The ILP completely dominated the executive of the Glasgow Labour Party: in 1920, 14 of its 18 members were ILP nominees.[18] At the grassroots level, the ILP's dominance of labour politics was even more profound. In 1919 the Labour Party's Scottish organiser observed with some exasperation that,

> Ninety per cent of the propaganda of the Labour Party is being carried out in Scotland by individuals who have joined the ILP. . . . And 75% of the Election work is done by them. On the other hand, members of Trades Unions . . . perform not more than 10% of the propagandist, and 25% of the electoral work.[20]

A combination of the structural weaknesses of the new Labour Party consistuency organisation and the indifference of affiliated trade unions undermined the attempt to constrain the ILP by constitutional fiat.[21] Until the early 1930s the ILP effectively was the Labour Party on the ground on Clydeside.

II

The labour vision of Clydeside socialists was inevitably broadened by the ideological ferment of the Great War. The boundaries of popular politics in the region were extended to encompass debate about property rights, workers' control and soviet democracy; topics which could not be contained within the boundaries of progressive liberalism. Within the ILP this ideological efflux was most clearly registered in the party's internal debate about post-war reconstruction and its platform and organisation for the general election scheduled for 1918. During the course of 1916 aggregate meetings of the Glasgow ILP, typically attended by over three hundred accredited branch representatives, moved from an electoral programme whose central planks were house building, communal land ownership and free education to a manifesto explicitly geared to winning workshop support.[22] For the ILP the immediate task was to forge a direct financial and political link between the local party and every workshop committee. To appeal to this factory constituency the Glasgow ILP's 'minimum programme' subordinated its long-established social demands to the primary aims of nationalising all manufacturing industry and establishing workers' control.[23] Grassroots pressure was clearly behind this shift in emphasis with the local leadership struggling to bridge the gap between the radical demands thrown up by the politicised industrial struggles of the Great War and the ILP's adherence to parliamentary politics.[24] As we shall see, maintaining a durable ideological hegemony was a constant problem for the ILP's local leadership, exacerbated by the disarray of party organisation caused by a membership explosion which further increased the heterogeneity of rank and file opinion.

Ideological confusion was both cause and effect of the virtual collapse of the ILP's established political infrastructure. Nor was the ILP's national organisation able to remedy regional shortcomings, a fact which left the party poorly prepared for the 1918 General Election.[25] The position was particularly acute in Scotland where wartime industrial and community activities had taken priority over branch organisation. Indeed, such was the disarray of the ILP's normal political infrastructure, and the vitality of workshop organisation, that the shop stewards' movement rather than party branches based in the community were considered the most effective vehicle for disseminating propaganda and raising funds for the coming electoral contest. Nor were these vital political activities restricted to ILP members: all 'known sympathisers' were issued with collection cards, irrespective of party affiliation.[26] Paradoxically, as Egerton Wake, the Labour Party's National Organiser reported in August 1918, exceptional levels of political activity had left Scottish Labour ill-equipped to fight a General Election.

> While the industrial and propaganda sides of the movement there has been a considerable activity . . . there has been a lack of concentration upon effective political organisation . . . There has not been sufficient time for the creation and development of that measure of constituency organisation necessary for Parliamentary campaigning.[27]

III

The General Election of December 1918 offered the Glasgow ILP leadership the opportunity to loosen the ideological and organisational links between the ILP and the shop stewards' movement. The ten ILP candidates in Glasgow had formed the nucleus of the party's pre-war leadership and it was they, rather than the lay membership, who were charged with devising a 'uniform platform'. Derived from Labour's national policies this uniform platform reversed the priorities established by ILP activists during the Great War; nationalisation and workers' control were removed from the ILP programme.[28] The defence of the 1915 Rent Restriction Act, not the democratisation of industry, was the crucial theme of the ILP's election campaign.[29] Despite this significant shift of emphasis, the shop stewards' movement co-operated fully in the ILP campaign.[30] Indeed, the Clyde Workers' Committee was persuaded to reverse its original intention to field its own candidates.[31] This is not surprising given the depth of the personal bonds and the still considerable overlap of policies between the factory movement and the Glasgow ILP.

Labour suffered a severe disappointment in the 'khaki' election of December 1918. Rather than winning between three and five Glasgow seats, as was widely anticipated, Labour won only one, Govan. On the face of it, Labour's failure to make its expected breakthrough in 1918 appears doubly surprising given that the election was the first fought under the terms introduced by the 'Fourth Reform Act' which created a mass, democratic electorate by enfranchising the overwhelming majority of adult males and, with some qualifications, females. For Iain McLean's influential history of *The Legend of Red Clydeside*, Labour's disappointing performance in 1918 is of the utmost importance.[32] McLean's overriding purpose is to demonstrate that there was a major break 'between wartime militancy and post-1922 Parliamentary radicalism'.[33] In short, Clydeside's unique experience during the Great War had little or no impact on post-war popular politics, save to establish an unwarranted 'legend' of proletarian class consciousness and a pantheon of radical heroes. More positively, McLean contends that Labour's poor showing in 1918 was attributable to the incomplete rapprochment reached between the ILP and the region's Irish community.

Conversely, Labour's sweeping success in Glasgow in 1922 was due, in large part, to the decisive post-war shift in Irish political allegiances, from Liberal to Labour. The basis for Labour's accommodation with the Irish community was that the ILP dropped their prohibitionism in return for the unqualified endorsement of Irish publicans and newspaper magnates. This support was consolidated by the ILP's assiduous courting of the Catholic church hierarchy and laity through political support for municipally financed denominational education. McLean maintains that as a result of the compromises made to secure Irish support between 1918 and 1922 the nature of the Glasgow ILP was gradually, but irreversibly, transformed from a principled radicalism to a calculating machine politics based on shadowy pacts between the leaders of the city's political machines.[34] Clearly, McLean's hypothesis has implications not only for our understanding of the timing of Labour's electoral breakthrough but also for the long-term development of Glasgow socialism. In particular, the emergence of Patrick Dollan as the principal power broker in city politics in the immediate post-war years assured his personal ascendancy in the Glasgow and Scottish ILP between 1928 and 1932, the period in which the ILP tore itself apart over the question of reconciling its socialist principles and continued affiliation to the Labour Party.

McLean's interpretation is of paramount importance both in terms of Labour's electoral progress and for the trajectory of the ILP as a whole. There are, however, a number of reasons for doubting the validity of McLean's thesis. First, the full impact of the new adult franchise was considerably muted by significant administrative deficiencies. In particular, a dated electoral register and inadequate arrangements for servicemen and non-householders combined to depress the Glasgow turnout in December 1918 which at 57 per cent was more than 20 per cent below that achieved in the 1922 General Election.[35] Most obviously, as earlier essays in this volume have demonstrated, there had always been a strong, if often stormy, affinity between Labour and the Irish in local politics. Equally, if the 1921 partition treaty conclusively ended the Irish community's historic support for the Liberals then the use of the universally reviled 'Black and Tans' in Ireland from 1916 had already severely eroded this impediment to a wholesale shift to Labour allegiance. Conjunctural factors explain why the Irish vote was not registered for Labour in 1918. The election of December 1918 found the Irish political machine in unprecedented disorder as a result of the war and the experience of the Easter Rising. The full weight of the United Irish League was mobilised behind only one Labour candidate, John Wheatley, who failed to win Shettleston by a mere seventy-four votes. Neither the secular nor the religious leaders of Glasgow's Catholic Irish were able to exert a decisive influence for or against Labour in the critical post-war period. If the former were disabled by tactical divisions over the pursuit of Irish home rule then the Church hierarchy was effectively silenced by the infirmity of its Scottish leadership and their fear of alienating communicants perceived as moving inexorably towards Labour support.[36]

In sum, there is little mystery in the limited advances made by the Glasgow left in the 1918 General Election.[37] The conjunction of a series of contingent and highly exceptional factors combined to artificially depress the Labour vote. To the inevitable, and temporary, swing in favour of Lloyd George and the coalition which had secured war victory was added organisational factors which limited the effectiveness of Labour's campaign. Given the seriously flawed administration of the contest there can be little doubt that the 1918 General Eelection left a considerable reservoir of latent support for Labour untapped. There is no justification for making Labour's poor performance in December 1918 the hinge of an interpretative framework which denies any continuity between the wartime experience of Clydeside and post-war politics and the beginnings of a manipulative machine politics which signalled the protracted death-knell of Labour radicalism.

Ironically, the ILP's disappointing electoral performance had beneficial side-effects for the party as it strove to consolidate member-ship gains and come to terms both with the reformed Labour Party and the extra-parliamentary left. The supine performance of the Parlia-mentary Labour Party in the first post-war parliament actually increased the salience of the Glasgow leadership's strategic argument for remaining within the labour alliance. The widespread failure of ILP candidates, especially the defeat of all its parliamentary leaders, exempted the ILP from culpability in the Labour Party's Westminster performance. The ILP was distanced from the weakness of official Labour and in a stronger position to argue that the inclusion of a sizable ILP contingent would radicalise the performance of Labour at Westminster.[38]

The initial disappointment of Glasgow Labour over the 1918 result was rapidly displaced by the perception that its exceptional nature made an electoral breakthrough a realistic medium-term prospect.[39] If this prospect shifted the gaze of leading Glasgow ILP-ers from the council chamber to Westminster then it equally demanded a different form of politics, a shift from extra-institutional agitation to electoral organisation. For the Glasgow ILP leadership this made it imperative that organisation be tightened, that ideological eclecticism give way to a defensible militant parliamentarism. It is well to recall the limits of the possible for Glasgow socialists before 1914. Before the Great War the ILP leadership had hoped for tighter party organisation, an effective dissentient voice in the city chambers and, at most, the extension of municipal enterprise until Glasgow became something akin to a socialist city state.[40] Now, however, they were confronted with infinitely broader horizons. The tantalising prospect of municipal and national power was the essential backdrop to developments in the Glasgow ILP before the 1922 General Election.

To the long-established belief in democratic rather than revolutionary political change was added a strategic imperative; avoiding any action which would jeopardise the untried promise of mass democracy. The major tactical problem confronting the Glasgow ILP leadership mirrored those of the national leadership: how to consolidate the advances made during the war period and maintain the fragile organisational unity within the party without endangering its links with the Labour Party. In this sense, any detailed exploration of the question of party aims could only exacerbate existing tensions within an already diverse and divided membership. Indeed, for the Glasgow leadership to initiate or sponsor widespread debate about party objectives could only hinder the pursuit of power. In such circumstances, the preservation and advancement of the party was consistently accorded a greater priority than the attainment of specific objectives. The anonymous author of *Forward*'s 'Catholic Socialist Notes' captured the disciplinary constraints which the pursuit of power imposed on the ILP:

> an excited raving mob will never be trusted. Our movement must display fitness for the task which is offered. We must realise in all sincerity that the ruling of a country requires great powers of self-control and mental balance, when the government has to be conducted against powerful reactionary gangs plotting for its destruction. Until now we have been mainly critics of the great governing class. . . . We are about to brush this class aside and take their place.[41]

It is not too fanciful to suggest that this injunction, on discipline and loyalty to the party rather than agitation, would have a double force for the ILP whose prospects of power were dependent upon the continued tolerance of the Labour Party. For the local ILP leadership, inadequate organisation was a major reason for the party's halting electoral advance. ILP branches had proved incapable of compensating for the inadequacies of factory activists in electioneering. In addition, widespread inexperience in managing an election campaign resulting from rapid membership growth was compounded by a degree of branch autonomy which made central co-ordination virtually impossible. In the aftermath of the khaki election the local ILP leadership finally disentangled itself from its lingering associations with the rump of the shop stewards' movement and moved to increase centralised control over rank-and-file debate, through allocating speakers and tightening procedural restrictions on policy-making bodies.[42] These efforts were not entirely successful. Attempts to prohibit sales of *The Worker*, now highly critical of the ILP in general and P.J. Dollan in particular, were similarly rebuffed by branch officials as an unwarranted intrusion on internal party debates.[43] In 1919, Dollan, secretary of the Glasgow ILP, noted ruefully that, 'the local autonomy of the Branches is so much emphasised that suggestions from the central organisation are not met with much heartiness'.[44]

IV

If post-war ideological developments within the Clydeside ILP cannot be attributed to authoritarian control then neither were they the result of personnel changes in the local leadership or a shift in the social composition of the membership. Unlike the national leadership, run by a circle of London-based intellectuals led by Clifford Allen, the position of the pre-war Glasgow leadership, particularly John Wheatley, Patrick Dollan and James Maxton was consolidated between 1914 and 1920. The virtually complete absence of centrally organised national campaigning during the war left open a space for local activism. Starved of national speakers and literature the Glasgow ILP was thrown back on its own resources.[46] Apart from Maxton and Dollan's brief spells in gaol in 1916–17 the leadership remained intact throughout the war.[47] The shared experience of pre-war political organisation, the peculiar mixture of wartime popularity for their role in the housing agitation and hostility for their pacifism served to bind the ILP leadership into a tight-knit social circle. Indeed, this intense

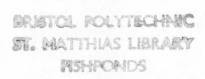

shared experience was vital to the personal loyalties which underlay the future notoriety of the Clydeside group in Parliament.[48] Crucially, there were no efforts to supplant the local leadership after 1918. The unofficial shop stewards' leadership, who could have used their wartime prominence as a springboard to post-war industrial or political influence, largely eschewed the opportunity of gaining positions in the trade unions or the ILP. The sole exceptions to this were David Kirkwood and John Muir both of whom had joined the ILP during the war under the influence of John Wheatley.[49] Similarly, with the exception of Helen Crawfurd none of the female leaders of the wartime rent strikes moved into the core of the local ILP leadership.[50] Wartime industrial and community unrest effected no permanent personnel changes in the ILP leadership none of whose central beliefs were transformed by their experience.

Unlike the personnel and ideological stability displayed by the Clydeside ILP leadership the party's membership underwent rapid change between 1918–22. Firstly, the party leadership was confronted with the problem of consolidating the membership growth which had begun during the war and continued in 1919. Secondly, partly because of this membership explosion, the party was confronted with a fundamental identity problem; the exigencies of war had blurred the distinctions between the socialist parties. Until the end of the Great War membership of one or other of the socialist parties on Clydeside was as much a matter of geographical chance as political conviction.[51] In the immediate post-war period the ILP encompassed a broad spectrum of radical opinion, from marxism to a vague commitment to social improvement. Thirdly, from 1920 the ILP experienced a sharp drop in membership. While the onset of recession was a major factor in this decline, a significant contributory factor was the completion of the process of realignment on the left. The formation of the Communist Party established a fault line on the ILP's left, an involuntary closure which compromised the ILP's historically open organisational style. While very few ILP-ers transferred to the Communist Party, the formation of the new party significantly altered the character of the ILP on Clydeside by crystallising latent tensions within the party.

From 1915 the ILP was aware that it was in the midst of a historic opportunity to massively increase its membership. Accordingly, in mid-1918 the Glasgow ILP established an Organising Committee with the dual purpose of accelerating membership growth and increasing ideological cohesion within the local party.[52] Not only would the ILP capitalise on the recruitment opportunities offered by public debate about post-war reconstruction, such a campaign was primarily designed to forestall the growth of the new Labour Party constituency parties. The Organising Committee – dominated by Dollan, Wheatley and Maxton – announced its intention of devoting the first month of winter campaigning to 'hurricane membership campaigns, in order to get 2,000 new members in this area'.[53] To judge from the results of the recruitment campaign, the Organising Committee were correct in their assessment that this intention was 'not an extravagant one, judging from the enthusiastic appreciation now dawning for the splendid stand made by the ILP for Socialism and Peace'.[54] Between November 1918 and January 1919 local membership rose by around 26 per cent.[55] Significantly, the 1918 'hurricane' membership campaign was conducted not by factory activists but by 'street captains' who were made responsible for organising Labour support in Clydeside tenements.[56] Clearly, the ILP's intimate involvement in the community based struggle to defend rent control was viewed by the local leadership as a more appropriate vehicle for building a broad-based party than reliance on shopfloor activists.

Rapid membership growth did not alter the social composition of the Glasgow ILP membership. Whereas the national post-war membership surge – from 30,000 to 45,000 – was, in large part, due to an influx of disaffected ex-Liberals and pacifists with an uncertain or, at best, untried affiliation to Labour and socialism no similar process unfolded in Glasgow. As in the pre-1914 period, the party membership faithfully reflected the industrial structure of the city but with one important difference: ILP members were overwhelmingly drawn from a new generation of skilled engineering, shipbuilding and textile workers politicised by wartime activism; their experience was of the immediacy of relentless agitation not the deferred hopes of building electoral constituencies.[57] In addition, a sizeable minority of ILP-ers were teachers, clerks and small traders, occupations whose literacy, numeracy and articulacy made them the natural intellectuals and administrators of the labour movement.[58] In Glasgow, however, administrative utility was not the basis of ideological dominance: the capacity to handle abstract concepts was not confined to a privileged minority with some measure of further education. On the contrary, the very nature of 'skill' on Clydeside carried with it implicit assumptions of the ability to translate abstract specifications into workable designs and finished products. Indeed, this facet of occupational experience was vital to the area's powerful tradition of working-class self-education. Between 1917 and 1920 local membership virtually doubled from 1,370 to 2,641 with the fastest rates of growth recorded in the artisanal communities of Govan and Partick, the heartlands of the 1915 rent strikes.[59] In 1919, the peak year for membership, the Govan ILP totalled 306, a third more than the second-largest branches in the east end wards of Bridgeton and Shettleston and ten times the size of the smallest ILP branches. The spread in branch size reflected the scope of ILP activity in the city, ranging from 'very active and experienced' branches such as Hutchesontown and Govan to those like Gorbals which were formed in the heady rush of the post-war organisation drive. Such small branches had much shallower roots in the community and only a thin layer of activists to maintain the routine of branch life – characteristics which left them vulnerable to sudden collapse.[60]

Between 1917 and 1920 women comprised around 20 per cent of the Glasgow ILP membership, a percentage which remained fairly constant irrespective of branch size or geographical location. By far the largest female contingent was located in the Partick branch with over one hundred female members, although even here they were outnumbered by more than four to one by their male comrades.[61] For the party leadership the paltry female membership represented a serious failure to capitalise on the recruitment opportunities thrown up by the wartime rent strikes and peace campaigns.[62] Despite their vital contribution to maintaining grassroots party organisation during the war, women were quickly returned to their subordinate role after the armistice.[63] Despite the continued importance of the rents issue the local leadership made no effort even to ensure that women's perspective on community issues was retained. Women were systematically under-represented on the Glasgow ILP's policy-making body numbering fewer than 10 per cent of branch delegates.[64]

Phenomenal membership growth posed a major problem for the ILP: how to retain the allegiance of newly enlisted members drawn to the party because of its industrial and community campaigning or by the particular excitement of a general election. Furthermore, these new recruits were unaccustomed to the rhythm of orthodox popular politics, the staccato pattern of long periods of mundane organisational and educational work interspersed by short, frenetic bursts of electioneering.[65] Nor could this be overcome by attendance at ILP election workers' training classes or abstract appeals to party loyalty. Ultimately, the local ILP leadership was forced to concede that it could devise no satisfactory organisational method 'to sustain the [new] members interest in the work of the Branch and of the Federation, and to destroy the apathy that leads to the lapsing of many members every year'.[66] It was not simply a matter of consolidating the allegiance of new members but also of transferring their commitment from one mode of politics to another, from constant activism to the intermittent political involvement of electioneering.

By the close of 1919 the ILP's national leadership concluded that the party had reached a membership plateau, the immediate task was to retrench and minimise future contraction.[67] Precisely because the Glasgow ILP drew the bulk of its membership from industrial workers it proved particularly sensitive to recession.[68] Organisational sensitivity to economic trends was further compounded by the party's decision to increase membership dues to a minimum of ninepence per month, a third above that levied on members of the new Communist Party. By late 1921 over one-third of the Glasgow membership were unable to pay their contributions and the party was forced to appeal for the assistance of middle-class sympathisers.[69] The sharp downturn in membership accentuated the uneven spread of ILP membership across the city, wiping out many east end branches and increasing the relative importance of Patrick Dollan's power-base in the Govan and Partick areas.[70] Membership loss drained the ILP branches of their vitality and as the social and educational dimension of branch life diminished so their activities became overwhelmingly focused on elections.[71] This qualitative shift in interal party life reflected not only falling membership but also the types of member lost to the ILP after 1920; particularly the women and young factory activists who were the party's dynamic links with the informal social networks so vital to the ILP's role in wartime popular politics. The shift in ILP membership was critical in determining the balance of opinion within the Glasgow party over a range of issues, from relations with the Labour Party to industrial and political democracy.

V

The great issue which had pushed the ILP to the fore of wartime popular protest was housing and rent control. Before 1915 the ILP had voiced moral outrage at Glasgow's appalling housing but with negligible practical impact and in the immediate post-war period consolidated its role as spokesman for tenant discontent. Above all, housing was an inherently unifying issue cutting across divisions of gender, ethnicity, religion, skill and locality. Tenant dissatisfaction at the failure of private landlords to provide sufficient and satisfactory housing at acceptable rents continued after 1918 while the nervous authorities anticipated that community unrest could prove an even more potent threat to public order than industrial conflict.[72]. In this charged atmosphere, the arguments of ILP-ers such as John Wheatley and Andrew McBride before government investigations into working-class housing in 1918–19 meshed with establishment fears and resulted in the extension of rent controls to higher-quality buildings and limited rent increases in controlled dwellings.

In his *Reply to the Rent Raisers* Wheatley justified the rent strike as a legitimate form of popular 'passive resistance' to a government which had surrendered its claim to democratic authority by ignoring its pledge to maintain the 1915 level of rent.

> When direct action or bloody revolution is mentioned, we are told that in this country, with its political liberties, the working class is the ruling class. The Imperial Parliament its Executive Committee. The voice of the people is the voice of Parliament, and, however much we may hate the law, we must obey that law, because it expresses the will of the people. But, what is our duty if a law is made – not only without popular sanction – but in direct violation of pledges on which its members were sent to Parliament? Surely we owe no allegiance, whatever respect, to members of Parliament, as individuals divested of their representative capacity? When they exceed the authority derived from the people they have no authority.[73]

Rising rents coincided with the onset of recession in mid-1920. Despite some initial success the ILP was unable to sustain a prolonged rent strike. In part, this failure was because of tactical differences within the local leadership as to whether rent should be withheld completely or only the increase.[74] More speculatively, perhaps the ILP's failure to retain the women members recruited during the war and the subordinate role of the remainder in the post-war party lessened its ability to galvanise such a social movement. Without organisation Glasgow tenants were gradually forced to pay higher rents or accept growing arrears, unified resistance continued only in Clydebank where the 'rent war' settled into a lengthy guerilla struggle against evictions.[75] The centrality of the housing question to Glasgow socialism and the failure of the 1920 rent strike to protect the legislative advances of 1915 confirmed the ILP's concentration on parliament as the key arena of post-war politics.

VI

Analyses of the Forty Hours' Strike of February 1919 have been obsessed with the street drama of the George Square riot and the arrival of the military to quell a revolution that never happened.[76] Our interest lies in the fate of the shop stewards' movement and its links with the ILP. Revolutionary and revisionist interpretations of the Forty Hours' Strike have drawn complementary conclusions. For both, February 1919 marks a decisive turning point in the development of Glasgow socialism, the final desperate fling of wartime radicalism. The 'failure' of the strike led to the profound disillusionment of the city's working class with direct action while victimisation sent the shop stewards' movement into terminal decline. This convenient fallacy obscures the complex realignment which occurred both within the factory strongholds of the wartime shop stewards' movement and the engineering union.

It was precisely the singularity of the working-class challenge to the rights of industrial capital and property that local elites feared most in the immediate post-war period. As prominent local employers such as William Weir appreciated, the danger to the established order lay neither with orthodox trade unionism, however militant, nor parliamentary socialism, but in the continuation of politicised industrial struggle after the armistice.[77] It was this awareness of the possibilities of working-class politics which underpinned the powerful local metalworking employers' associations determination that there should be a rapid and thorough dismantling of the last vestiges of wartime state regulation of industry.[78] The scope and vigour of the Clyde employers' covert activities, from securing tactic control over much of the city's popular press to co-ordinating the disruption of 'the best Socialist pitches' by Orangemen and ex-servicemen, suggests that the fear of social upheaval was not restricted to the fevered imaginations of metropolitan civil servants but common to significant sections of the employing class.[79] And yet in the wake of the Forty Hours' Strike the Clyde employers' associations made a tactical decision not to systematically cull shopfloor activists and to restrain their 'more willful members'.[80] To launch a concerted attack on the loose and shifting, but still influential, coalition of shop stewards in early 1919 would, the employers feared, serve only to consolidate their authority in the area. The employers concluded that with the transition to peacetime production the natural occupational allegiances of shop stewards to particular unions would quickly reassert themselves: 'the Wolf of Bolshevism' and industrial unionism would be limited 'to snapping at the factory gates'.[81]

It is clear that we must disentangle a number of overlapping, but distinct, processes to understand the industrial politics in the aftermath of the 1919 strike. For Iain McLean, 'the debacle of the 1919 strike broke the industrial power of the extreme left', discredited the philosophy and advocates of direct action and swung the Clydeside working class firmly behind parliamentary politics.[82] The reality was, however, considerably more complex than McLean's jaundiced revisionism allows. By no means all the activists involved in the 1919 strike drew pessimistic conclusions from their experience. John Paton recalled the exhilaration among the ranks of the ILP: 'although the strike failed, it had afforded a demonstration of mass strength that sent a thrill of excitement through all working class Scotland'.[83] Nor were the reputations of leading figures in the strike damaged.[84] The funds raised for the legal defence of those arrested during the George Square riot confirmed that the informal networks of shopfloor radicals remained largely intact.[85] Indeed, against the national trend, accredited membership of the unofficial shop stewards' movement actually increased on Clydeside throughout 1919.[86] Similarly, the number of authorised engineering union shop stewards remained stable until mid-1921 despite sharply falling employment.[87]

How then do we explain the undeniable collapse of the influence of radical shop stewards in this period? The return to commercial production entailed the rapid restoration of established skill hierarchies and demarcation lines while the 'ambiguous inheritance' of the craft tradition reverted to sectionalism.[88] In the shipyards and engineering factories of Clydeside, defensive craft sectionalism became more pronounced as recession deepened in 1920. All-grades bargaining policies were progressively marginalised not because of widespread victimisation but by the ascendancy of defensive sectionalism. Equally, structural changes in industrial bargaining undermined the autonomy of the shop stewards. In engineering, the 1919 Shop Stewards' Agreement was deliberately framed by the employers and the union executive to contain the shop stewards' movement and isolate individual radicals. As Allan Smith, the employers' chief negotiator, put it, union officials and employers shared a common purpose; namely, 'to give a definite status to the shop stewards and to constitutionalise the ' "Movement" '.[89] The Clyde engineering employers' association furthered this strategy by insisting that member firms formalise factory bargaining by recognising union representatives and by building durable, personal bonds with 'trustworthy individual employees'.[90] It was this gradual process which led to the growing antipathy between the shop stewards' movement and orthodox workplace trade unionists.[91] From 1919, therefore, the rank-and-file movement was engaged in an unequal battle within the union for scarce organisational resources and legitimacy. By 1920 such was the decline of the shop stewards' movement that a leading marxist, Robin Page Arnott, was bemused by Moscow's desire to win the movement for the fledgling Communist Party: 'It no longer exists. One might as well try to recruit the Chartists!'[92]

The demise of the shop stewards' movement was paralleled in Labour politics by the fate of the ILP Left, a small marxist group usually dismissed as an ineffectual pressure group advocating ILP affiliation to the Communist Party. But equally important for the ILP Left was the development of a specifically British marxism, attuned to British political conditions and possibilities. As the group's journal, *The International*, declared: 'We shall consider the application of Bolshevik principles to British economic and political conditions, and seek to formulate a course of action in accordance with our historical development'.[93] The leading figures of the ILP Left in Glasgow were Helen Crawfurd and J.T. Walton Newbold, a bitter opponent of John Wheatley.[94] While the ILP left had no significant presence within the Glasgow leadership or the party's organisational structure there was considerable minority support among the lay membership. The call to develop a marxism couched in 'the ordinary language of British political discussion' within mainstream labour politics exerted a powerful appeal in a party still torn between support for the 1917 revolution and parliamentary pragmatism.[95] The main thrusts of the ILP Left's policies echoed ideas with a wide currency among Glasgow socialists, particularly their advocacy of workers' and community councils as the distinctively British variant of the Russian experience. This reflected the widespread if diffuse perception among marxists that industrial organisation was inadequate in itself as the vehicle for social transformation. But the notion of social committees remained obscure, a still-born attempt to conceptualise the role of socialist parties in the formation of broad anti-capitalist alliances.[96] Just as the language of syndicalism remained a significant current within the early Communist Party so the ILP Left articulated a determination to sponsor grassroots control of the ILP.[97] In practical terms the ILP Left argued that the party should provide the organisational framework necessary to bolster the flagging unofficial shopfloor movement and to halt, if not reverse, the disintegration of activist networks.

> Here the ILP can render enormous aid – if its members will it. They can give to that new industrial movement, which is the force by whose support their political efforts will be made effective, the help of a great and experienced machinery of propaganda.[98]

For the ILP Left the party's role was not simply to provide a platform for advocates of industrial democracy but to actively resuscitate dissident factory unionism. This suggestion met with withering indifference from the Glasgow leadership. For the ILP to pursue such a strategy would inevitably draw the fire of the union leaderships 'who had declared open war' on the shop stewards' movement and who wielded such power within the Labour Party.[99] As an internal memo of the ILP's National Administrative Council put it, with admirable understatement: 'it would be unwise for the Party to go too much into the details of the organisation of the trade union movement'.[100]

Such were the tensions within the ILP, the uncertainties of the party's place in left politics, that John Paton described the Clydeside ILP as 'a rudderless ship drifting at the mercy of all currents in the political seas'.[101] If the Clydeside ILP had mounted a strategic defence of the decision to remain within the federal Labour Party then the departure of the ILP Left was symptomatic of the creation of clear ideological boundaries separating the ILP from marxism. To be sure, the local leadership deliberately abstained from any attempt to develop a systematic world-view, indeed, such a project would have been antithetical to the empirical tradition of 'labour socialism'.[102] Nevertheless, from the closing months of the war the party's leading figures made strenuous efforts to define the limits to, if not the substance of, ILP ideology. The first salvoes were fired by John Wheatley who heaped scorn on those millennial marxists for whom the Clyde Workers' Committee was a prefigurative movement, a rudimentary anticipation of a future soviet government. Conversely, Wheatley regarded the shop stewards' movement as a temporary expedient whose very existence was predicated upon an extraordinary – and purely temporary – industrial relations vacuum.[103] Equally, to focus exclusively on production as the fundamental axis of class relations was to neglect the politics of consumption and discount the experience of the popular struggle for peoples' housing. The final, decisive reason for rejecting the narrow focus on the factory as the critical arena for socialist politics was that it excluded, amongst others, distributive and technical workers and women, and this at a moment when the definition of citizenship had been massively expanded through the Fourth Reform Act. Not content with exposing weaknesses in productivist marxism Wheatley was equally impatient with strategies derived from a priori principles and not from political realities. The ultimate condemnation of 'honest but visionary enthusiasts who study phrases more than facts' was that it blinded them to the untried possibilities of mass democracy, 'forgetful of the fact that our problem now, is not to administer but to win socialism'.[104] Throughout this defence of radical parliamentarism Wheatley, in common with other ILP leaders, was careful not to reject marxism as an illegitimate participant in labour politics. However, it was equally clear that if marxists were to remain within the ILP then abstract principles had to be subordinated to political exigency.

The only concession the ILP leadership made to the syndicalist tradition was the acceptance of 'direct action' as a necessary complement to conventional politics.[105] In part, this reflected the result of the 1918 General Election which largely excluded the ILP from parliament and the general uncertainty over the party's future direction. In the immediate aftermath of November 1918 Tom Johnston grudgingly conceded that while industrial action 'was the longest way round and the roughest' the working class 'having missed the parliamentary opportunity' were left with little alternative 'meantime [but] to fight industrially'.[106] From the first, the ILP leadership made it clear that their endorsement of the strike as a legitimate political act was not a reversal of their long-held belief in the separate spheres of economic and political mobilisation. To the contrary, the prime political use of industrial action was to check the excesses of particular governments, not to challenge the authority of parliament in principle. In this respect, industrial action was an extension of the rent strike, a desperate tactic of civil disobedience, a demonstration of Labour's political weakness rather than its industrial strength. But the ILP made no attempt to develop this resigned, reactive position into a coherent proactive strategy. A combination of waning internal dissent, the decline of the shop stewards' movement and the proximity of fresh national elections after 1920 meant that this muted advocacy of direct action left no permanent mark on the ILP.

The protracted formation of the Communist Party of Great Britain (CPGB) and the question of which International the ILP should join crystallised wider differences of ideology and strategy. It was always a question of when, rather than if, the ILP withdrew from the conferences which ultimately created the CPGB. In Glasgow the most notable defector from the ILP to the CPGB was Helen Crawfurd, accompanied by a handful of branches convinced that 'the needs of electioneering have forced the party into reformism and opportunism'.[107] The ILP Left, frustrated by their inability to transform pro-bolshevik sympathies into active support for the Moscow Comintern or for the lonely task of forging an indigenous British marxism, seceded from the ILP to become a founding element of the CPGB. In April 1921 Patrick Dollan reflected on the impact the formation of the CPGB had had on the Glasgow ILP.

> The differences on policy within the Party, arising from the effects of the Russian Revolution on practice and theory, culminated in the withdrawal of a few members after the ILP had decided against affiliation with the Moscow International on the basis of the 'twenty-one conditions'. The defection of these few members has not weakened the organisation, which obtained peace to work out its policy in its own way. The membership is now united in aim and purpose.[108]

By early 1921 the situation within the Glasgow ILP had stabilised. The strategic and ideological vision of Wheatley and Maxton of a militant parliamentarism, a conditional acceptance of remaining within the

Labour Party had prevailed over anti-parliamentarism and those such as the ILP Left calling for closer links with the rump of the shop stewards' movement. The distinctiveness of the ILP, in but not of the Labour Party, democrats before parliamentarians, was clearly understood by the local party:

> A year ago there were signs of serious fissure. These signs have all but disappeared, and given a little tolerant good humour on non-essentials, there will be secession neither to the Labour Party Right, nor to the Underground Left.[109]

Forging this middle way between communism and reformism was, despite Dollan's bland summary, not entirely without cost. As we have seen, the realignment of the Glasgow left did not cause a mass exodus from the ILP but it did contribute to the loss of the women and young industrial activists which had given the party its wide social base and campaigning edge during the Great War. The formation of the CPGB signalled the total collapse of the interlocking networks of socialist activists which had linked 'the factory, the community and the state with a combination of direct action and institutional politics'.[110] This qualitative loss did not show up on any numerical balance sheet. In September 1920, the ILP National Administrative Council acknowledged the importance of this intangible factor in changing the nature of the party in areas such as Clydeside and Fife:

> The Committee is convinced that the failure of the Party to revise its programme in accordance with recent trends in Socialist thought has led to considerable discontent within the Party, and moreover, had kept out of the Party many of the energetic propagandists who have either stood aside from politics altogether, or have supported other organisations which stood for more modern conceptions of Socialism. The growth of Communist sympathies within the ILP, are important in this connection.[111]

VII

With the General Election of November 1922 the forward march of labour broke into an exhilarating quick-step. The administrative flaws which had dampened the Labour vote in 1918 were eliminated, a fact reflected in the 76 per cent turnout in 1922.[112] By 1922 party politics in the city had stabilised into a two-way division between Conservative and Labour, at the expense of the Liberals. Against a backdrop of mass unemployment and a union movement decimated by a series of major reverses, Labour won ten of Glasgow's fifteen seats. Another important factor was the re-emergence of housing as a central political issue as an ILP legal test-case secured a rent refund which held the promise of wholesale rebates if Labour won power. But 1922 represented not so much a breakthrough as simply the most dramatic demonstration of the consolidation of the Labour vote after 1918: the ILP pronounced itself satisfied but not surprised by its success.[113] Less dramatic, but also indicative of this process, was the doubling of the number of Labour councillors between 1919 and 1921 when forming a city administration became a realistic prospect, and this on a more restricted franchise than operated for national elections. Nevertheless, the emotional departure of the Clydeside MPs, cheered by tens of thousands of their fellow citizens, symbolised the arrival of Labour at the threshold of national government. For John Wheatley, November 1922 was a watershed in his political development, the moment which both confirmed his conviction that power could be won through elections and compelled him to revise his cautious evaluation of popular support for 'large-scale Socialist proposals':

> when we left Glasgow for London, the streets lined with hundreds of thousands of people . . . madly enthusiastic not for the MPs themselves, but for the Socialism for which they stood, it proved to me beyond doubt that the people were ready to respond to a bold Socialist lead. And so I gave expression to my changed view in Parliament.[114]

Notes

1 Phillip Snowden, Chairman's address to ILP National Conference, Glasgow, 6 April 1930.

2 See the exchange between James Hinton and Jean Monds, *New Left Review*, 97, 1976, pp. 81–104.

3 See James Hinton, *The First Shop Stewards Movement* (Allen & Unwin, London, 1973), pp. 125–7 for the image of separate industrial and community leadership. For a contrasting view see Joan Smith, 'Common Sense and Working-Class Consciousness: Some Aspects of the Glasgow and Liverpool Labour Movements in the Early years of the Twentieth Century' (unpublished PhD thesis, University of Edinburgh, 1980), pp. 461–2; and Bob Holton, *British Syndicalism 1900–1914. Myths and Realities* (Pluto, London, 1976), pp. 176–86.

4 Sean Damer, 'State, Class and Housing: Glasgow 1885–1919', in Joe

Melling (ed.), *Housing, Social Policy and the State* (Croom Helm, London, 1980), p. 105. For an evocative account of the intense personal connections between 'rebel networks' see Shiela Rowbotham, *Friends of Alice Wheeldon* (Pluto, London, 1986).

5 For the most famous example of fraternal animosity between John Maclean and William Gallacher, see Iain McLean, *The Legend of Red Clydeside* (John Donald, Edinburgh, 1983), ch. 12.

6 Robert Dowse, *Left in the Centre: The Independent Labour Party 1893–1940* (Longmans, London, 1966), pp. 35–8.

7 J.T. Walton Newbold, Manuscript Biography, n.d., n.p.

8 *ILP Conference Report*, 1918, pp. 21–2.

9 *Report to ILP National Administrative Council*, January 1919.

10 Gordon Brown, *Maxton* (Mainstream, Edinburgh, 1986), p. 89.

11 Ross McKibbin, *The Evolution of the Labour Party 1910–1924* (Clarendon Press, Oxford, 1974), pp. 91–106; Jay Winter, *Socialism and the Challenge of War: Ideas and Politics in Britain, 1912–1918* (Routledge & Kegan Paul, London, 1974), pp. 259–63, 273–4.

12 Christopher Howard, 'Henderson, MacDonald and Leadership in the Labour Party, 1914–1922' (unpublished PhD thesis, University of Cambridge, 1978), p. 175.

13 *Forward*, 14 February 1920; *Plebs*, XI, 5, 1919, p. 75.

14 See Smith, *'Common Sense and Working-Class Consciousness'*, p. 444.

15 *Forward*, 10 January 1920.

16 *Ibid.*; similarly, see Wheatley's Presidential address to the Scottish Labour Housing Association, *Glasgow Herald*, 3 January 1920.

17 John Foster, 'Scotland and the Russian Revolution', *Scottish Labour History Society Journal*, 23, 1988, pp. 8–9.

18 Howard, *'Henderson, MacDonald and Leadership'*, p. 187.

19 *ILP Conference Report*, 1920, p. 47.

20 *Labour Party (Scottish Division) Conference Report*, 1919, p. 21.

21 Ian Hutchison, *A Political History of Scotland 1832–1924: Parties, Elections and Issues* (John Donald, Edinburgh, 1986), p. 299.

22 Gordon Brown, 'The Labour Party and Political Change in Scotland 1918–1929: The Politics of Five Elections' (unpublished PhD thesis, University of Edinburgh, 1981), pp. 54–6; ILP National Organiser's Report to NAC, 10 June 1916, esp. pp. 20–1.

23 Glasgow ILP Federation, Aggregate Meeting, 30 November 1917.

24 *Forward* 3 February 1917.

25 Francis Johnson to Election Agents, November 1918; ILP Branch Circular, 15 January 1919.

26 Glasgow ILP Federation, Aggregate Meeting, 30 November 1917.

27 Labour Party, National Executive Committee, Minutes, 31 August 1918.

28 Glasgow ILP Federation, Election Committee, 8, 15 September 1918, 29 October 1918.
29 McLean, *op. cit.*, pp. 164–73.
30 *Forward*, 14 December 1918.
31 *Forward*, 16 February 1918. The SLP concentrated its efforts in three constituencies where particular propaganda points could be made about pensions, industrial conciliation and the Labour Party's co-operation with the wartime coalition government, see Raymond Challinor, *The Origins of British Bolshevism* (Croom Helm, London, 1977) pp. 206–8.
32 McLean, *op. cit.*, p. 154.
33 *Ibid.*, p. 157.
34 *Ibid.*, p. 184.
35 James Smyth, 'Labour and Socialism in Glasgow 1880–1914: The Electoral Challenge Prior to Democracy' (unpublished PhD thesis, University of Edinburgh, 1987), p. 329.
36 Tom Gallagher, *Glasgow The Uneasy Peace: Religious Tension in Modern Scotland* (Manchester University Press, Manchester, 1987), pp. 100–4; William Knox, 'Religion and the Scottish Labour Movement c. 1900–1939', *Journal of Contemporary History*, 1988, pp. 618–20.
37 Alastair Reid, 'Glasgow Socialism', *Social History*, 11, 1, 1986, pp. 92–3.
38 *Forward*, 22 February 1919.
39 Hutchison, *op. cit.*, p. 277; William Knox, *James Maxton* (Manchester University Press, Manchester, 1987), p. 29.
40 Samuel Cooper, 'John Wheatley, A Study in Labour History' (unpublished Ph.D. thesis, University of Glasgow, 1973), p. 77.
41 *Forward*, 22 November 1919; for a contrasting interpretation see, Christopher Howard, 'Expectations Born to Death: Local Labour Party Expansion in the 1920s', in Jay Winter (ed.), *The Working Class in Modern British History: Essays in Honour of Henry Pelling* (Cambridge University Press, Cambridge, 1983), p. 79.
42 Glasgow ILP Federation, Executive Committee, 15 November 1918.
43 *Ibid.*, 9 January 1920.
44 Glasgow ILP Federation, Annual Report, 1918–1919, p. 1; ILP Rule Book 1921.
45 See Catherine Cline, *Recruits to Labour: The British Labour Party, 1914–1931* (University Press, Syracuse, NY, 1963).
46 *Forward*, 9 March 1918.
47 Helen Corr and William Knox, 'Patrick Dollan', in William Knox (ed.), *Scottish Labour Leaders 1918–1939; A Biographical Dictionary* (Mainstream, Edinburgh, 1984), pp. 94–5.
48 Robert Middlemas, *The Clydesiders: A Left Wing Struggle for Parliamentary Power* (Hutchinson, London, 1965). pp. 98–9.

49 David Kirkwood, *My Life of Revolt* (Harrap, London, 1935). pp. 86–7; William Knox, 'John Muir', in Knox (ed.), *op. cit.*, p. 216.

50 Helen Corr, 'Helen Crawfurd', in Knox (ed.) *op. cit.*, pp. 83–4.

51 Joan Smith, 'Labour Tradition in Glasgow and Liverpool: *History Workshop Journal*, 17, 1984, p. 38; in 1917 Ben Shaw, Secretary of the Scottish Labour Party wrote to his London colleagues of his 'aggravation'; at 'finding so many organisations cropping up and appealing to our clientele and more or less overlapping ours', Shaw to Middleton, 3 April 1917, quoted in Brown, *The Labour Party and Political Change*, p. 55.

52 Glasgow ILP Federation, Organisation Committee, June 1918.

53 ILP Branch Circular, June 1918.

54 *Ibid.*

55 *Ibid.*, 22 November 1918, 30 January 1919.

56 Glasgow ILP Federation, Executive Committee, 23 January 1920.

57 John Paton, *Proletarian Pilgrimage* (Routledge, London, 1935), pp. 199–200; Dowse, *op. cit.*, p. 72; Hutchinson, *op. cit.*, p. 278.

58 Robert J. Morris, 'Skilled Workers and the Politics of the 'Red Clyde', *Scottish Labour History Society Journal*, 18, 1983, p. 13.

59 Glasgow ILP Federation, Annual Reports, 1917–1920.

60 Maxton to Allen, 28 June 1921, cited in Arthur Marwick, *Clifford Allen: The Open Conspirator* (Oliver & Boyd, Edinburgh, 1964), pp. 73–4; David Marquand, *Ramsay MacDonald* (Cape, London, 1977), p. 269.

61 Govan ILP, Monthly Report to Glasgow ILP Federation Organisation Committee, 20 November 1918.

62 *Ibid.*, 17 September 1918.

63 *Labour Leader*, 7 March 1918.

64 Glasgow ILP Federation, Aggregate Meetings, 1917–1922.

65 *Ibid.*, 19 June 1920; William Gallacher, *The Last Memoirs of William Gallacher* (Lawrence & Wishart, London, 1966) p. 117.

66 *Ibid.*, 18 March 1919.

67 NAC Report, Party Finance and Organisation, September 1919; Draft Report to ILP Policy Committee, 17 September 1920.

68 Glasgow ILP Federation, Annual Report, 1919–1920; for national trends see, Arthur Marwick, 'The Independent Labour Party, 1918–1932' (unpublished B.Litt. thesis, University of Oxford, 1960) pp. 30–39.

69 *Forward*, 15 November 1921.

70 Glasgow ILP Federation, Annual Report, 1920–1921.

71 *Ibid.*, 1921–1922.

72 David Englander, *Landlord and Tenant in Urban Britain 1838–1918* (Clarendon Press, Oxford, 1983), pp. 289–93.

73 John Wheatley, *The New Rent Act: A Reply to the Rent Raisers* (Glasgow, 1920), pp. 4, 8.

74 *Forward*, 3 July, 17 August 1920.
75 Sean Damer; 'State, Local State and Local Struggle. The Clydebank Rent Strike of the 1920's', Centre for Urban and Regional Research, Glasgow University, Discussion Paper 22, 1985.
76 See McLean, *op. cit.*, ch. 11 for description.
77 Alan McKinlay, 'Employers and Skilled Workers in the Inter-war Depression: Engineering and Shipbuilding on Clydeside 1919–1939' (unpublished PhD thesis, University of Oxford, 1986), pp. 84–5.
78 Gerry Rubin, *War, Law and Labour: The Munitions Acts, State, Regulation, and the Unions 1915–1921* (Clarendon Press, Oxford, 1987), pp. 242–3.
79 Scottish Economic League to Clyde Shipbuilders' Association, 16 November 1920, North West Engineering Trades Employers' Association, Case Papers.
80 McKinlay, *op. cit.*, pp. 68–70; Jim McGoldrick, 'Crisis and the Division of Labour: Clydeside Shipbuilding in the Inter-War Period', in Tony Dickson (ed.), *Capital and Class in Scotland* (John Donald, Edinburgh, 1982), p. 183.
81 Stephens Shipyard, *Works Magazine*, October 1919.
82 McLean, *op. cit.*, p. 139.
83 John Paton, *Left Turn!: An Autobiography* (Secker & Warburg, London, 1936), pp. 14–15; Harry McShane and Joan Smith, *No Mean Fighter* (Pluto, London, 1978), pp. 104–9; Tom Bell, *Pioneering Days* (Lawrence & Wishart, London, 1941), p. 72.
84 *Govan Pioneer*, Govan Central ILP, May 1919.
85 Smith, *'Common Sense and Working-Class Consciousness'*, p. 572.
86 Branko Pribicevic, *The Shop Stewards' Movement and Workers' Control* (Blackwell, Oxford, 1959), p. 103.
87 Elizabeth Lancaster, 'Shop Stewards in Scotland: The Amalgamated Engineering Union Between the Wars', *Scottish Labour History Society Journal*, 21, 1986, p. 32.
88 Hinton, *op. cit.*, p. 56.
89 Minutes of Special Conference, EEF and ASE, 12 December 1917, pp. 9–10.
90 'Memo on Shop Stewards', May 1919, NWETEA Case Papers.
91 *The Worker*, 10 July 1920, for an example of friction between radical and orthodox shop stewards.
92 Directorate of Intelligence, 16 December 1920, CAB/24/117/2316, cited in Martin Durham, 'The Origins and Early years of British Communism, 1914–1924' (unpublished PhD thesis, University of Birmingham, 1982), p. 59.
93 *The International*, 19 June 1920, p. 1; 'The Call of the Third International:

Declaration of the Left Wing of the ILP', *Communist International*, no. 11–12, June–July 1920; Paton, *Left Turn*, pp. 9–10.

94 Helen Crawfurd, unpublished autobiography, n.d., p. 225; McKibbin, *op. cit.*, pp. 196–204 for Walton Newbold.

95 *Forward*, 13 December 1919; *The International*, 8 July 1920, p. 4; Paton, *Left Turn!*, pp. 80–81.

96 See William Gallacher and John Campbell, *Direct Action* (Glasgow, 1919); Hinton, *op. cit.*, pp. 314–22.

97 See the constitutional amendment successfully moved by Neil MacLean (Govan), *ILP Conference Report* 1918, p. 63.

98 *Forward* 10 May 1919; ILP, Policy Committee, 11 June 1920.

99 *Forward*, 22 February 1919; *ILP Conference Report* 1920, pp. 61–2.

100 Report to NAC, January 1919, p. 20; ILP Policy Committee, 21 July 1920, p. 2.

101 *Forward*, 18 September 1919.

102 Stuart MacIntyre, *A Proletarian Science; Marxism in Britain, 1917–1933* (Cambridge University Press, Cambridge, 1980), ch. 2.

103 Glasgow ILP Federation, 17 January 1919; David Kirkwood, *op. cit.*, p. 171.

104 *Forward*, 6 April 1918; David Howell, *A Lost Left: Three Studies in Socialism and Nationalism* (Manchester University Press, Manchester, 1986), pp. 239–43.

105 Brown, *Maxton*, pp. 102–3; Graham Walker, *Thomas Johnston*, (Manchester University Press, Manchester, 1988), pp. 45–7.

106 *Forward*, 18 January 1919; 5 July, 20 September 1919.

107 *Forward*, 30 April 1921.

108 Glasgow ILP Federation, Annual Report, 1920–1921.

109 *Forward*, 8 January 1921.

110 Manuel Castells, *The City and the Grassroots: A Cross-Cultural Theory of Urban Social Movements* (Edward Arnold, London, 1983), p. 33.

111 Draft Report to ILP Policy Committee, 17 September 1920.

112 Smyth, *op. cit.*, pp. 330–1.

113 *The Times*, 'Socialism on the Clyde', 28 December 1922.

114 John Paton recalling Wheatley's statement after his death, *New Leader*, 16 May 1930, cited in Howell, *op. cit.*, p. 252.

SIX

'Ours is not an ordinary Parliamentary movement': 1922–1926

William Knox

The sweeping victory of November 1922, which saw Labour win ten of Glasgow's fifteen parliamentary divisions, generated an enthusiasm in the city that bordered on the millennial. Mass meetings to celebrate the electoral triumph were held all over Glasgow. On Sunday 20 November at St Andrews Hall a service of dedication was held at which the audience sang the 124th psalm: 'Had not the Lord been on our side'. The climax to the celebrations was the rousing send-off the victorious Clydeside MPs received at St Enoch's Station. Around 250,000 people packed the surrounding streets to see them off to London. The scene was almost biblical. The crowd sang some old Scots songs, 'Jerusalem', and finished with the 'Red Flag' and the 'Internationale'. James Maxton addressed the seething throng of people, warning the government that it could expect nothing from them but implacable opposition. David Kirkwood assured the workers that when they returned from Westminster the railways would belong to them. As Emanuel Shinwell recalled in his autobiography – *Conflict Without Malice* (1955) – the Glasgow workers had a 'frightening faith in us. We had been elected because it was believed we could perform miracles'.[1]

Yet, in spite of this initial enthusiasm and hope, within four years the realities of parliamentary politics and the continuing economic depression would see the labour movement become a demoralised and divided force. The sense of common purpose and direction would be lost amid bitter scenes of recrimination at the failure of the first Labour Government to alter the balance of wealth and power and the collapse of the General Strike of May 1926. Although this chapter will not deal directly with the General Strike or its consequences, it hopes to show that there developed in this period strong tendencies towards a reformulation of the role of the Independent Labour Party (ILP) within the wider labour movement which would lead it into conflict with the Labour Party. The actions of the Clydeside ILP and its parliamentary representatives exercised a crucial influence on these important developments, but the crisis of the labour movement and the part played by the Clydesiders cannot be understood solely within the context of the narrow territorial confines of the west of Scotland. The fierce debates which occurred within the Glasgow ILP Federation in this period concerning such questions as the leadership of Ramsay MacDonald, Communist affiliation, the futility or otherwise of gradualism, only mirrored similar conflicts taking place at a national level. Local issues once so vital in explaining the growth of the ILP and determining the ideology of the party increasingly became echoes of national issues and debates. Like other parts of the labour movement, the west of Scotland played both an active and reactive role in these struggles. Thus this chapter has a dual purpose; firstly, to emphasise the reaction of leading figures in the Clydeside ILP to events within the labour movement and societal developments in general; and, secondly, to show how the experience of these processes, and the conclusions derived from that experience, caused the leading elements to attempt to forge a new political direction not only for the west of Scotland ILP, but also for the British labour movement.

I

The Clydesiders were eclectic in their political approach with no clearly defined theory of human affairs. They were the product of competing and conflicting influences. Some claimed to have been influenced by Marx, but more claimed that their political philosophy was derived from the Bible and the poetry of Robert Burns.[2] What united them was a universal desire to do something about poverty and to do it quickly. In spite of the petty bourgeois and skilled background of many of the Labour leaders, all had had first hand experience of the poverty and squalor of the west of Scotland working class.[3] The export orientation of the heavy industries of the west made the economy vulnerable to shifts in world demand and led to periodic unemployment among skilled tradesmen. Those MPs who were teachers witnessed the poverty of Glasgow children on a daily basis and were appalled at the destitution. Maxton provided a graphic description of conditions at St James' School, Bridgeton, when he claimed that:

> In the school I was teaching I had a class of sixty boys and girls of about eleven years of age . . . thirty-six out of the sixty could not bring both heels and knees together because of rickety malformations.[4]

Those fortunate not to have personal experience of poverty came into contact with it in their time as members of the Glasgow Town Council, the parish councils and the education authorities. Thus when they arrived at Westminster they did not view themselves as MPs in the conventional sense, but as representatives of the impoverished Clydeside working class.

The poverty of their constituents was never far from their minds. Most of them used their maiden speeches to attack existing unemployment legislation and the failure of capitalism to improve the material condition of the working class. Concern over these issues was given a social touch when the Clydeside MPs refused to socialise with their political opponents or accept invitations from wealthy Labour Party members. Their actions in this respect were underpinned by the Glasgow ILP Federation, whose executive resolved that 'the Labour MPs and other public representatives can best maintain the dignity of Labour by abstaining from politico-social functions organised by those who have no sympathy with the working class movement'.[5] From the outset then the Clydesiders were at odds with smart London society and its potentially corrupting influence. They were also impatient with the ancient customs and ceremonies surrounding parliamentary life. All of this distracted from the real task: the abolition of poverty.

Although Labour had won 142 seats at the General Election, and was recognised as the official opposition, its parliamentary significance was minimal. This situation led to an immediate disagreement over parliamentary tactics between the leadership of the Parliamentary Labour Party and the Clydesiders. The latter had been partly responsible for the election of Ramsay MacDonald as leader of the Labour Party in 1922. MacDonald's stand against the First World War had endeared him to the Glasgow MPs and since the other leading contenders were J.R. Clynes and J.H. Thomas, both of whom were detested by the Clydesiders, they had little choice but to vote in the way they did. But they were soon to express doubts over their action as MacDonald sought to make Labour a respectable part of the mainstream of British political life. This involved a political strategy designed not to alienate support from the middle classes. Stress was, therefore, placed on moderation rather than confrontation. The problem was that MacDonald's strategy and his emotional attachment to the institutions of the Commons were incomprehensible to the likes of Kirkwood, Maxton and Wheatley, who tended to view parliament as 'territory occupied by the class enemy, as a capitalist institution and . . . remained sceptical of its value'.[6]

Kirkwood, at a later date, although it might have been articulated a few years earlier, summed up the difference between MacDonald and the Clydeside group when it came to parliamentary tactics:

> MacDonald himself can play the Parliamentary game in the most approved drawing-room fashion. But we don't all want to be Neroes fiddling while Rome is burning. . . . While MacDonald was worrying about the glorious traditions of the Mother of Parliaments there were other mothers suffering more. . . . I don't think it is a good business to be taming our movement. Ours is not an ordinary Parliamentary movement. It is a movement of fighters; of working men in revolt. . . . We insist on our right to fight and to shock the fine ladies and gentlemen, and to have as little regard for their old institutions as they had for our mothers. These institutions exist to keep my class in subjection.[7]

Harassment and confrontation became the keystones of Clydeside strategy in the Commons.

In keeping with their policy of confrontation they agreed to create some sort of scene on the floor of the Commons and follow this up with a nationwide campaign to highlight the position of the poor and hopefully force the Tories to do something about it. This was made clear by Wheatley in a retrospective article defending parliamentary disruption published in the *New Leader* on 29 June 1923. However, when the opportunity came it was totally unexpected. During a debate on the Scottish Health Board Estimates in June 1923, Maxton accused the opposition of murder in approving cuts in health grants to local authorities. When Sir Frederick Banbury, Conservative, objected Maxton called him the 'worst murderer' of all.[8] On an order to withdraw his remark from the Speaker Maxton refused. Standing his ground until overcome by physical exhaustion he sat down, only for his place to be taken by Wheatley, then Campbell Stephen and, finally, Buchanan, all of whom repeated the charge. After a Commons vote in which the whole of the Labour front bench abstained, MacDonald reputedly white with anger, the four MPS were suspended.

The suspension of Maxton and the others ignited a row within the Labour Party over parliamentary tactics. The leadership of the PLP was outraged. Such outbursts were seen as demonstrating to the Liberals and Tories that Labour was incapable of operating the parliamentary machine. The editor of the *New Leader*, H.N. Brailsford, dismissed the protest as a cheap stunt, which had not only served to 'discredit Parliament itself', but also 'weakened the prestige of Mr MacDonald'.[9] But the suspended MPs refused to apologise for their behaviour and for this they received the full backing of the Scottish ILP and labour movement. Tom Johnston, who acted as one of the tellers in the Commons vote, said that 'Every MP who took part in that shameful decision . . . was, in act and in deed, a murderer.'[10] His sentiments were endorsed in messages of support from the executive of the Scottish ILP, the Glasgow ILP Federation and the Glasgow Trades and Labour Council (GTLC). Even a strong MacDonald supporter like Patrick Dollan could say that 'every member of the movement was in whole-hearted sympathy' with the suspended MPs.[11]

The 'murderers' incident is important for two reasons: firstly, it shows that the Clydeside ILP was united in its stand on poverty, and in its support of those who were determined to do something about it, even if it meant embarrassing the leadership of the Labour Party; and, secondly, that there existed a different view of the conduct of the PLP and the role of the Labour Party between those on the MacDonald wing of the movement and those on the left. MacDonald's policy of conciliating the middle classes by pursuing responsible tactics and moderate political goals was unacceptable to the Clydeside ILP, who saw that Labour was in danger of becoming just another social reform party. As Tom Johnston put it:

> Unless we go ahead creating Socialist opinion and not merely an opinion that we are tame and harmless substitutes for the Liberal Party, we shall only get office and not power.[12]

The debate sparked off by Maxton's remarks in the Commons was to resurface some months later following the general election, but this time the significance of the debate was to be much greater.

II

The election of December 1923 was called on the issue of

protectionism versus free trade. Shortly before this Labour had done reasonably well in the municipal elections winning two seats from the moderates and 50.7% of the total valid votes cast, therefore, the party was fairly optimistic about its chances in the general election. The result saw Labour as the largest party in Glasgow with 51.4% of the poll and ten out of the fifteen seats.[13] A number of ILP candidates had opposed both protection and free trade and instead expounded a 'socialist' trade policy based on underconsumptionist ideas, but the national Labour Party was deemed free trade along with the Liberals. The election was interpreted as a defeat for protectionism and the Tory Party and it was left to the other parties to form a government. But what kind of government? Was it to be a coalition, or some other form of parliamentary understanding? Indeed, given the special circumstances should Labour accept office at all?

MacDonald argued that it was proper to accept office in such conditions as not to do so would constitute a missed opportunity for Labour. Office would allow it to prove the critics in the bourgeois press wrong by showing that Labour could carry on the King's government and that 'working men could hold the highest offices of state with dignity and authority'.[14] Moreover, if it did not accept office then the Liberals would be, with the Conservatives, the largest party in the Commons, the official opposition. All the advantages gained since 1922 would be lost and Labour's 'position in the country might be put back by a decade'.[15]

MacDonald's political strategy went against the radical grain of the Glasgow ILP. As early as March 1922 the executive of the Glasgow Federation had opposed any compromises between Labour and its political opponents, resolving 'That this executive of the ILP reaffirms its belief . . . in Labour's independence and emphatically repudiates any suggestion that there should be a working agreement between Labour and any other political party'.[16] For Glasgow activists long accustomed to confronting Liberals and Tories campaigning under a common banner of moderate at municipal elections the issue was clear-cut: socialism versus capitalism and in this struggle there was no difference between the establishment parties. With this in mind, Tom Johnston, shortly before the formation of the first Labour government, declared:

> There's going to be no Liberal/Labour Alliance or Coalition or Under-standing. . . . The Liberal Party is a Capitalist Party. . . . If the Labour Party . . . were to betray the working class by allying itself with a Capitalist Party, the Labour Party is finished.[17]

However, within the labour movement MacDonald's arguments were decisive. One day before Johnston's declaration the executive of the Glasgow ILP welcomed the decision of the Labour Party to form a government on 'independent' lines and expressed confidence in MacDonald as leader. The resolution mirrored the statements made to the executive by Dollan and James Stewart MP. Dollan had stated that the Glasgow ILP was 'whole-heartedly behind the Labour Party in its resolve to form a Labour Government', and Stewart had assured the executive that in MacDonald 'they had a leader on whose judge-ment they could rely'.[18] This unconditional statement of faith demon-strated MacDonald's sway over the Glasgow ILP, particularly among the local leadership, if not the city's parliamentarians. But, despite some reservations, most of the Clydeside MPs meeting in Cranston's tea rooms immediately prior to the announcement of a Labour govern-ment were in agreement with Kirkwood to 'gie the man a chance'.[19] Only Buchanan and Maxton explicitly linked their misgivings about MacDonald with their scepticism about the prospects of a Labour government, dependent on the Liberals for its survival, being able to do something to resolve the problem of unemployment. The inclusion of Wheatley in the Cabinet did something to sweeten the opposition and confirm the groundswell of goodwill towards Labour's first premier inside the party.

The debate, however, did not end there. Although it was generally agreed that Labour should accept the seals of office untainted by compromise or coalition, in the final analysis, it was still a minority government dependent on one or other of the parties to get its legisla-tive programme through the Commons. Given these conditions, the question was asked as to what strategy should a Labour Government adopt. The left wing of the ILP argued that once in office Labour should pursue a bold programme of social reform, and if this policy was rejected by the other main parties, it should resign and fight an election on the basis of Labour versus the rest. This would force a more 'natural' alignment of class and party in Britain and effectively end any supposed distinctions between the Liberal and Conservative Parties.[20]

The party system would, in turn, be transformed from a three-party one to a two-party one. Maxton had expressed the hope that the Liberals and the Tories would combine to form a government to protect 'private enterprise against Socialists'.[21] In the unlikely circumstances of the Commons accepting the radical package of reforms then Labour would reap the benefit at the next election. Such a view was not an extreme one and found support even among those on the right of the party. Phillip Snowden expressed the opinion that the PLP should force the creation of a 'Liberal Conservative Coalition', something which MacDonald himself had advocated in early 1923.[22] But in 1924 this form of confrontational parliamentary politics was rejected outright by MacDonald, who was more concerned to prove to the middle classes that Labour was fit to govern in the interest of the nation rather than the working class.

MacDonald's first Cabinet reflected his desire to project a moderate image. It was dominated by those on the centre-right of the Labour Party, but as a sop to the left John Wheatley and Fred Jowett were included, the former as Minister of Health. Some of the most talented of the Clydeside ILP were excluded. Tom Johnston, one of the gifted but discarded MPs, expressed alarm at the 'bouquets that it [the Labour government] was receiving from the enemy [the bourgeois press]'. But he consoled himself with the fact that:

> On housing we are assured of a march forward. So long as Wheatley is at the Ministry of Health we can be assured that the governing principle will be the production of houses and not a concern for the retention of lobby support from the Liberals.[23]

The omission of all but one of the Glasgow MPs did not automatically make the west of Scotland ILP hostile to the new government. Initially the reaction seems to have been one of encouragement and a high sensitivity to any hint of criticism of Labour's performance. Wheatley's *Glasgow Eastern Standard* declared that 'All the East End MPs are staunch supporters of the Labour administration. Not only are they standing four square in defence of the Government but they are enthusiastic about its work and capacity'.[24] Speaking on behalf of the rank and file Patrick Dollan was not just supportive but fulsome in his praise, claiming that Labour 'had achieved more for the working classes in three weeks than preceding Governments had done in so many years'.[25]

For some sections of the ILP this support, however, became increasingly conditional. *Forward* was prepared to admit the difficulties of a Labour government in 'office' but not in 'power' however, it felt that did not excuse it from radically departing from the spirit of Keir Hardie and socialism.[26] Early criticisms surfaced in the columns of the paper and on the floor of the Commons regarding such things as the wearing of court dress, and the appointment of Tories, such as Lord Chelmsford at the Admiralty and MacMillan as Lord Advocate, to important positions in government. The pacifist wing was unhappy over the decision to build a naval base at Singapore and the failure to reduce the size of the armed forces. Disquiet was also raised over the Trades Facilities Bill, which Johnston and Maxton criticised for providing overseas investors in the Sudan cotton industry with government handouts. There was a general unease over the fact that the government seemed to be rewarding capital and punishing labour. A feeling compounded when it became known that MacDonald was prepared to use the Emergency Powers Act against striking dockers and London tramwaymen. Indeed, the only things the left had to cheer about in the record of the government were the settling of the Ruhr dispute, the recognition of the Soviet Union, and, of course, Wheatley's Housing Bill.[27]

By April 1924 attacks on the moderation of the MacDonald government were becoming more widespread. Emrys Hughes, editor of *Forward* in Johnston's absence, issued a warning to the government regarding continued support for its actions, stating that:

> The ILP will support the Government loyally as long as the Government goes boldly to its task prepared to do big things. . . . But the ILP is not going to apologise for timidity or anything that savours of reaction or needless compromise.[28]

Campbell Stephen, shortly before this, also warned MacDonald that he could not take their support for granted, pointing out that 'the members from the Clyde . . . did not forget their loyalty to the people in the constituencies'.[29] But in spite of mounting criticism over its lack of dynamism, the MacDonald government was never under serious threat from its backbenchers or from revolt in the constituencies.

Although the overwhelming majority of the PLP were members of the ILP, it was the former which had first claim on their loyalty, even when support was demanded on matters which went against agreed

ILP policy. Outside the Commons MacDonald had the support of influential local figures like Dollan, who could write, as the attacks on the leader became louder, that 'No man has worked harder for any cause than MacDonald had worked for the Socialism of the ILP', and that the Clydeside workers 'have faith in the Premier, and are confident he extracts the utmost from the conditions within his control'.[30] Even strong critics like Maxton were afraid to take their opposition too far in case it might lead to the fall of the government or embarrass MacDonald unduly.

At a National Administrative Council (NAC) meeting in August 1924 a resolution was passed condemning the Dawes Report and affirming the ILP's stand on reparations. Maxton proposed and the NAC accepted that the resolution should not be published.[31] Moreover, attacks on MacDonald were limited by the fact that opponents such as Maxton were compromised by the positions they held within the PLP, which demanded some form of collective responsibility. Maxton himself was a member of the executive of the PLP. Wheatley, as a member of the Cabinet, was under the self-imposed gag of collective responsibility and only resignation could have lifted the ban but that would have endangered the passage of his Housing Bill. Therefore, whatever the opponents of the government felt in private, publicly they acted with some restraint when reviewing Labour's record. All Maxton could say by way of criticism was that 'it would have been a good thing if Labour had cut out the Buckingham Palace and similar functions of snobbery and maintained its social life among the common people.'[32] A little later he was claiming that the government 'had accomplished wonders'.[33]

Having to defend or conceal the shortcomings of the first Labour Government did not worry MPs for too long, as in October 1924 the Tories and Liberals combined to defeat Labour on a vote of confidence in the notorious J.R. Campbell case. In the election that followed the opposition was to set the agenda. As the defeated Labour candidate at Cathcart complained 'the whole time was taken up in explaining the Russian Treaty and the Loan. When we had got these cleared the Red Plot came'.[34] Four days before the election a letter was published in the *Daily Mail* under the heading 'Communist plots in Britain'. It was purportedly written by the president of Comintern, Zinoviev, to the Communist Party of Great Britain (CPGB) calling on them to increase pressure on the Labour government to conclude trade agreements with the USSR and step up the class war to overthrow capitalism. Labour, because of MacDonald's inept handling of the affair, was depicted by the press as a tool of Bolshevik foreign policy and there is no doubt that this was a major factor in losing it the election. The Russian situation created the basis for an electoral pact between the Liberals and Tories in Scotland and Labour was forced to fight an increased number of two-cornered fights in the constituencies. The outcome was that Labour lost Partick and Maryhill and all Labour majorities were reduced in Glasgow. Of the total valid votes cast Labour secured 197,406 votes, or 48.59% of the poll, in spite of an increased turn out.[35] In the November municipal elections the downturn in the Labour vote continued with only 45.84% of the total vote, although surprisingly winning four more seats.[36]

III

When the PLP met on the morning after the election MacDonald was re-elected party leader; however, not before he had come in for some savage criticism over his handling of the Zinoviev affair and the failure of the Labour government to achieve much in the way of constructive legislation, the Housing Act notwithstanding, Maxton was foremost among the critics. He proposed George Lansbury as leader but this proposal only received a derisory five votes.[37] Maxton accepted the decision and did not seek to further embarrass MacDonald over the Zinoviev affair. As a member of a party investigative committee, which also included William Graham and J.H. Thomas, Maxton exonerated MacDonald of any blame. In any case the affair was a relatively trivial matter to Maxton and his colleagues. What bothered them was the more serious question of the general political direction of Labour under MacDonald's leadership. During the Campbell case, John Scanlon disclosed to Maxton that the prosecution of Campbell might wreck the Labour government. Maxton acidly replied, that 'the sooner they are out of office the better, as every day they were in led us further from Socialism'.[38]

Sentiments such as those expressed by Maxton were signs of the beginning of a new political direction within the ILP. Wheatley succinctly summed it up when he claimed that Labour lost the 1924 general election because 'a timid "statesmanlike" attitude makes no appeal to a people struggling to emancipate themselves from poverty.

There can be no freedom for the toiling multitude under capitalism. Knowing that, we should fight to end it, and not mend it.'[39] Politically this involved the development of a dual strategy with the ultimate aim of capturing the labour movement for a more radical brand of Socialism than the gradualism of the MacDonald wing. On the one hand, gradualist ideology was to be combatted by the more dynamic underconsumptionist economic policies; and, on the other, the left wing of the ILP was to purge the party leadership of those elements close to MacDonald and to impose stricter discipline on those members of the PLP who were directly financed by the ILP or, at least, members of it. Almost immediately after MacDonald was re-elected leader of the party, Lansbury, Maxton, Wheatley and some other militants organised a left wing section of the PLP determined to pursue the principles and policies of the ILP even if it meant going against the Labour leadership. All three withdrew from the executive of the PLP 'as by accepting office they were more or less bound to respect Executive decisions'.[40] At the same time, the parliamentary group of the ILP was reorganised on a tighter basis. Membership was confined to those MPs the ILP was financially responsible for. Others were only admitted if they agreed to accept ILP policy as determined by party conferences. Divisional Councils were asked to nominate candidates for selection as parliamentary candidates only if they had shown proven service and ability in the furtherance of ILP aims and objectives. Later, in December 1925, the parliamentary group decided, on a motion of Fenner Brockway, to set up an inner executive consisting of seven members – Maxton, Kirkwood, Stanford, Scurr, Wallhead and two others – to direct ILP representation in the Commons.[41] The intention behind these moves was to achieve a tighter hold on the activities of ILP MPs and to ensure that their first loyalty was to it and not the PLP. Although the full implications of such a strategy were not apparent at the time, these actions were laying the basis for the development of a party within a party; something which eventually would become apparent after 1927 with the publication of the Cook–Maxton manifesto.

To strengthen the left wing of the labour movement resolutions were moved at various conferences in favour of Communist affiliation to the Labour Party. Communist influence had been growing within the Scottish labour movement since the formation of the CPGB in 1920. Membership of the party in Scotland stood at 2,000 in 1926 compared with 5,000 for the ILP and inroads were being made into the industrial and political wings of the labour movement.[42] The Miners' Minority Movement was openly challenging the orthodox miners' leadership in Fife and Lanarkshire. William Elger, secretary of the STUC, campaigned to reduce Communist influence at Congress. As trade council and trade union delegates Communists were also eligible for selection as delegates at Labour Party conferences and to stand as Labour candidates in elections. At the 1924 conference it was estimated that of 150 delegates 'not less than twenty Communists' were registered.[43] At the 1923 conference the affiliation of the Communist National Unemployed Committee to the Labour Party was supported. A year later Communist affiliation was accepted on the same basis as other organisations. Parliamentary elections were fought on behalf of Labour by avowed Communists, Aitken Ferguson and Alex Geddes, in preference to ILP nominees Dollan, Rosslyn Mitchell and Stephen Kelly, and in opposition to Labour Party policy, at Kelvingrove and Greenock in 1923 and 1924.[44]

Selection of Communist candidates by constituency parties against the wishes of the executive of the Labour Party inevitably led to disagreements as to the proper relationship between the Labour Party and the CPGB. Mirroring splits elsewhere in the labour movement, the ILP was deeply divided on the question of Communist affiliation. Dollan attacked 'left wing disrupters' whose intention, he claimed, was to 'smash the Labour movement'.[45] John McLure, secretary of the Glasgow ILP, argued that Aitken Ferguson was a 'counterfeit' candidate and this alienated working-class votes.[46] Local resentment was not shared by many of the Clydeside MPs. Maxton argued that, although he was opposed to the CPGB's insistence on armed struggle as the way to socialism, affiliation would not only cause the CPGB to work through constitutional channels, but also incorporation would allow the ILP to resume its position as the party of the left as the Communist challenge disappeared.[47]

Maxton's endeavours on behalf of the CPGB at the Scottish ILP Conference in January 1925 were defeated by 127 votes to 86 and it was significant that his main opponent in the affiliation debate was Dollan. Under his influence the CPGB was held at arms length by the Scottish ILP. This was clearly shown in February 1926 when the Glasgow Trades Council held a referendum among its affiliated organisations on whether or not to accept the 1925 Labour Party

Conference resolution which advocated the banning of all Communist affiliation with the party either as individuals or trades union delegates. Although the expulsion of Communists did not receive the support of Maxton, Wheatley, Kirkwood, Stephen, Buchanan, Mclean and, surprisingly, Johnston and Shinwell,[48] and in spite of a wave of sympathy for the CPGB in the labour movement following the arrest in October 1925 of Communist leaders on sedition charges, the referendum went in favour of the Liverpool decision.[49] The result was 60,227 in favour, with 18,780 against. Twenty-four ILP branches, with a combined membership of 1,978, voted for, with only seven branches, representing 314 members, voting against.[50] Interestingly, and a testimony to Dollan's influence, Communists received more support from Divisional Labour Parties and Trades and Labour Councils than they did from ILP branches. To counter Communist influence the Scottish executive of the Labour Party had to disband the Gorbals, Bridgeton, Paisley and Springburn Labour Parties in January 1926.[51] The events of 1925 showed quite clearly that it was Dollan, and not Maxton or Wheatley, who was the dominant figure in the west of Scotland ILP and that any strategic initiative had to command his support to have any chance of success. But after the 1925 Conference Dollan's support of minority dissent or broad left-wing alliances was increasingly uncertain.

Dollan's rise to prominence in the Scottish labour movement was made possible by the departure of the more charismatic Clydesiders to Westminster which allowed him, as chairman of the Glasgow ILP, the space with which to consolidate his hold on the local organisation. His power had been increasing due to his undoubted organisational ability. The victories in the 1920 local elections, which saw forty-five Labour councillors returned, and the 1922 General Election were in large measure a tribute to Dollan's shrewd political managership. Given the acknowledged weakness of Labour Party organisation and the general apathy of trade unions in Scotland to the question of parliamentary representation, control of the ILP's electoral machinery was an important basis of political power.[52] In the 1923 General Election 41 of the 43 Labour candidates were members of the ILP.[53] Dollan was also one of the few Clydesiders with an active trade union background. Prior to joining the ILP in 1908, he had been active in the Lanarkshire coalfields and this connection, as Tom Gallagher points out, was one which was of importance 'to him in later life when he was rallying the forces of moderation'.[54] During the First World War Dollan and Wheatley had built strong ties with the Clyde Workers' Committee and during the 1919 strike for the forty-hour week in Glasgow the former had edited the strikers' news sheet, the *Strike Bulletin*. Opposition to the CPGB strengthened his ties with trade union leaders as did his chairmanship of the Glasgow ILP's Industrial Policy Committee which was established in January 1925 to encourage greater ILP involvement in trade union affairs. The latter organisation staged industrial unity conferences, and campaigned for the nationalisation of the mines, but its organisation was based on union officials rather than the rank and file.[55] On top of this was his strong personal commitment to MacDonald which guaranteed him support from influential sections of the labour movement. By 1925 Dollan had thus become an increasingly important local power broker and a formidable opponent of left-wing dissent.

Although unsuccessful, much of the pressure within the official labour movement in favour of Communist affiliation had come from those associated with the National Left Wing Movement (NLWM). The NLWM was a broad-left organisation which included some Clydeside MPs such as Maxton, leading trades unionists like A. B. Swales, president of the TUC, leading Communists and was grouped round the Communist weekly, the *Sunday Worker*. There was no formal agreement and the movement was unofficial, but from May 1925 onwards it campaigned for Communist affiliation to the Labour Party and against the defeatism which continuing unemployment had engendered in the trade unions.[56] A more unified response to the downward pressure of capital on wages and employment was in line with the return to syndicalist-type action and greater optimism in the trade union movement following the success of 'Red Friday' in July 1925.

Coming from Glasgow, and having taken part in the industrial and political struggles of the war years, men like Maxton and Wheatley had stood out against the traditional separate spheres policy of the ILP. They spoke often on the need to supplement parliamentary activity with industrial, extra-parliamentary forms of protest. Maxton himself was convinced that 'capitalism [could be brought] to its knees by a well organised standstill . . . in a few weeks'[57] and Wheatley, following Red Friday, called for the establishment of workers' defence corps to defend workers from the government backlash.[58] This put the left at odds with Dollan who, like MacDonald, stressed the primacy of electoral politics over industrial action, but it meant that they were highly representative of the changing mood within the rank and file of the labour movement.[59] From a more determinedly radical position Maxton and his allies were able to win over a substantial section of ILP members from a cautious policy of gradualism and, in the process, initiate a struggle over the leadership of the party.

At this time the ILP was under the leadership of Clifford Allen who, through his social contacts, had built up party finances and by much individual effort transformed the ILP from a purely propagandist organisation into a policy-making one. However, his bourgeois manners and intellectualism did not endear him to the Clydeside element on the NAC, and neither did his close identification with MacDonald, who was increasingly seen as out of touch with the mood of the party. MacDonald had in fact used Allen's influence within the ILP to dampen down criticism of his leadership and Labour's policies, and it was this which Allen claimed, in a letter to C.R. Buxton, that undermined his control of the NAC.[60] The broader truth is that Allen's declining influence in the ILP was less the result of his friendship with MacDonald, and more to do with his passive style of leadership and his commitment to evolutionary socialism.

The issue that was to prove decisive in the power struggle within the ILP was that of compensation to former owners of property in the event of land nationalisation. Allen, in his capacity as chairman, initiated a series of commissions of inquiry into a wide range of economic subjects, such as agriculture and land, finance, unemployment, import boards and international trade. The commission on compensation, of which Maxton was a member, reported in favour of compensation in the event of the nationalisation of the land and this was ratified at the 1924 ILP conference. However, in a deliberately provocative move Maxton disregarded the decision of conference and cast his vote at the Labour Party conference later that year against compensation, arguing that to compensate former owners would only create a new class of rentier capitalists. Despite protests from Allen his actions were endorsed by the NAC. A few weeks later Maxton further embarrassed Allen when he proposed that MacDonald be relieved of his editorship of the *Socialist Review*. This was accepted by the NAC and Allen immediately resigned. The official reason was given as ill-health, but it is clear from his subsequent letter to Maxton that it was

169

the latter's behaviour at the Labour Party conference which forced Allen's hand. He wrote complaining bitterly that:

> Your POLITICAL actions at Liverpool were perhaps the most decisive factor in making me do what I did. . . . When I saw the future Chairman of the party revealing that he considered himself entitled to pledge the Party to Land Nationalisation without compensation in flagrant defiance of the recorded decision of the Annual Conference at York, I realised that the future of the Party was destroyed . . . I can't work with that kind of political irresponsibility.[61]

With Allen gone, Fred Jowett was elected temporary chairman until the 1926 ILP conference. But it was obvious that the left had won effective control of the party leadership; something even more emphatically underlined by Maxton's election by an overwhelming majority as party chairman in April 1926. In practical terms the desire to move the ILP away from gradualism had been a success. Although a reverse had been suffered over the issue of Communist affiliation, this was more than offset by the removal of the MacDonaldites from control of the NAC. But changes in personnel were hardly enough, if gradualism was to be eradicated from the political vocabulary of the labour movement it had to be replaced by a superior theoretical model of social change. The key to this was to be the 'living wage' programme, or, as it later became known, *Socialism in Our Time*.

For a number of years the Clydeside ILP, most notably Wheatley, had seen an imbalance between production and consumption as the cause of poverty and unemployment.[62] As a result of Allen's initiatives these views were given greater theoretical clarity in the 'living wage' proposals developed by H.N. Brailsford, J.A. Hobson, A. Creech-Jones and E.F. Wise. Although nominally a co-author of the programme, the influence of Hobson was paramount. Hobson's under-consumptionist economics stressed a demand-deficient cause of unemployment and poverty. He argued that the development of cartels and trusts had destroyed the free competition so beloved of nineteenth-century liberals and introduced highly restrictive market capitalism. Control of markets allowed entrepreneurs to take a bigger than normal share of national income. This surplus accruing to the capitalists increasingly took the form of unearned income and upset the 'natural' balance between savings and investment. Too much was being saved and not enough was being invested. As a result, wealth was not being channelled into productive activities, but was being wasted in conspicuous consumption or hoarded, or, worse still, being exported to more profitable investment opportunities abroad. This process led to a chronic tendency within the British economy to gluts and overproduction as the massive increase in the unearned income of the rich was incapable of absorbing the constant increase in output. At the latter end of the social scale there was a crisis of underconsumption. The huge surplus accruing to the rich resulted in a low standard of living for the working class, and their low wages and poverty, in turn, meant that there was a low level of demand for manufacturing products and services. The upshot of all this was that there existed a positive disincentive to businessmen to invest their surplus wealth in British industry. To reverse these trends and regenerate the economy Hobson advocated increasing the purchasing power of the working class through redistributive taxation and higher minimum wages. To guard against the dangers of inflation following a general increase in incomes there was to be a policy of direct credit control exercised through the nationalisation of the Bank of England and those industries which were important in controlling the direction and pace of economic growth.

Although the analysis and prescriptions were pre-Keynes rather than post-Marx, aimed only at erasing the worst defects of market capitalism, the *Socialism in Our Time* policy was more radical and dynamic than anything the official Labour Party had to offer. In spite of this, MacDonald dismissed it as hot air and 'flashy futilities' and did his best to misrepresent it in the labour movement. *Forward* was moved to describe him as 'The Lost Leader' for his opposition and accused him of 'grotesque' distortion of ILP policy.[63] The trades unions also opposed the programme because they felt it would interfere with free collective bargaining. However, most of them missed the real importance of *Socialism in Our Time*. For Maxton and others on the left of the ILP the point of the 'living wage' campaign 'was not to squeeze concessions out of a bankrupt system, but to force a conflict in which the system would be destroyed'.[64] As capitalism was on the verge of collapse, it could not possibly concede these demands without further deepening the crisis and hastening the collapse.[65] Brailsford, writing in the *New Leader*, stated that:

Our appeal is for a single challenge by the industrial and political movements acting together. Let them define their standard and then challenge the existing system to conform to it. With our eyes open we know we are asking for the impossible.[66]

John Paton, ILP organiser in Scotland, claimed that the *Socialism in Our Time* programme if implemented by a Labour Government would precipitate 'the real struggle for power and supremacy'.[67] Capitalism has survived deeper economic crises and shown in the post Second World War period that it is capable of absorbing more radical economic and social changes than those anticipated by *Socialism in Our Time*. However, it was an important part of the revived mood of working-class morale and militancy which preceded the General Strike and demonstrated the political distance between the left wing of the ILP and MacDonald.

It would appear, then, that within a short space of time the Clydesiders had moved from a supportive to a highly critical position on the MacDonald leadership, but did this mean the creation of an alternative political party, and if it did was the strategy a wise one? George Buchanan, in an unguarded outburst at the ILP conference in April 1926, declared that the Labour Party was being 'led by men many of whom . . . were retarding them, and until the party was courageous enough to change that leadership there was no future for it'.[68] Privately, Buchanan's views may well have been shared by Maxton, Wheatley and the others, but publicly it was the defeat of gradualism and the implementation of the *Socialism in Our Time* programme which remained the stated aims of the left. Maxton himself was opposed to splits in the Labour Party and saw the influence of the ILP as a unifying factor in the movement.[69] But the whole drift of the left's strategy was towards the creation of an alternative leadership. The imposition of greater discipline on the ILP parliamentary group, the new guidelines for the selection of prospective parliamentary candidates, the removal of MacDonald's men from the NAC, and the adoption of a radical economic programme, strongly suggested some conscious political plan. Moreover, as the measures were introduced over a period of eighteen months they had to be more than coincidences. Thus, although there was no attempt made to set up a rival party at this time, there was a clear, but unstated, policy initiative by the left to transform both the leadership and the political direction of Labour.

Certainly there were some grounds for optimism that this could be achieved. The success of 'Red Friday' and the leftward move of the trades unions seemed to indicate an emphatic rejection of the moderate policies of MacDonald and to herald a more militant political position among the rank and file. But the optimism was misplaced as the Maxtonite wing of the ILP failed to come to terms with political realities. Until Maxton's election as chairman the ILP had pursued a separate spheres policy and this had denied it a base within the trades union movement. This meant the ILP was incapable of drawing support from this crucial part of the labour movement – something which was clearly demonstrated in its failure to win support for the 'living wage' proposals and again in its inability to play more than a passive role during the General Strike. Even within the ILP there were crucial weaknesses undermining the Maxtonite strategy. As Labour was seen as the party of government it was natural that the politically aspiring should gravitate towards that part of the movement where power and patronage was held and with Maxton as chairman this ceased to be in the ILP. At the time of Maxton's election the number of branches stood at 1,075; just three years later it had fallen to 746 and decline was occurring in every Divisional Council. Even before 1926 the Liberal element which had been grouped around the Union of Democratic Control during the First World War had gone over to Labour in 1924. After this, middle-class support steadily ebbed away to the Labour Party denying the ILP their skill and knowledge. What increased the squeeze on the ILP was the fact the Communists were a serious rival for the dissident left-wing elements in the labour movement. The ILP could no longer claim to be the natural home of the left. These factors made it unlikely that any attempts from the left of the ILP to create an alternative leadership and policy for Labour would succeed. But how did the local ILP in the west of Scotland react towards these political manoeuvrings?

Although there had been serious divisions over the issue of Communist affiliation, both the adoption of the *Socialism In Our Time* policy and the election of Maxton as ILP chairman were warmly received. Dollan said of the latter that 'In some inexplicable way he is the embodiment of Socialist aim and activity. Scotland will rally to him as to no other.'[70] As long as the leadership of the ILP was prepared to work within the labour movement for change and their commitment to the eradication of poverty remained as strong as ever, toleration was extended to them. But it was clear that the real power broker in the west of Scotland was Dollan and not Maxton or Wheatley; therefore, support for new political initiatives was dependent on retaining the former's goodwill. As Maxton and Wheatley pulled further to the left after the General Strike and the publication of the Cook–Maxton manifesto this goodwill evaporated. If the price for dealing with the problems of poverty and unemployment was to be the break up of the Labour Party, then, for Dollan, party came before class. As early as January 1926 at the Scottish ILP Conference Dollan was warning that 'if public representatives did not keep party policy in mind, then the Party would have to impose a stricter discipline upon their statements'.[71] However, until the collapse of the General Strike it would seem that the ILP in the west of Scotland were only slowly becoming aware of the issues which divided them. The unity, which was the product of the universal desire to make electoral inroads into the hegemony of the Liberal Party, had been disturbed by the failings of the first Labour Government and the new political direction of the ILP. But it would take the events of May 1926 and the bitter recriminations which followed in its wake to shatter it.

Notes

1 Emanuel Shinwell, *Conflict Without Malice* (Oldhams, London, 1955), p. 77.

2 William Knox (ed.), *Scottish Labour Leaders, 1918–1939: a Biographical Dictionary* (Mainstream, Edinburgh, 1984), p. 37.

3 *Ibid.*, pp. 16–21.

4 *New Leader*, 27 December 1941.

5 *Glasgow Herald*, 17 March 1923.

6 Robert E. Dowse, *Left in the Centre: The Independent Labour Party, 1893–1940* (Longmans, London, 1966) p. 93.

7 *Glasgow Eastern Standard*, 10 July 1926.

8 *Hansard*, 27 June 1923.

9 *New Leader*, 6 July 1923.

10 John McNair, *James Maxton: the Beloved Rebel* (Allen & Unwin, London, 1955), p. 123.

11 *Glasgow Herald*, 8 December 1923.

12 *Forward*, 7 July 1923.

13 *Glasgow Herald*, 8 December 1923.

14 David Marquand, *Ramsay MacDonald* (Jonathan Cape, London), 1977, p. 312.

15 *Ibid.*, p. 298.
16 *Glasgow Herald*, 15 December 1923.
17 *Forward*, 15 December 1923.
18 *Glasgow Herald*, 15 December 1923.
19 Emrys Hughes, Rebels and Renegades (heavily amended unpublished autobiography), Emrys Hughes Papers, National Library of Scotland, Dep. 176, Box 10, ff. 1–2.
20 Dowse, *op. cit.*, p. 82.
21 *Forward*, 18 December 1923.
22 Dowse, *op. cit.*, p. 82.
23 Hughes, *op. cit.*, ch. 2, ff. 5–6.
24 *Glasgow Eastern Standard*, 1 March 1924.
25 *Glasgow Herald*, 15 February 1924.
26 *Forward*, 1 March 1924.
27 Dowse, *op. cit.*, p. 93; *Glasgow Herald*, 11 February 1924.
28 *Forward*, 26 April 1924.
29 *Glasgow Eastern Standard*, 22 March 1924.
30 *Forward*, 28 June 1924; 23 August 1924.
31 Dowse, *op. cit.*, p. 113.
32 *Daily Herald*, 25 August 1924.
33 *Glasgow Herald*, 6 September 1924.
34 *Forward*, 8 November 1924.
35 *Glasgow Herald*, 31 October 1924.
36 *Ibid.*, 5 November 1924.
37 William Knox, *James Maxton* (Manchester University Press, Manchester, 1987), p. 54.
38 John Scanlon, *Decline and Fall of the Labour Party* (Peter Davis, London, 1932).
39 *Forward*, 8 November 1924.
40 Scanlon, *op. cit.*, pp. 87–8.
41 Knox, *Maxton*, p. 79.
42 Gordon Brown, 'The Labour Party and Political Change in Scotland 1918–1929: the Politics of Five Elections' (unpublished PhD, Edinburgh, 1982), p. 380.
43 *Ibid.*, pp. 309–10.
44 *Ibid.*, p. 312; *Forward*, 25 October 1924.
45 *Ibid.*, 23 June 1923.
46 *Ibid.*, 31 May 1924.
47 James Maxton, *Twenty Points for Socialism* (Glasgow, 1925).
48 Brown, *op. cit.*, p. 382.
49 Leslie J. MacFarlane, *The British Communist Party. Its Origin and Development until 1929* (MacGibbon & Kee, London, 1966), pp. 49–50.

50 *Forward*, 20 February 1926.
51 Brown, *op. cit.*, p. 383.
52 *Ibid.*, pp. 246, 392.
53 *Ibid.*, p. 248.
54 Tom Gallagher, 'Red Clyde's Double Anniversary', *Scottish Labour History Society Journal*, 20, 1985, p. 4.
55 *Forward*, 31 January 1925, 7 March 1925.
56 MacFarlane, *op. cit.*, pp. 149–50.
57 *Glasgow Herald*, 17 August 1925.
58 *Forward*, 22 August 1925.
59 Rejecting the collapse of capitalism thesis put forward by the CPGB, Dollan declared 'The walls of Capitalism are more likely to collapse as a result of the patient sapping and organised efforts of the ILP': *Forward*, 14 June 1924.
60 Dowse, *op. cit.*, p. 110.
61 Martin Gilbert, *Plough My Own Furrow. The Story of Lord Allen* (Longmans, London, 1965), pp. 194–5.
62 John Wheatley, *Starving in the Midst of Plenty* (Glasgow, 1923).
63 *Forward*, 17 April 1926.
64 Marquand, *op. cit.*, p. 453.
65 *Ibid.*
66 *New Leader*, 17 April 1925.
67 John Paton, *Left Turn!: An Autobiography* (Secker & Warburg, London, 1936), p. 236.
68 *Glasgow Herald*, 5 April 1926.
69 *Forward*, 10 April 1926.
70 ILP *Journal*, May 1926.
71 *Forward*, 16 January 1926

SEVEN

The end of 'the agitator workman': 1926–1932

Alan McKinlay and James J. Smyth

Between the end of the General Strike and 1932 the tensions within the ILP over political strategy erupted into crisis over the party's relationship with the Labour Party, a controversy which ultimately resulted in the ILP's disaffiliation in 1932. Importantly, none of the developments discussed in this chapter was the result of rank-and-file pressure: there was no groundswell of grassroots opinion which stimulated the launch of the Cook–Maxton Manifesto nor was there widespread enthusiasm for disaffiliation. On the contrary, for Maxton the first purpose of the Manifesto campaign was to reverse the ILP's demoralising membership decline while disaffiliation was resignedly accepted rather than enthusiastically embraced. Unlike other vital moments in the ILP's history when the discretion of local and national leaderships was checked by membership pressure, the conflicts between 1926–32 were primarily at the leadership level. For Glasgow's labour politics this process hinged on the contrasting positions of three individuals: Patrick Dollan, James Maxton and John Wheatley. Of the leadership cohort which had dominated the rise of the ILP in the decade before 1922 only Dollan remained wedded to local rather than Westminster politics. While Maxton and Wheatley were building their power-base at Westminster and on the ILP's National Administrative Council (NAC) Dollan was consolidating his privotal place in labour politics in Scotland. Until the departure of the ILP parliamentary contingent in November 1922 Dollan had simply been an able organisational adjutant to the more charismatic figure of Maxton and the more capable political general, Wheatley. But while Maxton and Wheatley were radicalised by their dispiriting personal experience of Westminster politics Dollan remained determined to maintain the alliance between the ILP and Labour at all costs and convinced of the worth of Labour representation and administration as an end in itself.

Crucially, it was Dollan who filled the organisational vacuum left in city politics by their departure and he who cultivated the personal ties with local union officials to strengthen his position within the Glasgow Labour Party. By the late 1920s, therefore, the phenomenal personal popularity of Maxton and Wheatley was in inverse relationship to their power in the Glasgow ILP.

I

Although the Glasgow ILP was not involved in directing or advising miners' leaders during the General Strike or the seven month lock-out, it threw itself wholeheartedly into supporting the mining communities on the city's borders. The Glasgow Federation's Annual Report for 1926 stated, 'during the entire seven months our Glasgow organisation was devoted to Miners' Relief'.[1] In some ways the uncomplicated certainties of the miners' struggle came as a relief to ILP activists as they tried to come to terms with the legacy of the first Labour Government and, in Glasgow, confronted the immensely difficult task of ousting the entrenched moderate city council. Fund raising and manning soup kitchens was a welcome psychological respite for activists complaining of their isolation within communities beset by 'the apathy of poverty', or worse, 'in a very critical and somewhat tired frame of mind, as a result of the reaction immediately following the brief experience of a Labour Government'.[2] There was no such consolation for the Clyde MPs whose distance from both local involvement and influence in metropolitan decision-making was doubly frustrating. For both Maxton and Wheatley their own powerlessness betokened wider failings of labour politics, a belief which further eroded the validity of their conditional commitment to the Labour Party, an allegiance severely tested by their experience of the 1924 minority administration.[3]

The miners' lock-out was the prime focus of ILP activity throughout 1926 to the extent that vital party affairs were held in abeyance. In August 1926 the Scottish Division did not even have 'tentative proposals' for delegate conferences to discuss *Socialism in Our Time*, the innovate set of ILP policies geared to regenerating industry and reducing inequality by increasing working-class consumption. John Paton, the Party's national organiser, concluded that the campaign to popularise the new policies should proceed although its impact would inevitably be 'very much less important in scope and effect than was originally contemplated.[4] Moreover, Paton acknowledged that the ILP membership was itself grudging in its support of the Living Wage campaign:

> there has not been the consistent and energetic propaganda of the new programme which might perhaps have been expected. Many branches have taken this programme too lightly and have imagined that support could be taken for granted; others have dismissed the proposals as 'stunts' and 'slogans'.[5]

In Glasgow the contrast between dismissive and generally supportive branches broadly reflected the political geography of the city's ILP. While the east end branches were the most supportive of *Socialism in Our Time* it was they, because of their proximity to the mining areas on the city's outskirts, which bore the brunt of the party's time-consuming involvement in supporting the locked-out colliers. And as these branches abandoned all their normal propaganda activities for the duration of the mining crisis the *Socialism in Our Time* campaign was abandoned by default.

But the debacle of the General Strike and the defeat of the miners did not cause Maxton and Wheatley to abandon their belief in transitional politics centred on legislation. However, the experience of the hope and dismay of 1926 did drive a further wedge between the ILP left and the Labour leadership. The growing gulf between Maxton and Wheatley and MacDonald and the Labour front bench was not one of revolution versus reform, but rather between rival forms of gradualism. For MacDonald, socialism was to be achieved painlessly and over generations by a Labour Party which had first to conclusively prove its fitness to govern. While accepting that political action was the only feasible route to socialism in Britain Wheatley emphasised that a Labour Government's first priority must be to effect 'a constructive but *rapid* transition'.[6]

If the experience of minority government had persuaded Wheatley that the Parliamentary Labour Party as presently constituted was unlikely to prove the vehicle for socialist transformation then the General Strike disillusioned him about the established leadership of the trade union movement. After May 1926 Wheatley redoubled his criticism of MacDonald and there was the first glimmer of an alternative political strategy in his warning that 'since trade unionism has been mortgaged to its enemies a new form of organisation may be necessary'.[7] Wheatley's conditional allegiance to the Labour Party had been irreversibly damaged; the problem was how to transform personal disenchantment into a viable alternative strategy for the ILP as a whole. The search for a strategy which would pitch the ILP against the Labour front bench and the apolitical quiescence of the union leadership was to dominate the lives of the Clydeside MPs and the Glasgow party until disaffiliation in 1932.

II

A central feature of the Glasgow ILP before 1922 was the openness of its organisational and ideological boundaries. Indeed, we argued that the ILP's vitality and popular appeal was built on its pivotal role in building and sustaining a dense network of radical activists across a broad range of issues. After 1926, however, a key characteristic of the ILP was how remarkably self-contained it had become. After the Great War we noted the untidy dissolution of the overlaps between the ILP, factory activists and community protest. The Glasgow ILP's transition from being an umbrella organisation sheltering a number of social movements to a clearly bounded political party, which began in the immediate aftermath of the Armistice, accelerated throughout the 1920s. By 1926 the party not only had no such energising connections with grassroots protest movements, it determinedly avoided creating them through, for instance, formal participation in the nascent unemployed workers' movement or the National Minority Movement (NMM) inside the unions. But the decentralised nature of the ILP's organisation left slivers of political space for temporary alliances with other left activists at branch level. Despite this, in Glasgow the managerial logic of Dollan's leadership was seldom frustrated as he wielded ever-greater disciplinary powers including expelling individual militants and closing recalcitrant branches. For Dollan, of course, this was a virtuous circle as each expulsion strengthened his hand on the Glasgow executive.

Between 1926 and 1928 the Glasgow ILP's membership remained around 5,000, a relative stability which contrasted starkly with the sharp decline of the party's national membership which plummeted from 34,000 in 1925 to under 21,000 in 1929.[8] This made the dominance of the Scottish Division, or at least its leading figures such as Maxton, within the national ILP unassailable: a dominance much resented by fading ILP heartlands such as West Yorkshire which were being inexorably eclipsed by the rise of the Labour Party at constituency level.[9] But beneath this apparent constancy the Clydeside party was subject to an increasingly rapid membership turnover, especially amongst its new recruits. Nor did the Glasgow ILP's tireless support of the miners' cause result in a major influx into the party. Unlike the Communist Party, the local ILP increased its paid membership by a mere one hundred during 1926.[10]

Nevertheless, despite its difficulties the ILP remained paramount within the Labour Party throughout Scotland. So deeply entrenched was the ILP in Glasgow that it left little opportunity for constituency Labour Parties to become firmly established, far less flourish. In 1926 Ben Shaw, the Labour Party's Scottish Secretary, suggested that this anomalous situation would only be reversed by reducing the representation of affiliated organisations which would both limit the ILP's control and reduce the opportunities for the Communist Party to build left-wing groups in Glasgow constituency Labour parties. In short, without the active involvement of individual Labour Party members Labour's constituency parties were little more than mediums through which the ILP and, to a much lesser extent the CPGB, pursued their interests. The haphazard attendance of trade union delegates was no match for the diligence of committed ILP and disciplined CPGB groups, especially in the city's east end. But Shaw's proposal met with a frosty response from the Labour Party's national executive: 'an attempt should be made to increase the individual membership in Scotland'.[11] As recession gave way to the depression of 1930–32 the pressure on the Labour Party to increase its individual membership to make good the loss of affiliated trade union branches intensified.[12] But Shaw's concern evoked little sympathy among local ILP organisers whose first priority was to arrest the decline of their own organisation. Although Dollan shared the Labour Party's concern with left-wing influence at grassroots level he remained protective of the ILP's premier position in the city's labour politics. Dollan consistently refused to collaborate in any moves to increase the Labour Party's individual membership, curtly advising Shaw that he should direct his efforts to areas with no political organisation rather than attempting to supplant established ILP branches.[13]

This determination to maintain the ILP's significant *political* influence within the 'Labour alliance' underpinned Dollan's hostility to renewed calls for the ILP to submerge its identity within the Labour Party or, as Phillip Snowden suggested, disband completely.

> Have we created something better than ourselves – in Mr Snowden's words, 'a far greater and more powerful instrument for establishing the Socialist State', so that we ought to summon ourselves to disband, like a Christmas Club that has already shared out its shortbread and its geese?[14]

Just as the type of members enlisted and then lost to the ILP between 1914 and 1922 was a vital factor in determining the party's political balance so the changing character of the Glasgow membership was critical in shaping the party's response to the controversies of 1926–32. As a result of the demise of ephemeral activity of many branches the ILP's geographical coverage of the city was gradually curtailed. The perennial problem of retaining new recruits was compounded by the additional complications of emigration and the gradual, natural loss of older party stalwarts who had joined the party around the turn of the century and who often held important posts at branch level.[15] If a generation gap had emerged as a result of the membership explosion of the war years then it was exacerbated during the years of slow decline. Not only did ILP 'stalwarts' complain of younger members' indifference to mundane organisational matters but also of their quite different political attitudes. The political socialisation of recruits during the 1920s differed significantly from those of the pre-war generation. While the vision of the 'stalwarts' was of a long, slow haul to the New Jerusalem the political horizon of the rising generation, formed during a period of rapid advance and heroic defeat, was much more immediate. As we shall see, the absence of any basic empathy between these two political generations was one of the fissures within the ILP laid open by the disaffiliation debate.

In 1929 a survey of Scottish branches revealed eighty changes of secretary and forty-nine lapsed branches over a six-month period, losses which the ILP's decentralised structure made enormously difficult to stem.[16] The loss, whether by death or flitting, of an experienced secretary often meant the collapse of the entire branch with little prospect of reactivation. The political impact of this insidious membership crisis was as profound as its organisational effect. Indeed, local officials feared that the democratic fabric of the Glasgow party as a whole was seriously threatened:

the Federation had a tendency to lose its power by the constant change of delegates. He appealed to those appointed to retain Executive office for at least one year and to have as full an attendance as possible.[17]

By late 1929 the Glasgow ILP's finances were in a parlous position with fast-mounting debts and no cash assets. In effect, the party was locked into a vicious cycle of decline; lack of finances prevented large-scale campaigning which in turn limited the opportunities to raise fresh funds and mount effective recruitment campaigns.[18] Again, the ILP's loose organisational structure hindered the efforts of the national and local leaderships to tap into branch finances. The first loyalty of the individual ILP-er was to his or her branch, not to the city or national organisation. Branch delegates to the Glasgow Federation were regularly chastised by the city party's three full-time organisers for their parochial allegiances and their failure to convince their party constituents of their financial obligations towards the parent organisation.[19] Deepening recession was, however, the prime cause of membership loss.[20] In four months in mid-1930 the ILP secretary, William Regan, recorded a loss of 349 men and 64 women, a total of around 10 per cent of the total Glasgow membership. This 'big falling-off' was not ascribed to any extraordinary disappearance of several ward parties but to a more general malaise:

> he attributed this falling-off mainly to industrial depression which was discouraging all kinds of Organisations. There was also a dissatisfaction with the Labour Movement and a lack of incentive to members to continue active Socialist propaganda.[21]

Implicit in Regan's assessment was the assumption that campaigning and recruitment were activities principally, if not exclusively, conducted during election campaigns. The rhythm of the ILP's political practice was now set by municipal and parliamentary electoral calendars, not by the type of intimate involvement in the daily lives of working people which had characterised ILP politics before 1918. The clearest example of this shift was the ILP's refusal to participate in unemployment agitation because this would have involved co-operating with communists, despite Maxton's support of joint campaigning on specific issues. Criticisms that it was the ILP's failure to provide political leadership to the unemployed which limited the party's appeal outside elections were brushed aside by Dollan's assurances that 'all things considered, our position was nothing to be alarmed about in view of the very acute unemployment.[22] The decimated east end branches, including Maxton's own Bridgeton constituency, advocated collaboration with communists through the National Unemployed Workers' Movement and that reduced subscriptions be used to enable recruitment among the unemployed. But, as the Parkhead branch was tartly reminded, reduced membership dues for the unemployed were not for recruitment but retention: 'The spirit of this rule is undoubtedly that the unemployed stamp is only to be used for the purpose of retaining old and trusted members who are temporarily unable to pay their dues'.[23] Because of the overwhelmingly working-class composition of the Glasgow ILP the party's membership was severely hit by the collapse of the city's metalworking industries between 1929 and 1932. In 1930 at least 50 per cent of the party's membership was unemployed while branches in the shipyard districts were even more severely hit; by late 1931 only six of the remaining thirty six members of the previously flourishing Partick branch were in work.[24] By mid-1932 the Glasgow membership had shrunk to 1,200, under a fifth of the peak of 1920, and such was the shortage of funds that it was forced to cut the wages of its three employees to balance the books – 'a matter of shame'.[25] As we shall see, the decline in ILP membership and the strict limits on its ability to pursue an independent strategy within the Labour Party were important, complementary factors in shaping the *form* of Maxton and Wheatley's open challenge to MacDonald's leadership in 1928.

III

The Cook–Maxton Manifesto of 1928, a joint project between James Maxton, Chairman of the ILP, and A.J. Cook, General Secretary of the Miners' Federation of Great Britain, has been dismissed as a Quixotic venture borne of overblown egos and political naivety. While nobody could accuse John Wheatley of being a political ingenu his involvement in the Manifesto and readiness to attack long-term colleagues such as Tom Johnston has been ascribed to a deeply embittered personality, rather than a coherent political strategy.[26] To the contrary, we shall argue that the Manifesto was consistent with the thrust of Maxton and Wheatley's post-war political strategy while the nature of the campaign itself reflec' d both the strengths of the

ILP's popular appeal and the limits of their understanding of political mobilisation.

The Clyde group was drawn to Cook not only because of his charismatic leadership of the miners' union during the long months of the 1926 lock-out but also by his refusal to be constrained by administrative proprieties, most apparent in his readiness to leak details of the secret Mond–Turner talks between the TUC and business leaders.[27] Equally, Maxton and Cook shared a leadership style based on the immediacy of their contact with their constituency, their ability to articulate the collective unconscious of their most active followers. The authority of both men rested on this intangible basis and accompanied an almost wilful disregard for conventional organisational power-broking.[28] Just as Cook spoke 'straight to the people' so Maxton pursued a similarly unconventional vision of party leadership. As one close observer remarked, Maxton displayed.

> a strong aversion to the ordinary idea of leadership, he declines to attempt to impose his will on the Party or any of its sections. He conceives it to be his function to ascertain the mind of the Party and then to give it powerful expression on the platform.[29]

Both Cook and Maxton were popular yet isolated figures – 'Ishmaels' – their authority utterly dependent upon the special relationship struck with their respective membership.[30] The singular nature of Maxton's personal authority determined the nature of the Manifesto campaign. For Wheatley, the instigator of the project, the labour movement was in 'a state of apathy, almost hopelessness' after 1926 which could only be dispelled by Maxton 'appealing to the masses over the heads of his own organisation'.[31] Just as Cook rejected metropolitan trade union officialdom as a peer group so Maxton disdainfully eschewed the approval of Labour's parliamentarians. Equally, neither Cook nor Maxton was in full command of his executive nor, in the latter's case, was he in charge of the party machine in his native Glasgow. But if collaboration with Cook was a desperate attempt by the Clydesiders to overcome the ILP's historic weakness within the trade unions then it was misconceived since Cook's isolation became more complete not only within the TUC but even inside the leadership of the miners' union.[32] Indeed, by participating in the Manifesto campaign Cook became even less trusted by his fellow trade union leaders while his commitment to the return of a Labour Government drew the fire of his erstwhile communist supporters.[33] Nevertheless, there is a consistency of approach in the careers of both Cook and Maxton which cannot simply be dismissed as the outcome of 'maverick' personalities but which reflects their leadership style and their peculiar position within popular politics and trade unionism.

The Cook–Maxton Manifesto was devised behind the closed doors of a Westminster committee room, not the open forum of Glasgow socialists which had congregated in Miss Cranston's tea room in Sauchiehall Street to discuss tactics in the years before 1922. Nor were any representatives of grassroots opinion represented in these secret discussions, an absence which signified the degree to which the Clydeside parliamentary group had become estranged from the local political organisation. This was compounded by the fact that the campaign was planned without consulting the ILP's national leadership. As a consequence, even sympathetic individuals on the NAC, such as Paton, the general secretary, regarded the campaign as an unconscious attack on the ILP itself.[34] Despite such misgivings the ILP national leadership narrowly agreed to endorse the Manifesto in principle, although because the party had no directive power it stopped short of practical support. The Scottish ILP, dominated by Dollan, did not even go this far, accepting only the 'spirit and purpose' of the campaign while insisting that *Socialism in Our Time* could best be promoted through official party channels.[35]

The Manifesto was launched in July 1928 at a packed Glasgow meeting where neither Maxton nor Cook lived up to their reputations as orators; the former giving an evasive speech careful to stress his continued loyalty to the Labour Party, while the latter delivered an arid marxist diatribe.[36] Wheatley, by all accounts, was enraged by the poor speeches and immediately withdrew his promise to underwrite the campaign. What was at issue, however, was not so much the quality of Maxton's oratory but a fundamental disagreement over the Manifesto's ultimate purpose. Wheatley, Maxton's political mentor, apparently regarded the campaign as a way of gauging the feasibility either of launching a new socialist party or, at the very least, of restructuring the parliamentary Labour Party through grassroots pressure.[37] The measure of the popular appeal for this venture was to be the purchase of pledge cards which would form a national register of prospective supporters. *Forward* was scathing in its dismissal of the Manifesto pledge cards:

Have we ever before in the history of the British Socialist Movement been asked to sign anything so vague and sentimental, a pledge to blindly follow two individuals in which there was no clearly defined programme. Who drafted this pledge? Surely not Maxton and Cook. Do they really think that the Socialist rank and file are much the same as reformed drunkards who can only be kept up to scratch by signing pledges at the Band of Hope or the Good Templars?[38]

Maxton, on the other hand, clearly opposed any break with the Labour Party: his vision of the campaign was more diffuse and its political purpose unclear. Indeed, the very language Maxton used to justify the Manifesto campaign suggests a complete absence of any theoretical understanding of what the project involved. Time and again Maxton used religious language to explain his intention: it was to be a spiritual revival, evangelical in style and ecumenical in appeal. Maxton's speeches were saturated with references to the vision of socialist pioneers such as Keir Hardie, invoked as an emblem of recovery of both personal conviction and a form of popular politics.[39] In effect, the Cook–Maxton Manifesto was an attempt to return to the agitational politics of the pre-1918 era. During these years, as Joan Smith has reminded us, the ILP was the hub of a vibrant network of socialist organisations which routinely shared platforms and collaborated in a broad range of political activities. It was in such a milieu of daily co-operation across party lines, premised on a tolerance of difference and opposition, that Maxton and the east end ILP's politics were formed. Even at the height of a Manifesto demonstration in the Bridgeton Olympia moved to 'the wildest enthusiasm in the whole history of East End politics' A. J. Cook's refusal to condemn MacDonald as a 'renegade' received the loudest applause of the evening, a reaction entirely consistent with the local ILP's political tradition.[40] Indeed, Maxton explicitly recalled the collaborative and mutually beneficial relationship between the ILP and the Clyde Workers' Committee during the Great War as the model he was attempting to recover.[41] In itself, this goes some way to explaining Dollan's hostility: his politics was no longer that of the street corner agitator but that of the council chamber and committee room power broker. For Dollan, the campaign was not so much a revival or recovery but a regression to the politics of defiance, not the politics of power. Moreover, Maxton's insistence that the ILP should act as an intermediary between the Labour Party, the Communist Party and other social movements was anathema to the tidy minds of party managers, difficult if not impossible to discipline and control. Broad-based alliances would necessarily blur the boundaries of official Labour politics during a period when the full weight of executive power in both the Labour Party and the unions was being mobilised to clarify organisational parameters as a bulwark against Communist Party influence.[42] In short, the Manifesto campaign held the promise of an organisational as well as an ideological challenge to gradualism.

In October Cook and Maxton issued a second campaign pamphlet – *Our Case for a Socialist Revival* – which was based on quite different demands from those of the original Manifesto or, indeed, *Socialism in Our Time*.[43] In particular, *Our Case* condemned the 'enlightened Liberalism' of official Labour policy and MacDonald's determination to make Labour a national rather than a working-class party. To this criticism was added specific demands including complete taxation at death of all wealth over £5,000, a doubling of the housing subsidy and the abolition of the monarchy. But the speed with which the original Manifesto demands were radically altered suggests not uncertainty or confusion but that the specifics of the Manifesto were secondary to its overriding purpose of mobilisation. In Glasgow, only the east end branches fully supported the Manifesto campaign which opponents ascribed to Maxton's popularity rather than the attractions of the Manifesto. But the east end branches were consistently to the left of the Glasgow Federation as a whole. For example, the Bridgeton branch, usually regarded simply as Maxton followers, included NMM activists well-known in local factories and supporters of the Left Wing Group in the Divisional Labour Party. East end ILP-ers such as Tom Clark, a former CWC activist, sustained the NMM presence on the district committee of the engineering union during periods when communist delegates were excluded and led effective local protests against executive attempts to limit political debate within the union.[44] Maxton's readiness to co-operate with the Communist Party on specific projects was not, therefore, merely personal idiosyncrasy but reflected and reinforced the practice of the east end ILP.

Despite the relative success of the set-piece demonstrations addressed by Maxton and Cook, the Manifesto failed to establish any significant organisation. Even in Glasgow there is no evidence of any lasting benefit for the left wing of the ILP, far less the basis of a more broadly-based movement. That is not to say the Manifesto was unimportant. On the contrary, it clarified the divisions between the Maxton faction and mainstream opinion and deepened the hostility of the Labour front bench to the ILP. The cool reception the Scottish ILP gave to the Manifesto confirms a paradoxical reversal in the power base of the Clyde MPs. Before 1922 Wheatley and Maxton had been commanding figures in the Glasgow party but their election to Westminster and Maxton's chairmanship of the national party gradually undercut their local strength. Patrick Dollan, by contrast, reinforced his already formidable power base in city politics by courting local union officials and the Co-operative Party and, on the Scottish Divisional Council, by carrying the support of rural ILP branches.[45] While the Clyde MPs moved leftwards the Glasgow party under Dollan remained wedded to the task of securing Labour administration, locally and nationally. For Maxton and Wheatley, however, socialism was much more than a legislative programme but a faith founded in experience, and they viewed the ILP as custodian of a political tradition whose roots lay in a moral, not just economic, critique of capitalism. These divergent understandings of the purpose and traditions of the ILP were vital in deciding the response of ILP-ers to the disaffiliation crisis which finally came to a head in 1932.

IV

The disaffiliation of the ILP was a seminal moment in the strengthening of the centralised managerial authority of the Labour Party's National Executive Committee after the fall of the first Labour Government. Central authority within the Labour Party was buttressed by a growing armoury of disciplinary powers, from the proscription of organisations to centralised control over the selection of parliamentary candidates. The anomalous position of the ILP under the 1918 Labour Party constitution left it unclear how far the ILP and its members were subject to the final authority of the Labour Party. Unlike other affiliated bodies the ILP was a fully fledged political party with the full apparatus of conferences, executive, policy agendas and parliamentary group. As we have seen, the allegiance of ILP-ers such as Wheatley and Maxton to Labour was always conditional and strategic rather than unreservedly loyalist. Whilst the Labour Party remained in opposition the clashes between these fundamentally different political visions was containable. But, as the previous chapter demonstrated, after the experience of the 1924 minority government the die was cast: the collapse of the 1929 Labour Government and MacDonald's formation of the National Government in 1931 crystallised organisational and ideological conflicts which had remained latent from 1918. From 1928 onwards it was a question of when and on what terms, rather than if, secession would take place.[46]

Discipline and doctrine were the twin cores of the dispute between Maxton's ILP and the Labour Party. From early 1926 a small group of ILP MPs centred around the Clyde group and Fenner Brockway was formed to direct the ILP's parliamentary strategy. The drive to maintain a coherent, distinctive – if numerically reduced – identity for the ILP was extended in 1928 when Maxton insisted that the ILP would finance only those MPs who would support *Socialism In Our Time* at Westminster. Within two years the ILP parliamentary group was reduced from 140 to 18 MPs, 4 of whom were from Clydeside. This tight-knit parliamentary group was the basis for the Maxton group's capture of the NAC. Organisational and ideological distinctiveness was further accentuated by the publication of the Labour Party's *Labour and the Nation* in 1928, a document bereft of any concept of class or vision of socialism as an attainable prospect. Beneath its moralistic endorsement of parliamentary reformism *Labour and the Nation*'s one positive assertion was that Labour was no longer the spokesman for the narrow interests of the working class but was now the party of the whole community. The contrast between MacDonald's complacent gradualism and Wheatley's impatient stress on class politics could not be more marked:[47] 'Our movement, whether we like the description or not, is a class movement as distinct from a national movement.'

But it was MacDonald who was the commanding Labour personality and Wheatley who struggled vainly to gain a respectful hearing for the ILP's alternative policies at Labour Party Conferences.[48] The return of a minority Labour Government in May 1929 enhanced MacDonald's authority still further while his opponents were additionally handicapped because they now courted accusations of disloyalty to a fragile Labour Government. The exclusion of Wheatley from the cabinet, despite his success in the 1924 administration, was depicted by John Scanlon, an intimate political associate, as an important symbolic event in the evolution of Labour politics:

The dropping of Mr. Wheatley . . . was more than the dropping of one man. It was the end of an epoch in Labour politics. It was a public intimation that the Party had reached the end of the agitational Keir Hardie period, and was now committed to Fabian respectability. . . . In 1929, when the Socialists acquiesced in the dropping of the agitator workman, they made their choice.[49]

While it is something of an exaggeration to depict 'the dropping of Mr. Wheatley' as the moment which signalled the end of an era in popular politics, Scanlon was correct to regard these years as a decisive turning-point; an end to tolerance of organised ideological hetero-geneity, an expectation that the first allegiance of the Labour member should be to the party and not some vision of socialism. Such expectations were contrary to the ILP's traditional decentralised organisational structure, protected by constitutional safeguards against centralised control, which encouraged ideological diversity. All of these tensions were heightened by the MacDonald govern-ment's adherence to a strict economic orthodoxy based on maintaining the gold standard and a belief in sound money. Above all, the belief that government had only a very limited role to play in reducing unemployment was anathema to men such as Wheatley whose formative experience of municipal politics had been of an expanding economic and social role for the local state to redress the failings of competitive markets. This interventionist instinct found economic expression in *Socialism In Our Time* whose central tenet was the need to increase working-class spending power to end the immoral obscenity of 'poverty in the midst of plenty' and regenerate British industry.[50]

The reconstruction of the ILP parliamentary group and their increasingly open opposition to MacDonald's government, especially over unemployment benefit, was condemned by Dollan. As a result of Maxton's reforms the Labour Party was now confronted by a disciplined opposition group in parliament rather than individual mal-contents, a situation which the host party could not tolerate with equanimity. It was on these grounds, the inevitability of inter-party conflict, that Dollan opposed Maxton's reforms.[51] In December 1929 Dollan called for a special party conference to reformulate parliament-ary strategy and dismantle the collective controls over individual MPs enforced by the Maxton group. But this plea, endorsed by the Scottish Divisional Council, was overwhelmingly rejected by the ILP NAC and the 1930 national conference, a contrast illustrative of Dollan's local and Maxton's national strength.[52] Dollan responded to this reverse by broadening his attack to include not just Maxton but also those regions, especially London, whose limited electoral success was the basis of their conviction that the ILP's main purpose was to act as the socialist conscience of the labour movement, not to remain an integral part of Labour administrations.

> Much of the weakness of the ILP today was not only due to unemployment but to bad tactics. . . . There had been a period of excommunication. In Scotland the ILP was not only a propaganda organisation; it was also a political organisation. The people who have no MPs could go on excommunicating but the ILP branches would stand behind the MPs who were excommunicated.[53]

Dollan's position in the debate over the relationship between the ILP and the Labour Party was entirely consistent: he was equally opposed to the ILP being subsumed within the Labour Party and to the self-imposed exile from mainstream labour politics which he regarded as the inevitable consequence of Maxton's strategy.

In contrast to the ILP's unchallenged dominance of Glasgow's Labour Party politics before 1924 the differing reactions to the experience of minority government and the General Strike had undermined the coherence of the ILP delegation to the Borough Labour Party. From 1926 the Glasgow ILP Federation's inability to exercise effective control over Parish and Town councillors was symptomatic of the uncertain constitutional status of city-level organisation within the party. ILP delegates to the city Labour Party were nominated by their branch not the Federation which made it difficult for local officials to keep track of which individuals on the Trades and Labour Council were ILP-ers.[54] In particular, branch activists were acutely concerned that they had extremely limited knowledge of, far less control over, ILP councillors: one east end branch appealed to:

> All Town Councillors who are members of the ILP to report to the Branches in their Ward, at least once per quarter, thereby enabling the Branches to have a regular account of their members' stewardship in the Town Council.[55]

Even this mild injunction was rejected by nineteen votes to eight, again a division which reflected the political geography of the Glasgow ILP. Backed by all but two of the ILP councillors, Dollan insisted 'that administration points should be left to public representatives'.[56] This narrowest of majorities exaggerated the left's influence within the Glasgow ILP as the vagaries of attendance exposed Dollan to periodic embarrassment but never lasting defeat. The controlling group of councillors around Dollan had confirmed its dominance of the city's ILP leadership after 1926 to such an extent that by 1929 there was an air of desperation about the efforts of east end branches to recover even a limited accountability from ILP members on the town council. This feeling of impotence and mutual distrust runs through the proposal – again unsuccessful – that John McLure the party's local organiser stand for a council seat in order to guarantee at least ILP surveillance of the Labour group:

> it is in the best interests of the Party that the Secretary should be allowed to stand for the Town Council. Some years ago the Federation decided that the Secretary should attend the fortnightly meetings of the Town Council Labour Group. The object of the decision was to keep the Party in touch with what was being done by the Group. The Secretary has carried out this instruction. He attends the meetings of the Group but merely as an onlooker. He has no standing in the meetings and cannot take part in any discussions even when questions affecting the Party or electoral organisation in the City are under consideration. Further, he dare not report outside what has transpired or he is accused of carrying tales and at the subsequent meeting is made to feel, by the atmosphere of suspicion, that he is there on sufferance. Thus the purpose that the Federation had in view in asking him to attend is frustrated. The only remedy is for the Secretary to be a bona fide member of the Group just as the Secretary of the Borough Labour Party.[57]

Dollan's Glasgow ILP was far removed from Maxton's vision of the ILP as a broad-based organisation whose first purpose was to construct coalitions of socialist opinion irrespective of party allegiance. And, as we have shown, Maxton's vision reflected his reading of the ILP's role in the Glasgow labour movement before 1922, especially during the Great War. More than this, however, it was in the city's east end that this tradition of creating alliances between diverse and fragmented constituencies remained alive although with a limited impact on city politics. For ILP delegates from Bridgeton and Shettleston to the Trades and Labour Council to support Communist Party nominees for the Labour ticket in council by-elections in 1927 was, therefore, an open challenge to Dollan's hegemony which, in this sense, *anticipated* the logic of the Cook–Maxton Manifesto. To counter this challenge

Dollan engineered the expulsion of those ILP-ers who had supported communist candidates and disbanded three Parkhead branches who protested at the imposition of a written pledge 'to give every possible assistance to official Labour candidates and to abstain from actively supporting any sectarian or anti-Labour candidate in all Local and Parliamentary elections'.[58] Naturally, each round of expulsions strengthened Dollan's grip on the Glasgow party. Immediately after the purge of the east end branches Dollan's support on the ILP's city Federation soared to approximately five times that of his left-wing opponents. It was to take a full year of negotiations with the ILP national leadership before Dollan was forced to withdraw the loyalty pledge.[59]

Conflict between the ILP and the Labour Party increasingly spilled over into local politics. Vitriolic squabbles continually broke out at grassroots level. The dispute between the ILP and the Labour Party in 1931 over the candidates for local elections typified the squabbles which disfigured labour politics in the city. The Gorbals Divisional Labour Party accepted an ILP-er as their candidate but refused to allow the local ILP branches to manage the campaign. By running an ILP candidate the Labour Party hoped to secure the ILP's commitment whilst it would retain control of the direction of the campaign. In reply to this charge Ben Shaw, the Labour Party's Scottish Secretary, argued that internecine fighting within the ILP had crippled its ability to campaign effectively:[60]

> The Gorbals Branch was not competent to run an election, due to inefficiency. They incurred excessive expenses and jeopardised the ILP position in the whole District and the Branch itself was divided. There were two sections, each trying to clear the other out. A section of the members were using the Branch for ulterior motives; they had purposefully created an impasse so that they could make way for another Candidate through a Trade Union.

In the four years after 1926 the uneasy coalition within and between the ILP and the city's still rudimentary Labour Party was increasingly strained. The fissures within the labour alliance could not be contained by calls for loyalty to the minority Labour Government. This was particularly true for ILP-ers who were expected to subordinate their party's distinctive policies to the economic orthodoxies which dominated Labour Party thinking.[61] Equally, the sense of powerlessness which motivated the Maxton group's reconstruction of the parliamentary party was paralleled at local level. The fate of these analogous processes was, however, completely different. In Glasgow, left-wing attempts to extend control over representatives on civic bodies emanated from east end activists in the ILP Federation, a body with uncertain powers, and had no backing from city councillors. These attempts were either easily rebuffed or, if pressed to the limit, served only to strengthen Dollan's hold on the Glasgow ILP. In short, the shifting balance of power in the Glasgow ILP was a mirror image of changes at national level.

The death of John Wheatley in May 1930 dealt the ILP left wing a hammer blow. Wheatley's stature as a national figure was guaranteed after his success as Minister of Health during the first Labour Government. Unlike many Labour ministers Wheatley could not be criticised as an opportunistic Liberal convert to the Labour Party. Ministerial success and Wheatley's long record as a Labour councillor could have provided the basis for further personal advancement within the parliamentary party. Yet, Wheatley's main role after 1924 was as one of the most astringent critics of Labour policy and of MacDonaldism and his effectiveness led to his increasing isolation within the Labour Party.

For the ILP left Wheatley's loss was manifold. Not only was Wheatley a politician of national stature and a shrewd political operator – witness his 'hidden' role within the Clyde Workers' Committee – he was also the most capable proponent of the alternative underconsumptionist economic strategies developed during the 1920s. Further, he commanded a considerable personal fortune and a popular weekly paper, the *Glasgow Eastern Standard*, which supported the ILP left. There is little reason to suppose that had Wheatley lived the trajectory of the ILP would have been significantly different. The compulsive logic of Wheatley's position after 1924 pointed towards an eventual break with the Labour Party, not just with MacDonald.[62] In the short term, the most important consequence of Wheatley's death was that the ILP's poor showing in the resulting by-election was attributed to the candidate, John McGovern's, endorsement of his predecessor's criticism of the Labour Government.

From the General Election in 1929, when Wheatley secured 60 per cent of the poll and a majority of 6,724 votes, to the by-election in June 1930 the Labour vote fell by almost 9,000 votes. Two related reasons were advanced to explain this collapse of the Labour vote: the unpopularity of the ILP left's criticism of the Labour Government and local antipathy towards McGovern, particularly the Catholic Church's hostility to an atheist, ex-catholic. But other reasons are probably more germane. The Shettleston result was part of a general swing against the government and consistent with other by-election results in England.[63] Unlike the General Election when Wheatley had a straight fight against the Conservative, McGovern also had to contend with a Scottish National Party candidate and with Saklatvala for the Communist Party who, although he lost his deposit, still received 1,459 votes. Despite having held the seat for Labour, McGovern was immediately attacked by the leadership of the Glasgow Labour Party as unfit to be a Labour MP. The deep political divisions and bitterness within McGovern's constituency party were revealed by accusations that he had packed the selection meeting with supporters using false credentials and that he had rejoined the Catholic Church to win the nomination.[64] Once in Parliament McGovern ignored an undertaking to honour PLP standing orders and joined the Maxton group. In 1931 McGovern comfortably held the seat, despite the opposition of an official Labour Party candidate.

By voting against the MacDonald government the ILP parliamentary group had overstepped the limits of the Labour Party's tolerance of dissent codified for the first time in the host party's 1928 standing orders whose conscience clause permitted abstention only. Relations between Labour Party managers and the ILP had become increasingly strained from 1928 but the standing orders controversy added a disciplinary dimension to doctrinal questions. The formation of the 1931 National Government strengthened the ILP critics of gradualism as a political philosophy and insulated them from indulging in personal criticism of MacDonald. The political crisis of 1931, therefore, did nothing to draw the ILP and the Labour Party together. Despite parliamentary independence, however, Maxton remained conciliatory towards the Labour Party and rejected immediate disaffiliation.[65] It was only in November 1931 – after the nineteen ILP MPs had been refused Labour Party endorsement for the General Election, after Henderson, the new Labour Party leader, had resisted Maxton's conciliatory overtures for a relaxation of standing orders, and with the ILP's membership plummetting – that Maxton became an advocate of disaffiliation. *Forward*, for so long an open forum for the Glasgow left, was overtly critical of Maxton's leadership and the prospect of the ILP becoming 'a sort of half-way house between the Communist Party and the Labour Party, a sort of Mahomet's coffin suspended between heaven and earth'.[66] The disaffiliation question dominated the Scottish ILP Divisional Conference in January 1932. Maxton was the main speaker for disaffiliation arguing that the experience of the decade from 1922 had demonstrated how impervious the Labour Party was to socialist argument but that the decisive reason for disaffiliation was the disciplinary controls which required ILP MPs to submerge themselves 'body, soul and intellect' in the Labour Party.[67] Despite Maxton's personal standing the Scottish Conference voted by almost two to one for reconciliation with the Labour Party, a decision echoed by all but three of the other ILP Divisional Conferences.[68] Two months later the national ILP conference endorsed continued affiliation subject to a negotiated resolution of the standing orders dispute, albeit with a much reduced majority. But given the entrenched positions of the Labour Party and the ILP national leaderships this only delayed the final reckoning which came at a specially convened national conference in Bradford in July 1932.

There was little evidence of self-delusion among the delegates to the Bradford conference. Indeed, there was widespread acceptance that the inevitable consequence of secession in the short term would be marginality. Of the Clyde MPs only George Buchanan voiced optimism about the prospects of the ILP replacing Labour as the dominant working-class political party. Speaker after speaker, including Maxton, acknowledged that disaffiliation began a journey into, but not necessarily through, a political 'wilderness'. The image of a collective and personal 'wilderness' signified the beginning of a moral as well as a political process. Disaffiliation was understood as the beginning of an indefinite period of purgative oblivion and spiritual renewal, a symbolic rejection of the compromises required of the ILP because of its relationship with the Labour Party. In effect, collective disaffiliation would permit individual party members to renounce the routine bad faith required of them; no longer would the ILP-er be compelled to sustain a 'double personality'. The religious imagery which pervaded the disaffiliationist argument reflected the durability of ethical socialism in Scotland where, as William Knox has observed, it 'continued to shape the mood, programme and rhetoric of the Labour movement until the outbreak of the second world war'.[69]

It is impossible to offer any reliable estimate of the support for disaffiliation among the Glasgow ILP rank and file. Dollan's control of the city party machine and *Forward's* partiality stifled opposition to the local leadership. But at least eleven city branches supported disaffiliation, contrary to Dollan's confident assertion that he controlled a homogeneous Glasgow block vote for continued affiliation.[70] The most notable cleft in the Glasgow ILP was generational. 'The young people', Dollan remarked patronisingly, 'seemed to have a disposition towards disaffiliation due . . . to their lack of experience and knowledge'.[71] The Bradford conference also marked the final disintegration of the group which, in different ways, had dominated the Glasgow ILP from the eve of the Great War. With John Wheatley gone and Patrick Dollan, Tom Johnston and David Kirkwood remaining loyal to the Labour Party, James Maxton stood alone. Not only did the Bradford conference vote for disaffiliation by 241 to 142 votes it also approved a 'clean break' policy which meant that ILP branches withdrew from constituency Labour Parties and members stopped paying the political levy to their trade unions.[72] Of 44 Labour members on the city council, 40 were ILP-ers but only 7 disaffiliated.[73] In Glasgow, the bitterness of the years after the General Strike ensured that the rival factions moved quickly to build their separate camps.

Within a month of the fateful conference Dollan had formed the Scottish Socialist Party which claimed to have carried 107 ILP branches and around 50 per cent of the membership.[74] Conversely, despite attracting an audience of over three thousand to a 'disaffiliationist' conference Maxton proved unable to rebuild the shattered ILP which was overwhelmingly concentrated in Glasgow's east end. ILP representation on the city council, which varied between 5 and 10 councillors in the 1930s, was based on just 4 wards: Calton, Dalmarnock, Parkhead and Shettleston and Tollcross. These wards comprised much of the east end where the Maxton wing was strongest and where the ILP held two of its parliamentary seats, Bridgeton and Shettleston. A pattern quickly established itself between the two parties: Labour remained by far the larger but unable to completely remove the ILP which retained its presence on the city council without being able to significantly increase its representation.[75] Ironically, the potentially devastating division in the Labour ranks was overshadowed by a bizarre turn of events which installed the first Labour administration in the City Chambers. While Labour became Glasgow's majority party in parliamentary terms in

1922, at the local level it reached its limit in 1920 when a net gain of 20 seats gave it a total of 44 councillors, some way short of an overall majority.

Labour's breakthrough was due to the emergence of militant Protestantism as an electoral force in the shape of the Scottish Protestant League (SPL). The SPL was a temporary phenomenon in Glasgow politics but it effectively handed power to Labour by splitting the right-wing vote which had been united behind the Moderates. The SPL first made an impact in the local elections of 1931 when it won almost 12 per cent of the poll while contesting only 11 wards. In 1933 the SPL reached its zenith when it won another 4 seats and secured 23 per cent of the total vote, just 1 per cent less than the moderate poll. Of the 7 seats taken by the SPL in these years, 6 were gained from the moderates while only 1 was taken from Labour. As a result of the SPL drawing moderate votes Labour made 12 net gains, sufficient to form a minority administration in 1933.[76]

Disaffiliation left a vacuum in Scottish politics: in 1932 the Labour Party was little more than a shell organisation still dominated by the ILP. As Arthur Woodburn, the newly appointed secretary of the Scottish Labour Party reflected, his task was not so much of putting flesh on the party skeleton but 'practically to build from scratch'.[77] Dollan proved an unreliable ally, determined to preserve his fiefdom through the Scottish Socialist Party. More importantly, the shift from the ILP to the Labour Party as the pivot of labour politics in Glasgow marked not just an organisational transition but a seminal change in the nature of working-class political organisation. The limited organisational functions of the constituency Labour Party contrasted strongly with the much larger purpose of the ILP branch: to build socialist representation and through the social, educational and cultural activities of the branch to anticipate the citizenship of the Socialist Commonwealth:

> Many of the ILP-ers who had remained attached to the Party of their youth were not prepared to follow Maxton into the wilderness and yet did not want to begin a new interest in the Labour Party. This all did immeasurable harm. The ILP also had another great advantage over the Labour Party in the form of its organisation. Its branches were enthusiastic individuals who worked together as a team, socially, friendly, and with their interests centred on their branch. The Labour Party is a federal party and when a Constituency Party meets it is a group of delegates from branches of trades

unions, local labour parties and ward committees. The main power of the Labour Party is therefore exercised by delegates who have only a periodic association and little possibility of permanent or social association. The ILP was small and intimate. The Labour Party by its very size could not have this advantage.[78]

VI

The years after 1926 crystallised the inherent tensions within the ILP's relationship with the Labour Party. In this period Labour Party federalism was tempered by a new managerialism intolerant of an ILP insistent on its autonomy and distinctiveness. Politically, there was a narrowing of possibilities on the left with the ILP being squeezed between the stultifying gradualism of the Labour Party and the dead hand of Communist Party sectarianism. And yet features of *local* political traditions in Glasgow were vital in shaping the ILP's response to these national changes. The historic strength of the Glasgow ILP had been its capacity to act as a broker between a range of social and political movements. The ILP's catalyctic role in the housing and industrial movements of the Great War were the touchstones of Maxton's politics and underpinned the unsuccessful Manifesto campaign of 1928. After 1926 the Glasgow party was torn between those such as Maxton who attempted to recover the fluidity and openness of the pre-1918 period and the local leadership grouped around Dollan for whom such ideas were abhorrent. For Dollan, the arrival of the mass franchise meant that the ILP's prime role ·was the politics of representation rather than mobilisation. The disciplinary dimension of ILP disaffiliation laid down the boundaries of legitimate dissent within the Labour Party which remains in force today: the ILP was the last legitimate 'party within a party'.

Notes

1 Glasgow ILP Federation, Annual Report, 1926–7, p. 1.
2 *Ibid.*, 1925–6, p. 3.
3 Robert E. Dowse, *Left in the Centre: The Independent Labour Party 1893–1940* (Longmans, London, 1966), p. 129; Samuel Cooper, 'John Wheatley, A Study in Labour History' (unpublished PhD thesis, University of Glasgow, 1971), p. 276.
4 ILP, Scottish Divisional Council, Organising Report, August 1926, p. 3.

5 *Ibid.*, pp. 3–4.
6 David Howell, *A Lost Left: Three Studies in Socialism and Nationalism* (Manchester University Press, Manchester, 1986), p. 264, our emphasis.
7 *Glasgow Eastern Standard*, 22 May, 1926; Gordon Brown, *Maxton* (Mainstream, Edinburgh, 1986), p. 189.
8 Gordon Brown, 'The Labour Party and Political Change in Scotland 1918–1929: The Politics of Five Elections' (unpublished PhD thesis, University of Edinburgh), 1981 p. 401.
9 Jack Reynolds and Keith Laybourn, *Labour Heartland: A history of the Labour Party in West Yorkshire in the Inter-War Years 1918–1939* (Bradford University Press, Bradford, 1987), pp. 67–71.
10 (Glasgow ILP Federation, Executive Committee, Minutes, 22 November 1926.
11 Labour Party, National Executive Committee, Organisation Sub-Committee, 26 April 1926; E. Wake, 'Report of the NEC Re Liverpool Resolutions and Communist Activities', 26 July, 1926.
12 Labour Party, Scottish Council, Annual Conference, 5 April 1930, pp. 38–9.
13 *Ibid.*, p. 38.
14 *Forward*, 7 January, 1928.
15 *Glasgow Eastern Standard*, 12 May 1928, for example.
16 ILP, Scottish Divisional Council, Organising Report, August 1929, pp. 1–3; East End ILP, Annual Report, 4 July 1928.
17 Glasgow ILP Federation, Executive Committee, Minutes, 23 April 1926.
18 *Ibid.*, 4 November 1929.
19 *Ibid.*, 8 August 1930.
20 Glasgow ILP Federation, Management Committee, Minutes, 18 January 1929.
21 Glasgow ILP Federation, Organiser's Report, 8 August 1930.
22 Glasgow ILP Federation, Executive Committee, Minutes, 22 August 1930.
23 *Ibid.*
24 *Ibid.*, 13 November 1931.
25 *Forward*, 9 April 1932.
26 Graham Walker, *Thomas Johnston* (Manchester University Press, Manchester, 1988), pp. 87, 93–4.
27 John Hannan, *The Life of John Wheatley* (Spokesman, Nottingham, 1988), p. 163.
28 Keith Middlemas, *The Clydesiders: A Left Wing Struggle for Parliamentary Power* (Hutchinson, London, 1965), pp. 212–13.
29 John Paton, *Left Turn: An Autobiography* (Secker & Warburg, London, 1936), p. 288.
30 John Paton, *Proletarian Pilgrimage* (Routledge, London, 1935), p. 335.

31 *Glasgow Eastern Standard*, 22 October 1927; Egon Wertheimer, *Portrait of the Labour Party* (Putnams, London, 1929), p. 124.
32 Howell, *op. cit.*, p. 276.
33 Paul Davies, *A.J. Cook* (Manchester University Press, Manchester, 1987), pp. 148–52.
34 Paton, *Left Turn*, pp. 296–97.
35 *Forward*, 14 July 1928.
36 *Glasgow Herald*, 9 July 1928.
37 Hannan, *op.cit.*, p. 164; Fenner Brockway, *Inside The Left: Thirty Years of Platform, Press, Prison and Parliament* (Allen & Unwin, London, 1942), p. 195; William Knox, *James Maxton* (Manchester University Press, Manchester, 1987), pp. 75–6.
38 *Forward*, 14 July 1928.
39 *Forward*, 30 June 1928.
40 *Glasgow Eastern Standard*, 23 February 1929.
41 Brown, *op. cit.* (1986), p. 210.
42 Roderick Martin, *Communism and the British Trade Unions 1924–1933: A Study of the National Minority Movement* (Clarendon Press, Oxford, 1969), pp. 93–101.
43 Cooper, *op. cit.*, pp. 331–7 argues that a series of Commons speeches by Wheatley inspired these reformulated demands.
44 Alan McKinlay, 'Employers and Skilled Workers in the Inter-War Depression: Engineering and Shipbuilding on Clydeside 1919–1939' (unpublished DPhil thesis, University of Oxford, 1986), pp. 147–9.
45 Tom Gallagher, *Glasgow The Uneasy Peace: Religious Tension in Modern Scotland* (Manchester University Press, Manchester, 1987), p. 201; *Forward*, 15 January 1927.
46 Eric Shaw, *Discipline and Discord in the Labour Party: The Politics of Managerial Control in the Labour Party, 1951–87* (Manchester University Press, Manchester, 1988), pp. 16–21.
47 *Glasgow Eastern Standard*, 12 March 1927.
48 David Marquand, *Ramsay MacDonald* (Jonathan Cape, 1977), p. 456.
49 John Scanlon, *Cast Off All Fooling* (Hutchinson, London, 1938), pp. 190–1.
50 John Wheatley, *Socialise the National Income* (Glasgow, 1929); Adrian Oldfield, 'The Independent Labour Party and Planning, 1920–26', *International Review of Social History*, XXI, 1976, pp. 23, 25.
51 Arthur Marwick, 'The ILP, 1918–1932' (unpublished B.Litt. thesis, University of Oxford, 1960), p. 298.
52 Glasgow ILP Federation Minutes, 14 November 1930; ILP Conference Report, 1930, pp. 102–3.
53 ILP Conference Report, 1931, pp. 99–100.

54 Glasgow ILP Federation Minutes, 21 August 1931.
55 *Ibid.*, 14 November 1927.
56 *Ibid.*, 3 May 1929.
57 *Ibid.*, 29 November 1929.
58 *Ibid.*, Executive Committee, Minutes, 18 December 1927.
59 *Ibid.*, 4 May 1928, 15 June 1928.
60 *Ibid.*, 21 August 1931.
61 *Forward*, 18 January 1930.
62 Knox, *op. cit.*, pp. 100–101.
63 Ian Donnachie, 'Scottish Labour in Depression: the 1930's', in Ian Donnachie, Christopher Harvie and Ian Wood (eds), *Forward!: Labour Politics in Scotland 1888–1988* (Polygon, Edinburgh, 1989), p. 53.
64 William Knox (ed.), *Scottish Labour Leaders 1918–1939: A Biographical Dictionary* (Mainstream, Edinburgh, 1984), p. 177.
65 Dowse, *op. cit.*, pp. 177–8; Brockway, *op. cit.*, pp. 215–16.
66 *Forward*, 16 January 1932.
67 *Forward*, 31 January 1932.
68 *New Leader*, 29 January 1932.
69 William Knox, 'Religion and the Scottish Labour Movement c. 1900–39', *Journal of Contemporary History*, 23, 4, October 1988, p. 626.
70 ILP Conference Report, 1932, pp. 5–6; *Forward*, 6 August 1932.
71 *Ibid.*, p. 17.
72 *New Leader*, 15, 22 July 1932.
73 John McNair, *James Maxton: The Beloved Rebel* (Allen & Unwin, 1955), p. 231.
74 *Forward*, 27 August, 3 September 1932.
75 *Forward*, 5 November 1932; *Glasgow Eastern Standard*, 5 November 1932.
76 Tom Gallagher, 'Protestant Extremism in Urban Scotland 1930–1939: Its Growth and Contraction', *Scottish Historical Review*, LXIV, 1985, pp. 162–4.
77 Arthur Woodburn, typescript ms, p. 68.
78 *Ibid.*, pp. 76–7.

EIGHT

Traditions, myths and legacies: the ILP and the Labour left

David Howell

Left-wing factions within the Labour Party claim a commitment to the radical remaking of society, but they are also creatures of tradition. They look to their predecessors both for inspiration and for tactical lessons: their opponents similarly interpret the past to justify their activities. If the idea of the invention of tradition can be applied to nations, it can also be applied to parties of the left.[1] Labour's traditions are not just contested; they are relatively recent. It was only in the years after 1918 that a distinctive Labour identity clearly emerged. Within this forging of a Labour identity, the controversies surrounding the Independent Labour Party played a significant part. A durable memory of the age of MacDonald is of James Maxton, in appearance almost the caricature of a Labour critic, condemning the Labour leadership for its deviations from Socialist principle. Yet such images and the traditions of which they form a part may contain powerful myths. The force of the tradition must be appreciated since it helps to explain subsequent behaviour; but the uncritical acceptance of powerful traditions need not make for good historical understanding.

One strand in Labour characterisations of the ILP in the years prior to disaffiliation was that these were the Clydesiders, a radical parliamentary group whose politics were somehow moulded by a distinctively Glaswegian experience. This characterisation incorporated the emotions of the 1922 election victories, the parliamentary scenes that followed; the estrangement from the Labour leadership. It survived disaffiliation and the long, hard years as a separate and declining party. Even in 1945, Glasgow kept alive the ILP's parliamentary presence. James Maxton and Campbell Stephen had no official Labour opponent whilst John McGovern finished ahead of Conservative, Labour and Communist challengers. Lack of support for the war seemed to be no handicap and it is tempting to argue that there existed some kind of special relationship between sections of the Glaswegian working class and a radical and pacifist ILP.

Such a presentation can be found at first sight within the measured prose of the first Nuffield election study. When one of the authors visited Glasgow during the 1945 campaign, her experience of the city anticipated Labour's relatively small advance: 'In this city where Labour had made so much progress in its early days, saturation point seemed now to have been reached . . . Meetings were thinly attended. Gone were the soap-box orators of former days.'

She found one exception. Only in Bridgeton was there the old enthusiasm, with Maxton addressing a packed meeting on a soaking wet evening:

> When at last he rose to speak, an intense silence settled upon the hall. He charmed and delighted his hearers with one story after another, speaking little of election politics. However, the burden of his speech was – 'Twenty years ago you sent me to Parliament to protest. I have protested for you, and I will protest for you till I die.' He was in the very truth, the father of his people.[2]

Here is the image of the incorruptible radical drawing his strength of purpose from the support of his electors.

Yet even this instance promotes scepticism. In fact, Bridgeton was not notable for political enthusiasm in the Glasgow of 1945. Its poll ranked next to the lowest in the city. The characterisation of Maxton's oratory is hardly that of a left-socialist offering a principled alternative to the limitations of the Labour Party. Rather it seems a folksy appeal that owed little to a distinctive political position.

The theme deserves a more extensive analysis. The origins of British Labour politics lay in diverse initiatives; each group had to adapt to its immediate political environment, exploiting the weakness of older parties and paying due regard to their strengths. Locally dominant trade unions had to be considered: the susceptibilities of their officials and activists had to be understood. So Labour politics emerged often working with the grain of existing local culture.

Scotland had its own distinctive pattern – the early emergence of the Scottish Labour Party, its amalgamation with the ILP, the contribution of the Scottish TUC and the formation of the Scottish Workers' Parliamentary Elections Committee. Precocious organisational development was perhaps in part a substitute for a generally weak trade unionism. Scottish Liberalism had little immediate need to make electoral concessions, the MacDonald/Gladstone Pact did not include Scotland, and Labour's limited parliamentary advance – just three seats prior to 1914 – necessitated in each case the initial defeat of a Liberal candidate.

Within this Scottish distinctiveness, Glasgow had its own specific politics, influenced by the concentration of skilled workers, the early drive for municipalisation and the urgency of the housing issue. The emphasis on local diversities is important. It was after all during this pre-1914 period that the men and women who came to dominate Glasgow ILP politics between the wars were serving their political apprenticeships. Typically they were born in the 1880s with only John Wheatley coming from an earlier generation.

Against these localisms, Labour politics contained increasingly powerful centralising tendencies. The development of a national – that is British – Labour Party was underpinned by the desire of trade unions to establish all-British standards. In the coalfields, after 1918, it was the coal owners who were economic Home Rulers. Amalgamations meant that economic decisions were taken increasingly in England rather than in Scotland. When the Clydesiders made their celebrated journey to the South in November 1922 St Enoch's station had only a few more weeks as the terminus of a specifically Scottish railway company. Increasingly Labour's bid for power was interpreted as a drive for control of a centralised British state – a strategy given credibility by superficial interpretation of electoral trends. Within the Labour Party, the 1920s were the prime decade of that dedicated centraliser and rationaliser Arthur Henderson, loyally backed by the National Agent, Egerton Wake. Inevitably the aspirations of Glasgow ILP politicians were cast in the British context.

The Glasgow MPs who became thoroughly identified with the left were influenced decisively by their post-1922 experiences. They became disillusioned with MacDonald, and to varying degrees with the Labour Party. The process was cumulative – the first Labour Government, the General Strike and its aftermath, the production of *Labour and the Nation*, the pusillanimity of the 1929 government. Yet not all Glasgow ILP-ers followed that path. Against Maxton and Wheatley, there must be placed Tom Johnston. *Forward* had been viewed widely as the authentic voice of the Glasgow ILP and Johnston did not respond to the difficulties of office – even a close association with

Jimmy Thomas – by shifting to the left.[3] Alongside Johnston, there was Patrick Dollan, the one who stayed behind, his objective not Westminster, but the council chamber. For so long a close associate of Wheatley, he remained heavily involved in the ILP until disaffiliation, but never contemplated a personal breach with the Labour Party.

Even as the dispute between the ILP and the Labour Party escalated, the West of Scotland provided discordant signals. The dispute focused on ILP criticism of the parliamentary party's standing orders. In the autumn of 1930, Tom Irwin was denied endorsement as Labour candidate in the East Renfrew by-election because he took the ILP side in the controversy. Six months later David Hardie faced with the same choice at Rutherglen, signed an appropriate letter dictated by Labour's National Agent and was endorsed as an official Labour candidate.[4] The diversity extended beyond specific personalities. The ILP's Scottish Division was the strongest in the party. In 1931, it claimed 273 branches out of the ILP's total of 712.[5] Dollan's industry and organisational ability helped to ensure that the Division failed to support many of the positions taken by the more radical parliamentarians. Ironically, the growing dominance of a group loosely referred to as the Clydesiders owed something to the backing of the ILP's non-Scottish and weaker Divisions. The point was made sardonically by Dollan in the spring of 1932 as the ILP's relationship with Labour moved near to breaking point.

> The revolutionary centres like Winchester, Truro, Marylebone, Westminster, Newton Abbot supported the motion for disaffiliation. They indeed must be disappointed with the apathy of the Clyde.[6]

Easy generalisation about the impact of local experiences on the emergence of the ILP as a left faction should be avoided.

Similar cautions should characterise any attempt to understand the ILP as a left opposition within the Labour Party. At one level it may be illuminating to compare successive Labour lefts – Maxton's ILP, the Socialist League, Keep Left and so on. Such comparisons must be subject to two qualifications. One is an appreciation of the way that beliefs about the weaknesses of earlier factions influenced subsequent strategic choices. The inherited beliefs might be fallacious, but they could be nonetheless powerful. Certainly the disaffiliation of the ILP and its aftermath had a considerable impact on subsequent factionalism.

Something of this legacy will be examined later, but immediate attention will be given to the second qualification – that each left faction must be understood in a specific context of wider Labour Party politics. The ILP's strategic predicament in the late 1920s must be appreciated within the party world that emerged from the constitutional changes of 1918. It was not simply that the internal operations of the reformed party had no readily available blueprint and that procedures developed through trial and error. There were significant legacies from the pre-war party in terms of organisational forms, ideas and personnel, but the element of novelty in the 1920s was crucial.[7] It was not merely a question of a revised constitution. It stemmed also from the inflation of political expectations. Optimism was buoyed up by an electoral system that exaggerated Labour's strength at a time of complex party competition – and then was deflated by the chastening experience of office.

Within the remodelled party the ILP was an anomaly. The normal presentation of the constitutional changes does not penetrate to the root of the question. The reform of the Labour Party's National Executive removed the sectional protection for ILP nominees but did not end the ILP presence on the executive. Throughout the 1920s a prominent ILP-er was returned within the National Societies section alongside the nominees of the major unions. For several years the successful ILP nominee was Fred Jowett, a member of the party since the very beginning. Moreover, for some years the prominent Glasgow ILP-er Agnes Dollan stood successfully for a seat in the Women's Section. The judgement that the commitment to establish Divisional Labour Parties (DLP) with individual members represented a threat to the traditional role of the ILP should be assessed in the context of what happened in the 1920s. Clearly the new organisational pattern could undercut the place of the ILP as the avenue through which individual socialists entered the Labour Party; but in practice the network of DLPs developed slowly. In weaker areas initial optimism gave way to stagnation. Often DLPs were little more than Trades and Labour Councils and many individual members continued also within the ILP with the smaller body as the focus for much of their energies.[8]

The fundamental anomaly was rather that the ILP was a potentially discordant element because of its thorough and separate structure. It affiliated to the Labour Party as a Socialist Society but it was quite unlike any other affiliate within this section. In 1925 the other six organisations had a combined affiliation of 6,397; in contrast the ILP had one of 30,000.[9] Only the ILP had the organisational resources that might make credible a claim for some degree of effective autonomy.

Many of the affiliated trade unions had the resources and on occasions the inclination to make such a claim. This comes through clearly in the complex manoeuvres aimed at drawing a clear line between the Labour Party and its Communist counterpart. This problem preoccupied Labour Party leaders and administrators for almost a decade and left an enduring mark on the party's managerial practices. Overwhelming opposition to Communist affiliation was secured readily, but it proved very difficult to exclude Communists from every level of Labour organisation. The fundamental obstacle was the convention of trade union sovereignty; that such an affiliated organisation should be free to nominate anyone who paid into the union's political fund, irrespective of that individual's party membership. To do otherwise would undercut the whole concept of affiliated membership through the political levy. The consequence was that until 1927 prominent Communists such as Harry Pollitt and Arthur Horner were accepted as trade union delegates to the national Labour Party Conference. Only in 1928 with Communist and anti-Communist factions much more antagonistic in many unions, could the Labour Party succeed in excluding Communist trade union delegates from Labour Party institutions. The terms of the exclusion certainly gave the Labour Party hierarchy more influence over the political affairs of affiliated unions, yet crucially the final break only happened when many unions were prepared to champion it for their own internal reasons.[10]

If Labour's leaders could accept some degree of autonomy for unions who were often supportive of the party leadership, it did not follow that an equivalent tolerance would be afforded to the ILP. The relationship of give and take with the unions was based in part on a belief in the feasibility of a demarcation between industrial and political affairs. A rift between the Labour Party and the ILP could emerge only if the latter was in *political* disagreement with the larger organisation. In such an eventuality indulgence was unlikely to be granted. In short, the ILP in the 1920s was a political affiliate with some of the organisational attributes of an industrial one.

Its emergence as a left faction that could reveal the anomaly crystallised slowly. Pre-1914 there had always been a left within the ILP. In the 1890s, this had advocated unity with the Social Democratic

Federation; after 1906 it had kicked against the limitations of the alliance with the unions and electoral and parliamentary deals with the Liberals; it had sympathised with the spectacular protests of Victor Grayson and in general had caused much annoyance to an ILP leadership committed to the compact with the unions and to ultra-respectability. The war of 1914–18 had done much to reunite the ILP around a platform of opposition to conscription, militarism and secret diplomacy. It appeared more plausible as a left within the Labour Party and was attacked by patriotic trade union leaders as an unrepresentative middle-class grouping. Yet the ILP's membership remained politically heterogeneous. The war attracted new recruits; others retained membership cards for old times sake. In the post-war world, the ILP could attract the politically ambitious. Hugh Dalton, on the look-out for a parliamentary seat noted in July 1923:

> I got a letter from Fenner Brockway saying the ILP Branch at Huddersfield want to nominate me and asking me if I am a member of the ILP. I thereupon join or rather rejoin after a lapse of years.[11]

The 1918 revision of Labour's Constitution inevitably provoked debate about the ILP's future role. One response associated with Clifford Allen developed the idea of the party as a socialist think-tank preparing policies for application by the wider movement. The extent of members' commitment to such a strategy is questionable. For many, the ILP seems to have remained essentially a propagandist and electoral organisation, not an instrument for devising and publicising detailed policies. Moreover, the experience of the 1924 government brought the neat specification of function into question. What was the value of developing detailed policies, if the Labour Party leadership was so cautious? One response was that the mere provision of policy was insufficient; a political battle had to be fought.

The emergence of the most significant policy statement *The Living Wage* was more or less concurrent with a decisive shift in the ILP leadership. Allen resigned the chairmanship in October 1925; Maxton and his allies came to control the National Administrative Council, the National Conference, most of the Divisional Organisations and with Brailsford's replacement by Brockway, the editorship of the party paper, the *New Leader*.[12]

The new leadership was equipped with a party policy that has often secured retrospective praise. The underconsumptionist diagnosis and proposals of *The Living Wage* could be presented as a case for a reformed capitalism, a credible alternative to the stultifying orthodoxy of much of the Labour leadership. However, the newly-dominant group within the ILP interpreted the proposals not as a route to a more humane and efficient capitalism, but as a potentially speedy method of moving towards socialism. 'Socialism in Our Time' became the catch phrase for the radical ILP.

A drive to win wider support for these policies faced serious obstacles. Any attempt to secure the backing of the Labour Party Conference faced the hostility or indifference of many unions. One of the very few union leaders who had a close relationship with this ILP leadership was A.J. Cook of the miners. Recriminations over the collapse of the General Strike and then over the Mond–Turner talks meant that this connection was no recommendation for many union officials. But the problems went much deeper than the frictions generated by individuals. Industrial defeat had led to many union leaders placing more reliance on a Labour electoral victory. This meant suppressing doubts about MacDonald and some of his colleagues and characterising critics as harmful to Labour's chances. The growing antagonisms within several unions could facilitate a ready identification of any group on the left as disruptive and sympathetic to the Communists. Policy controversies could be cashed into the simple world of internal union rivalries. More specifically the ILP's 'Living Wage' policy with its insistence that wage standards should be laid down by government and that family allowances should supplement wages, could be condemned as an attempt by some politicians to invade the unions' own sphere. Beneath all the specific arguments there lay a gulf between divergent styles articulated and on occasions exploited by Ernest Bevin:

> With regard to our refusals to talk to you and people in your category in the movement, believe me, we have very good reasons. . . . the 'superior class' attitude is always there in relation to the trade union leader who comes from the rank and file and we feel it.[13]

The consequence of this balance of forces was apparent in the years after 1926. The Living Wage proposals were passed to a joint Labour Party/TUC Committee which focused on one divisive question, family allowances, and eventually ceased to meet. The discursive Labour Party document *Labour and the Nation* was squared with major unions prior to its consideration at the 1928 party conference.[14] This assembly was organised efficiently behind the MacDonald leadership and ILP critics were swept aside.

If ILP policies could not secure support at Labour Party Conferences then one alternative was to articulate them in the House of Commons. The pursuit of this strategy soon raised the question of the ILP's relationship to the wider party. Many Labour MPs carried ILP membership cards. The significance of this varied between individuals. For some it was purely formal; for others it indicated a major focus of their political activity – and perhaps their ultimate political loyalty. A smaller group had a closer connection with the ILP. They were sponsored members with the ILP taking responsibility for their electoral finances. Both categories of MP were entitled to attend meetings of the ILP parliamentary group.

In the 1929 parliament the sponsored MPs included many of those who were committed advocates of the increasingly radical ILP policy – Maxton, Campbell Stephen and Wheatley from Glasgow. Wise and Brockway from elsewhere. But it was far from a politically homogeneous group. It included Tom Johnston and Shinwell both of whom were critical of the emerging ILP position and several others who had never allied themselves with the left. Any attempt to mobilise an ILP parliamentary group behind a policy critical of the broader Labour leadership would expose this heterogeneity. The problem was articulated by the ILP pacifist Alfred Salter early in the 1929 parliament:

> We are bound to the ILP by ties of conviction, interest and sentiment and we do not want to see our movement come to an inglorious end or degenerate into a little rump of 'rebels' and quasi-communists engaged in pinpricking and harassing the Labour Party and its chief.[15]

The origins of such a radical mobilisation lay in a decision at the ILP's 1929 conference shortly before the election of the second Labour Government. Already there were disagreements amongst delegates reflecting the growing estrangement between the ILP's new leadership and the dominant sentiments within the wider Labour Party. The conference rejected an attempt to give the National Administrative Council a significant role in the decisions of the ILP parliamentary group. However, new regulations governing the acceptability of ILP candidates included a requirement that marked the beginning of a dispute that ended in disaffiliation: 'Proposed candidates should give an undertaking that they accept in general the policy of the Party as determined by Annual Conference, and if elected, will be prepared to give effect to it in the House of Commons.'[16]

The conservatism of the 1929 Labour Government soon left its divisive mark on the deliberations of the ILP parliamentary group. When members discussed the government's very limited proposals for reform of unemployment insurance a majority wished to back the government. Maxton argued that he had a more fundamental loyalty to ILP Conference decisions: 'He stated it as his intention, whatever the decision of the Group, to table and vote for amendments incorporating ' "The ILP Minimum Demands".'[17]

A predictable response came at the ILP's 1930 conference. Party discipline had to be heightened and a resolution was passed overwhelmingly. This instructed the NAC: 'to reconstruct the ILP Parliamentary Group on the basis of acceptance of the policy of the ILP as laid down by the decisions of Annual Conference and as interpreted by the NAC and to limit endorsements of future ILP Parliamentary candidates to nominees who accept this basis'.[18]

The consequence was a fall in the membership of the parliamentary group from around 140 to 18, some directly sponsored, but others ILP members who were sponsored by other organisations.[19] The implication of this step was emphasised by one sponsored MP who stayed out of the reformed group: 'If the ILP continued its affiliation to the Labour Party, it could not do so without accepting all the implications of that affiliation'.[20]

In terms of formal decisions the impact of the reformed ILP parliamentary group was trivial. It could hope to have little influence on the outcome of votes, given the loyalism of many Labour backbenchers and the stylistic distance of several trade union officials who had their own criticisms of government policy. But in the administration's increasingly beleaguered state, with unpredictable parliamentary and electoral prospects, a tough response to dissent could discourage other potential critics.

During the lifetime of the 1929 government disciplinary pressures gradually intensified. The party constitution as amended in 1929 required that Labour MPs 'accept and conform to the Constitution, Programme, Principles and Policy of the Party'. In the same year the PLP acquired a set of standing orders, but at first, this seemed to be little more than a formality. As the government's difficulties increased and criticism grew, so the question of party discipline became more immediate.[21] The ILP insistence on organising to forward its own proposals provoked a hostile response. By the end of November 1930, the Labour Chief Whip was elevating party unity as the primary virtue: 'He would rather see the Parliamentary Party do the wrong thing unitedly than to see what is going on today – a small group maintaining the right of criticism inside and outside of the House, posing as custodians of principle.'[22]

Alongside the increasingly acerbic exchanges within the parliamentary party, negotiations between the ILP and the Labour Party began in the summer of 1930 over the implications of the former's new requirements for candidates. The pace of the exchanges was leisurely and there were times when the differences seemed trivial.[23] Yet the Labour refusal to endorse Irwin's candidacy at East Renfrew was a demonstration of the dispute's potential for division. Eventually the formal point of disagreement came down to the ILP's refusal to accept the parliamentary party's first standing order: 'Any member who has conscientious scruples on any matter of Party policy shall be free to abstain from voting.'[24]

The ILP case rested on a debatable interpretation of the past. The ILP had always presented itself as the socialist conscience of the Labour Party and it was argued that such a standing order, restricting permissible dissent to matters of individual conscience, frustrated such a role. Thus Fred Jowett, a much less combative figure than Maxton and several others within the leadership, justified his support of the ILP position by arguing that the new disciplinary regime marked a breach with previous practice. There had been earlier episodes where ILP members had adopted a distinctive line within the parliamentary party – attempts to limit Labour's entanglements with Edwardian Liberalism and specifically the National Insurance controversy of 1911, and of course the stand taken by some ILP members during the war.[25]

The argument from continuity perhaps exaggerated the extent of earlier ILP solidarity. The pre-1914 controversies had been as much within the ILP as between the ILP and the wider party; the ILP position on the war had not been backed by all its sponsored members and the sympathetic ones had generally taken care to maintain their links with the Labour Party. The attempt to legitimise ILP actions by reference to the past also faced the problem that many ILP MPs disputed this interpretation, suggesting that the change was within the ILP rather than within the wider movement. Such a presentation tended to ignore the vehemence of earlier disputes, but made the effective claim that priorities had changed and that for the first time, a radical leadership was prepared to use the ILP organisation in a combative factional strategy.

A further justification for the ILP's position advanced by the party's General Secretary, John Paton, effectively spotlighted the underlying anomaly:

> The ILP claims no more than would be claimed by a Trade Union affiliated to the Labour Party. If the Annual Conference of a Trade Union instructed its Parliamentary Members to vote in a particular way on a special issue, the Trade Union concerned would expect its Members to carry out the mandate given. . . . In the last resort, no Trade Union would surrender this right.[26]

Any response by the Labour Party hierarchy was tempered inevitably by the fact that the ILP had a well-established legitimacy within the movement. It had been one of the prime movers in the formation of the Labour Representation Committee. It had supplied several of Labour's parliamentary leaders and it continued to provide the organisational strength in many constituencies. There was no way that an easy ideological demarcation could be made between the two organisations. There were no simple parallels with the previous controversies over Communist affiliation and involvement within Labour organisations. In 1931 the ILP still counted as a somewhat contumacious member of the Labour family.

The official Labour line was presented by Henderson, a firm disciplinarian who was nonetheless very aware of the complex balance that was the Labour Alliance. His criticism of the ILP centred on the distinction between an individual conscience and organised dissent; in effect it disputed the ILP claim that their position was consistent with their past record. His published correspondence included a phrase that would become celebrated as a loyalist indictment of the ILP position and which would be employed as a charge against subsequent left factions. The ILP's new conditions for candidates were creating 'a party within a party'.[27]

The sensational exit of MacDonald and a few colleagues did not end the dispute. Six weeks after the collapse of the Labour Government.

Henderson was yielding no ground to the ILP: 'I know of no way of carrying on a great party in the House of Commons . . . but either voting according to the decisions of the Party or abstaining according to the dictates of your conscience.'[28]

The debate about standing orders was increasingly a short hand for a widening gulf over policy. It was all too easy for mainstream Labour politicians to blame those who had defected to the National Government for the failures of the 1929 administration. Brockway, speaking to Labour's 1931 conference, had indicted not just the absent few but the entire strategy of the recent government: 'Unless it is understood that there was that fundamental difference of view during the last two and a half years, the particular issues which are involved cannot be understood.'[29]

Such an exhibition of virtue was perhaps unlikely to gain much sympathy from those who had kept their doubts private until the sensational events of the preceding August.

One sign of the increasing estrangement came during that 1931 conference. With a General Election pending and ILP candidates to be refused endorsement, Labour's National Executive gave permission for Constituency Parties to initiate official candidacies against the dissenters. The option was taken up only in Shettleston where McGovern's style had perhaps widened the gulf, but the mere granting of permission was one more signpost down the track that ended nine months later with the ILP disaffiliation.[30]

As the rupture came closer, the tensions within the ILP dominant group increased. By Easter 1932, Brockway was arguing that the earlier policy of 'Socialism In Our Time' was inadequate in the context of what seemed like a terminal crisis of capitalism. The earlier contrast between ILP and Labour was redundant:

> We must concentrate upon securing and retaining such power that we will be able to carry through the decisive change from Capitalism to Socialism without fear of effective interruption or obstruction. . . . This policy inevitably means a break with the gradualism of the Labour Party.[31]

Against this expectation that economic crisis could produce a mass radicalisation, some of those who had backed the ILP position in the previous parliament expressed their opposition to a break with Labour. Kirkwood acknowledged that he had responded positively to a request from his union that he accept PLP decisions.[32] Joseph Kinley argued that they should work within the Labour Party to expose the failures of 1929–31;[33] E.F. Wise suggested that the behaviour of those favouring disaffiliation was at odds with their diagnosis:

> According to Cullen & Brockway they were within some months' distance of the complete breakdown of capitalism which did not know where to turn. Was that the time to be occupied in rows about the Standing Orders?[34]

Already the battle lines were drawn. The July 1932 decision to disaffiliate splintered the left that had dominated the party since 1926.[35] The subsequent decline of the ILP served as a warning for later left factions.

The legacies of this estrangement did not influence merely the left. The traumas of the second Labour Government left powerful memories. Dissent had come not just from the ILP but also from the small group around Sir Oswald Mosley. The latter element had split early in 1931 to form the short-lived New Party. And the targets of much of the dissent, MacDonald and Snowden, had been associated closely with the ILP for several years. The splintering of the party – the Mosleyites, the defectors to the National Government, the ILP – all strengthened the sentiment in trade union circles that intellectuals of whatever tendency could not be trusted. Their enthusiasms were brittle; they were not constrained by trade union disciplines; they were supercilious; they confused their own egos with the interests of the labour movement. The example of Mosley and his political instability was used to indict later left critics. A miners' official attacked Sir Stafford Cripps in 1937.

> Sir Stafford Cripps is a rich man with rich pals around him and they are the biggest danger to the Labour Party in this country. You will find these chaps where Mosley is before much longer.[36]

Anti-intellectualism ran through Labour Party controversies in the 1930s. At the end of the decade, an as yet unknown Constituency delegate, George Brown, could be found fulminating from the conference rostrum about 'a small and noisy section of intellectuals'.[37]

Such sentiments were backed by increasingly firm managerial controls, a response in part to the disasters of 1929–31 and in part to the shift of the Communist Party back from the isolation of the Third Period to the strategies of the United and Popular Fronts. The increasingly tough regime was backed by the major unions keen to prevent a repeat of 1931. In particular, the two large General Unions were increasingly significant actors within the party; the weight of their votes showed a proportional increase and their leaderships were firmly committed to the new regime. It was in this unpropitious climate that the left attempted to reform after the disaffiliation of the ILP.

Those responsible for the Socialist League, effectively the ILP's successor, attempted to learn from the failure of the earlier faction. The attempt was unsuccessful. The ILP from the mid-1920s until disaffiliation had combined a radical leadership and programme with a politically heterogeneous membership; similarly the much smaller league began as a marriage of two groups each with its own style and priorities. The ILP's internal arguments had revealed the existence of a significant group including Patrick Dollan and E.F. Wise who were determined that the left should retain its presence within the Labour Party. Dollan's subsequent involvement in the Scottish Socialist Party was paralleled by Wise's activity in the National ILP Affiliation Committee. This latter group combined with the Society for Socialist Inquiry and Propaganda, founded by G.D.H. Cole. This was a response to the inadequacies of the 1929 government; it was envisaged by its advocates as essentially a research group loyal to the Labour Party, a role perhaps not too far from Clifford Allen's vision for the ILP a decade earlier.[38]

The combination of the Affiliation Committee and the SSIP to produce the Socialist League was marked by a revealing disagreement. Bevin had been chairman of the research grouping but was replaced by Wise within the combined organisation. The disenchanted Transport Workers' leader wrote off the new initiative: 'I do not believe the Socialist League will change very much from the old ILP attitude.'[39]

The lack of significant trade union supporters was an obvious weakness of the league. It helped to ensure that like its ILP predecessor, the League faced overwhelming obstacles in winning the Labour Party for its ideas. Indeed the social ethos of the League was perhaps even more distinctive than that of the ILP. The ILP rebels had included men with trade union backgrounds such as Buchanan and Kirkwood whilst advocates such as Maxton could speak credibly for the Glasgow working class. Aginst this, the League's dominant figures included the affluent Wykehamist Sir Stafford Cripps whilst several others came from the Public Schools and Oxbridge. The trait lent itself to easy lampooning by critics, as a substitute for substantive argument.

Despite its concern not to follow the ILP's slide to disaffiliation, the League emulated its predecessor in one fundamental respect. It affiliated to the Labour Party as a Socialist Society and attempted to develop a network of branches. Its affiliation to the Labour Party was always much more modest than that of the ILP and never exceeded three thousand. No attempt was made to sponsor parliamentary candidates, so one potential source of friction with the wider party was absent. The overwhelming impression is of the organisation's weakness. Several of its branches were very small; many were ephemeral; its relative stronghold was in London which provided a high proportion of the limited membership and some London-based individuals had a strong influence on the organisation's strategy.

Labour politics in the 1930s were perhaps at their furthest left at the party conference of October 1932 just as the League was beginning its turbulent career. Reaction to the events of 1931 and the impact of the recession made some unions more open to left-inclined policies such as the public ownership of the joint-stock banks. The tone of the conference seemed more critical of established leaders. When Sir Charles Trevelyan moved a resolution instructing a future labour government to stand or fall by its Socialist commitment, Henderson responded critically and was interrupted. The chairman's response was revealing: 'I must ask delegates to hear Mr. Henderson. It is unusual for you to behave in this way when he is speaking.'[40] The lack of deference offered some support to those who had argued within the ILP that the Left should stay inside the Labour Party and fight for its ideas – but decisions at this conference owed little if anything to effective left factionalism.

The Leicester conference was a summit for the left in the 1930s. Gradually over the next two years the major unions achieved more unity of action in the pursuit of modest policies and the limitation of left influence. As this cohesion developed so the League began to be characterised increasingly by loyalists as a disruptive faction whose intellectual leaders gratified their own vanities by radical postures and damaged the party by electorally embarrassing pronouncements. For those on the left, the prospect of change that had opened up after 1931 receded as the party leadership and above all, most major trade union officials responded to domestic and international challenges with a crippling lack of imagination.

The consequence was that the Socialist League shifted gradually to a thoroughly oppositional stance. The early emphasis on research and propaganda gave way to the advocacy of distinctive policies on immediate issues. The emphasis developed by Cripps at the League's 1934 conference was remarkably close to the style of the ILP's demand for 'Socialism in Our Time'. Socialist policies were not a matter of 'some vague utopia in the far-distant future but of quick action to accomplish that change'.[41]

Such an insistence, necessitated that the Labour Party adopt radical policies. Indeed the official document produced in 1934, *For Socialism & Peace*, was much more substantial than *Labour and the Nation*. Nevertheless, the League criticised the statement because of its limited proposals on public ownership, its lack of support for workers' control and its approach to disarmament. But League attempts to radicalise the document were as fruitless as the ILP's efforts to inject some substance into *Labour and the Nation*. A mass of seventy-five amendments was pruned by the conference's Standing Orders Committee to a few critical and lengthy alternative sections. The conference platform backed by the votes of the major unions overwhelmingly defeated the League's challenges. The organisation was marginalised as a group of naive, impractical but potentially divisive visionaries. A passage from Hugh Dalton's memoirs presents a patronising characterisation:

> He had a dream in which he saw himself at a Labour Party Conference moving a resolution to nationalise the Solar System. This was at first regarded as a brilliant idea, but towards the close of the debate, a Socialist Leaguer got up at the back of the hall and moved an amendment to add the words 'and the Milky Way'.[42]

This 1934 Labour Conference was perhaps a decisive moment for the League. Attempts to change policy through established party procedures had produced overwhelming rejection. Over the next two and a half years, the League moved to agitation on a wider platform, eventually seeking links with other left organisations in a 'Unity Campaign'. Ironically this involved the prospect of work with the much diminished ILP, but more seriously for the League's future, it involved co-operation with the Communist Party. This marked a sharp contrast with the ILP in the pre-disaffiliation period, when Maxton and his colleagues faced not just the criticism of official Labour, but also the dismissive sectarianism of Third-Period Communism. By the mid-1930s, the advance of fascism had radically changed Communist policy and the emergence of credible Popular Fronts in France and Spain seemed to offer an effective alternative to earlier political failures. For their part leading Socialist Leaguers were realistically sceptical that they could win votes within the Labour Party and were ready to explore an alternative.

Any suggestion of links with the Communist Party produced predictable responses within the Labour Party and many trade union hierarchies; at the 1936 party conference both Communist affiliation and the United Front policy were rejected decisively.[43] Once the League had voted early in 1937 to sign a 'Unity Manifesto' with the ILP and the Communist Party, the NEC's response was draconian. First, it disaffiliated the League – a more severe step than any taken against the ILP. Yet this step simply denied the League any organisational standing within the party. League members could still be individual members of the Labour Party. Finding that disaffiliation did not put an end to the support for the 'Unity Campaign', the NEC went much further and placed the Socialist League on the party's list of proscribed organisations. In order to avoid loss of Labour Party membership, the League therefore dissolved itself in the spring of 1937. The attempt to maintain an organised faction affiliated to the party but avoiding the fate of the ILP had failed.[44]

The tough and decisive intervention of the party managers contrasted with the slowly-developing rupture with the ILP. Yet the League's challenge was if anything less substantial than that of its predecessor. The tougher line was in part the product of managerial interpretations of the past. One reading of 1929–31 was that the party had been critically weakened by divisive factions and personal vanities. Moreover, the party's dominant culture meant that it was typically easier to exercise discipline when the Communist Party was an element in the controversy. Anti-Communism was deeply entrenched in some sections of the party and in many unions; the Labour Party leadership had spent much energy distinguishing its ideological position from that of the Communists, and several of the party's organisational controls had developed as a result of earlier attempts to deal with Communist involvement in the party. Such left factionalism had none of the penumbra of legitimacy that had surrounded the ILP until the end. Moreover, appeals for a united or subsequently a popular front ran counter to a basic optimism within Labour politics, the belief that whatever the recent failures, Labour could triumph electorally without any pacts or understandings. It was easy to indict such critics for their unnecessary pessimism.

The crushing of the Socialist League did not end the argument. Sections of the Labour left alarmed at the international situation, the policies of the Chamberlain Government, and the responses of the Labour Party continued to agitate for a broader alliance. But in the spring of 1939, this whole agitation ended with the expulsion of three MPs Cripps, Bevan and Strauss. Their crime was to continue the advocacy of a popular front after the National Executive Committee had decided to reject any such initiative. The controversy demonstrated the extent to which the scope for debate had been reduced. Two of the expelled MPs highlighted the dilemma:

> individual members of the Party have the duty and privilege to attempt to change the decisions of the Conference . . . It is almost impossible to make any impact on a Party consisting of millions of members, if all co-operative activity by the minority is proscribed.[45]

Against this stood the robust presentation of Dalton, a protagonist for the tougher regime: 'If . . . comradeship was to be effective and true, minorities must submit with good grace, to majority decisions.'[46]

These limits on legitimate left factionalism proved durable. Labour's wartime involvement in the Churchill coalition generated disagreement over the alleged willingness of Labour ministers to acquiesce in cautious policies and over the limiting consequence of the electoral truce; but the distinctiveness of wartime politics produced no equivalent of the ILP or the Socialist League. Equally the postwar years of majority Labour Government were not marked until the closing stage by the frustrations and recriminations that had characterised Labour's previous period in office. This did not mean that the Attlee Government lacked critics within the party.[47] Several of the younger MPs had cut their political teeth in the controversies of the 1930s. In particular, the government's failure to follow a distinctively Socialist line in foreign affairs, the estrangement from the Soviet Union, the advent of the Marshall Plan and of NATO all provoked criticism from the left within both the PLP and many Constituency Parties. But the dissent had no significant impact on either government or party. Critics were themselves split between dedicated supporters of Soviet policy, those who hoped for a third way between Stalinism and

American capitalism, and those who evinced unhappiness about armaments and alliances without articulating an alternative. Moreover, the focus of dissent was often limited to international issues. Ministers could point to substantial achievements in industrial and social policy and indeed in retrospect the left has generally portrayed the Attlee Government in more positive tones than either its successors or its predecessors. The political arithmetic was unambiguous. Majorities within the PLP, the Party Conference and the NEC remained steadfastly loyal to 'their' government.

Within these majorities, the trade unions played a key role. In the post-war years the miners and the two major general unions were firm supporters of the Labour leadership. Yet from one perspective the trade union world was perhaps less monolithically on the right than it had been in the mid and late 1930s. The engineers, the railwaymen and the shop workers all contained well-organised left factions. With Labour in office, their influence was curbed by an underlying loyalty to the political side of the movement; but once this constraint was removed, the trade union voice could be more discordant. However, the basis of the left's increased strength in some major unions was also a curb on its impact. Much of the left's expansion was the result of increased Communist influence in several unions during the wartime alliance with the Soviet Union. Ironically this left secured some trade union influence just as the intensification of the Cold War was facilitating a more virulent anti-Communism. The polemical equating of trade union left politics with Communist priorities was thus an effective way of limiting that influence.[48]

Until the spring of 1951 the Labour Party's internal politics remained relatively calm. The standing orders that had been the formal breaking point for the ILP had been suspended in 1946. Parliamentary rebellions could provoke pained or aggressive response from loyalists. Four MPs were thrown out of the party on the grounds that their politics were indistinguishable from those of the Communist Party. Organised left-factionalism was limited. The 'Keep Left' group, small and largely middle-class, produced two well-publicised pamphlets. Its regular meetings discussed policy matters in considerable detail, but in comparison with earlier episodes, 'Keep Left' was a very cautious grouping. In no way was it a faction concerned to promote policies fundamentally at odds with those of the government: it made few attempts to campaign for its viewpoint within the wider party. In fact 'Keep Left' members spoke with more than one voice on the most controversial area of all, international affairs.

Perhaps memories of earlier failed factions had an influence. Some on the left suggested that there were other more diplomatic paths to influence. Richard Crossman insisted early in 1950 that effective political work was best pursued 'behind the scenes in committee rooms upstairs, or even over a glass of beer'.[49] There were some within the parliamentary party who had been centrally involved in the ILP debates. Jennie Lee and from 1950 Fenner Brockway had backed the ILP policy in the 1929 parliament and had stayed with the ILP. Emrys Hughes had campaigned through the columns of *Forward* against a breach with the Labour Party. With the memory of what disaffiliation had involved, all the ex-ILP-ers were insistent that such a breach should not be repeated.[50] Hughes for example emphasised:

> There is no use remaining aloof and dividing yourselves into isolationists and sects. Yes I know all you are likely to say about the 'yes-men' and the careerists and the office-seekers turned into the worst reactionaries. They come and go, but remember it is your movement and not theirs.[51]

But in April 1951 the Bevanite controversy began with the resignation of the three Ministers, Bevan, Wilson and Freeman. For four years Labour Party exchanges were dominated by intense factional antipathies.

The accession of the three ex-Ministers strengthened the old 'Keep Left' not just because of their own involvement, but because it was followed by some expansion of the group's membership. Nevertheless the Bevanite group of MPs remained relatively small and members showed varying and fluctuating levels of involvement. Some on the parliamentary left never joined. Either they showed no interest or were excluded on personal or political grounds. This small parliamentary group was backed by two journals, *New Statesman* and more significantly, *Tribune*, and by a popular programme of Tribune Brains Trusts in the constituencies. Certainly the Bevanites had support in key party institutions far beyond that of the ILP or the Socialist League. Bevanite causes could secure the support of more than one-fifth of Labour MPs: from October 1952, Bevanites occupied all but one of the places reserved for Constituency Parties on Labour's National Executive. In making this advance, they had pushed off the executive two of the 1945 government's leading figures – Morrison and

THE ILP AND THE LABOUR LEFT

Dalton. Bevanite support within the constituency parties was accompanied by some significant strength amongst the unions. On an untypical issue, German Rearmament, the Bevanites and their allies came close to winning at the 1954 party conference. Generally amongst the Unions the Bevanites could gain support from at least some of the larger organisations with substantial left factions and also backing from smaller unions where the left were firmly in control. But they always faced the firm opposition of the two general unions and the miners.[52]

These strengths have to be placed in perspective. There was no chance that the Bevanites could be more than a substantial minority within the Parliamentary Labour Party. The chance of securing a majority in the party conference was always slim; when Bevan fought Gaitskell for the party treasureship with conference as the electorate he was defeated in successive years by an increasing majority. Within the National Executive the Bevanites were an easily identifiable minority: 'The table is three sides of a square and at the bottom of one end sit six little Bevanites with 19 members of the Executive and about 10 of the staff all ranged round against them.'[53]

Given the limits of Bevanite strength the draconian responses of their opponents seem in retrospect surprising. Personal antipathies clearly played their part but it is significant how loyalist reactions sometimes harked back to the old controversies over the ILP. The Bevanites were after all the most formidable challenge yet to the party regime that had been influenced by the controversies of 1929–31.

Early in March 1952, the Bevanites led the revolt of the so-called '57 varieties', a breach of a three-line whip on the defence estimates proposed by the recently-elected Tory Government. The issue linked back to the controversy that had occasioned the previous year's resignations. The response of the Labour leadership was severe. The Chief Whip advocated the expulsion of leading rebels: such apparently organised flouting of a PLP decision was virtually unknown since the days of Maxton's purged ILP group – and this revolt was on a bigger scale. All the deeply-rooted sentiment advocating acceptance of majority decisions came to the surface laced with the abrasive accents of Cold War politics. Yet the reconciling elements within the PLP proved decisive. Expulsion would be hard to justify constitutionally given that standing orders had been suspended for six years, and would be politically inept since it would fragment the party further. The move for expulsion was blocked and standing orders were reintroduced.[54]

This passage of arms was modest compared with the fiery emotions of that year's Morecambe conference. It was not just the advance of the Bevanites in the NEC elections but also the evidence of many delegates' lack of respect for cautious parliamentarians and trade union officials. Stung by critical speeches and by interjections from the floor, loyalists such as Arthur Deakin of the Transport Workers attacked the left, not least on the issue of factional organisation:

> Those people within the Party who have set up a caucus. . . . Let them get rid of their whips; dismiss their business managers and conform to the Party constitution. Let them cease the vicious attacks . . . abandon their vituperation and the carping criticism which appears regularly in the *Tribune*.[55]

Predictably, Morecambe's emotions presaged an attack on the Bevanites. A PLP meeting to debate a proposal for a ban on organised groups featured references to the ILP as a precedent. Attlee suggested that it indicated the limits of the acceptable: 'Groups are all right for special purposes but what I disapprove is an omnicompetent Group like the ILP used to be.' Morrison also employed the parallel indicating how such a faction could discomfort loyalists: 'The Bevanite Group has had a function, the same function as the ILP and it creates the assumption that only some Members of Parliament are good Socialists. I resent that.'[56] The prohibition on unofficial groups was carried by 188 votes to 51. The consequence was a ban on such activity for more than a decade. The impact of the Bevanites was blunted. Differences within the group's erstwhile members became more significant as some leading figures moved towards a rapprochement with the party leadership.

Attempts were made by the right within the PLP and the Unions to curb Bevanite activity outside parliament. *Tribune* criticisms of trade union leaders brought heavy-handed reactions: an attempt – ultimately abortive – was made to ban the Tribune Brains Trust. The trade union leader who initiated this employed Henderson's characterisation of the ILP: 'The next logical thing to do is to examine the Tribune Brains Trust and see if they are a party within a party.'[57]

There were limits to this disciplinary regime. *Tribune* journalists produced effective defences of their right to criticise trade union leaders. Their appeals to liberal sentiments could find a favourable response beyond their customary political sympathisers. In the spring of 1955 an attempt to expel Bevan failed narrowly. Yet the fact that the failure owed something to complex voting patterns on the NEC and the willingness of several senior Labour politicians to advocate the removal of a leading colleague also demonstrate the extent to which a tough style of party management retained its grip. The obstacles to an effective left politics within the Labour Party perhaps help to explain Bevan's eventual uneasy reconciliation with Gaitskell and his public and decisive breach with the unilateralists at the 1957 conference. Avoidance of the fate of the ILP meant either that kind of difficult accommodation or a potentially embittering marginalisation within the party.

Even following the 1957 conference, the weakened left ran foul of the party's disciplinary approach. An attempt was made to compensate for recent setbacks including the breach with Bevan by rehabilitating a small pressure group, *Victory for Socialism*. However the proposals included its conversion into a mass membership organisation with branches and with facilities for developing its own policies. The parallels with the ILP and the Socialist League were obvious; the response of the Labour Right was predictable and effective. The NEC issued a warning to Constituency Parties: 'it was unwise to introduce . . . an element which would distract and confuse the membership and cause a duplication of effort'.[58]

The organisational blueprint was not pursued; VFS activities were limited to an energetic but less structured campaign. The limiting of this initiative was one more example of a management of left factionalism that had its roots in the experiences of the late 1920s and the challenges posed then by the Communist Party and the ILP.

Yet by the late 1950s changes were beginning that would eventually transform the factional world of Labour politics. One generation of party leaders was giving way to another. Attlee quit the leadership in 1955; Morrison and Dalton retired as MPs in 1959; Bevan died in 1960. All of this group had not just been in the front rank in the 1945 government, but had been in the 1929 parliament. The failures of MacDonald's government had helped to form them as politicians. Indeed by the time that Labour returned to office in 1964 there were only six members of the PLP whose careers went back to the party meetings where Maxton and his colleagues had stood out against government failure and backbench loyalty.[59] As the radical years of the ILP moved thoroughly into the realms of history and often of myth so the disciplinary regime that had dominated party life for so long began to be transformed.

Personnel changes in the PLP helped to produce a more liberal regime after 1966 with Crossman as Leader of the House and Silkin as Chief Whip. A parallel development occurred in the party administration where retirements and new appointments meant an end to the old unbending view of party loyalty. Moreover the political environment changed as mounting opposition to several of the Wilson government's policies meant a much less manageable party. By the late 1960s many trade union leaders were openly critical of the Labour Government; the old belief that enough stalwart unions would protect the parliamentary leadership was eroding fast. Gradually the NEC ceased to be a forum in which the party right could guarantee a majority. The consequence was an end to predictability in party affairs: left-factionalism bloomed. This was facilitated by a widely held view of the 1950s as a decade in which party relationships had been blighted by the intolerance of leading politicians, trade unionists and party officials. It was a precedent to be avoided.

The climax came after 1979 with the left achieving an influence within the party that would have astounded Maxton and his colleagues. The constitutional changes of 1980 and 1981, the shift to the left on policies, the close-run deputy leadership contest between Benn and Healey, even the defections to the Social Democratic Party – all demonstrated a very different party from that of Maxton and MacDonald – or of Bevan and Attlee.

But countervailing forces soon developed and the left's influence receded. Divisions within the left surfaced as early as the spring of 1981 when Benn rejected the position of the majority within the Tribune Group, that he should not stand for the deputy leadership. The 1981 and 1982 elections to the National Executive reduced the left's membership, a decline that would leave its impact on disciplinary decisions. These early indications were followed by dramatic developments. Electoral disaster in 1983, Kinnock's election as party leader, controversy over the miner's strike, the permanent crisis that was Liverpool politics, electoral disaster again in 1987 all helped to weaken the left. Within all sections – unions, the PLP and the local parties – some modified their positions in pursuit of electoral success and perhaps from a belief that traditional perspectives furnished a misleading guide to contemporary complexities. The result was the gradual isolation of a much smaller left often supportive or tolerant of the Militant Tendency.

There were superficial similarities with the ILP. Once again the distinctive experiences of a city became linked with controversies over left-wing factionalism, and once again there was no simple connection between the two. One of the fundamental charges against Militant was that it was, to borrow yet again Henderson's 1931 phrase, 'a party within a party'. Yet there was a massive difference between Militant's clandestine organisation with its commitment to democratic centralism and the ILP's open conspiracy, between an organisation that claimed not to exist at all and one that had been an affiliate of the Labour Party since the beginning. Equally there were those on the National Executive in the 1980s who hankered after the certainties of an older disciplinary regime – but any such ambitions were frustrated. Attempts to reconstruct central control of dissent were limited severely by a radically changed political environment.[60] Both left and right drew selectively on the party's history to justify immediate decisions. Sometimes the parallels might illuminate, but all too often they obscured the extent to which for Labour Party factionalism, 'the past is a foreign country: they do things differently there'.

Notes

1 On this theme see Eric Hobsbawm and Terry Ranger, *The Invention of Tradition* (Cambridge University Press, Cambridge, 1983).

2 R.B. McCallum and Alison Readman, *The British General Election of 1945* (Oxford University Press, London, 1947).

3 For Johnston's politics see Graham Walker, *Thomas Johnston* (Manchester University Press, Manchester, 1988).

4 *Labour Party National Executive Committee Minutes*, 23 June 1931 for the Hardie case; correspondence between the ILP and the Labour Party over Tom Irwin is in *Independent Labour Party Conference Report*, 1931, pp. 43–51. See also *Labour Party Conference Report*, 1931, pp. 302–3.

5 See *Independent Labour Party Conference Report*, 1931 for breakdown of branches by divisions.

6 *Independent Labour Party Conference Report*, 1932, p. 35.

7 On Labour's as yet developing management structure in the 1920s see Eric Shaw, *Discipline and Discord in the Labour Party* (Manchester University Press, Manchester, 1988), pp. 1–15.

8 On local Labour Parties in the 1920s see Christopher Howard, 'Expectations Born to Die: Local Labour Party Expansion in the 1920s' in J.M. Winter (ed.), *The Working Class in Modern British History* (Cambridge University Press, Cambridge, 1983).

9 See *Labour Party Conference Report*, 1925, pp. 134–5.

10 See Shaw, *op. cit.*; Ross McKibbin, *The Evolution of the Labour Party 1910–24* (Clarendon Press, Oxford, 1974), pp. 191–204.

11 See entry for 7 to 13 July 1923, Ben Pimlott (ed.), *The Political Diaries of Hugh Dalton* (Jonathan Cape, London, 1986), pp. 34–5, and also the entry for 6 February 1924: 'I have told the ILP that I will do a lot of propaganda speaking for them in the future, in good areas where it would be well to be known', *ibid.*, p. 37.

12 On these changes see Arthur Marwick, *Clifford Allen: The Open Conspirator* (Oliver & Boyd, Edinburgh, 1964); Martin Gilbert (ed.), *Plough My Own Furrow* (Longmans, London, 1965); Fenner Brockway, *Inside the Left* (New Leader, London, 1942); F.N. Leventhal, *The Lost Dissenter: H.N. Brailsford and his World* (Clarendon Press, Oxford, 1985).

13 Leventhal, *ibid.*, pp. 196–7. The specific occasion was the *New Leader's* attitude to trade union leadership during the General Strike.

14 See *Labour Party National Executive Committee*, Minutes, 26 October 1927 and then 2 May 1928 with reference to forthcoming consultation with the Miners' Federation.

15 *New Leader*, 7 December 1929 cited in Fenner Brockway, *Bermondsey Story* (Allen & Unwin, London, 1949), p. 148.

16 *Independent Labour Party Conference Report*, 1929, p. 66: the more far-reaching proposal was rejected by 214 to 124.

17 See *Independent Labour Party Conference Report*, 1930, pp. 5–6 for the division within the parliamentary group; see also Dollan at pp. 79–80 for his concern about some MPs' activities.

18 See *ibid.*, p. 76 for text. Dollan perhaps diplomatically, supported this proposal, but opposed a rigid party discipline.

19 The members of the reformed group were John Beckett, W.J. Brown, W. Hirst, Fred Jowett, David Kirkwood, Jack Lees, James Maxton, Eli Sandham, John Strachey, E.F. Wise, Fenner Brockway, Robert Forgan, T.F. Horrabin, Joseph Kinley, Jennie Lee, John McGovern, Campbell Stephen and R. Wallhead. Three of these – Brown, Strachey and Forgan – left the Labour Party with Mosley early in 1931.

20 *Independent Labour Party Conference Report*, 1930, p. 81 (T.W. Stamford).

21 See Shaw *op. cit.*, pp. 15–21; also R.K. Alderman, 'The Conscience Clause of the PLP', *Parliamentary Affairs*, 19, 1966.

22 *Joint Meeting Labour Party National Executive and Parliamentary Labour Party Consultative Committee*, 26 November 1930.

23 For the correspondence see *Labour Party Conference Report*, 1931, pp. 293–302.

24 For text of standing orders see *Labour Party Conference Report*, 1931, p. 298. See also in *ibid.*, p. 33, the proposal to make refusal by a candidate to accept or act in accordance with the standing orders, into a violation of the Party constitution.

25 See Fred Jowett, *The ILP Says No To The Standing Orders of the Labour Party* (ILP, London 1932).

26 John Paton to Arthur Henderson, 30 July 1931, cited in *Labour Party Conference Report*, 1931, p. 300.

27 Arthur Henderson to John Paton, 27 July 1931, cited in *ibid.*, p. 300.

28 *Ibid.*, p. 176. The ILP's attempt to refer back the section on party discipline in the NEC's report was defeated by 2,117,000 votes to 193,000.

29 *Ibid.* pp. 174–5.

30 *Labour Party National Executive Committee*, Minutes, 7 October 1931.

31 *Independent Labour Party Conference Report*, 1932 pp. 10 and 16.

32 *Ibid.* p. 29.

33 *Ibid.* pp. 41–2.

34 *Ibid.* p. 47. Cullen was the delegate from the Poplar ILP and urged immediate disaffiliation.

35 The disaffiliation issue was debated at the ILP's 1931 conference: see *Independent Labour Party Conference Report*, 1931, p. 96, for votes; at the annual conference, Easter 1932 the decision was for conditional affiliation; then at the special conference in July 1932 where the decision to disaffiliate was taken.

36 *Labour Party Conference Report*, 1937 p. 160. This speaker, John McGurk, was a Lancashire Miners' Offical and had been party chairman in 1919. See also Dalton's comment on Bevan at a PLP meeting in April 1951. 'This is Mosley speaking', Pimlott, *Political Diaries*, p. 539.

37 *Labour Party Conference Report*, 1939, p. 235.

38 For the Socialist League see Ben Pimlott, *Labour and the Left in the 1930s* (Cambridge University Press, Cambridge, 1977), ch. 5.

39 Cited in *ibid.*, p. 46.

40 *Labour Party Conference Report*, 1932, p. 204.

41 Cited in Pimlott, *Labour and the Left*, p. 53.

42 Hugh Dalton, *Memoirs Volume 2. The Fateful Years 1931–45* (Muller, London, 1957), pp. 58–9.

43 *Labour Party Conference Report*, 1936, pp. 207–11 and pp. 250–57.

44 For the NEC's statement see *Labour Party Conference Report*, 1937, pp. 25–8 and for the debate, pp. 156–64.

45 *Labour Party Conference Report*, 1939, p. 50: letter from Bevan, Strauss, Edgar Young and Robert Bruce to the NEC.

46 *Ibid.*, p. 231.

47 See Jonathan Schneer, *Labour's Conscience: The Labour Left 1945–51* (Unwin Hyman, London, 1988).

48 See on trade union politics Martin Harrison, *Trade Unions and the Labour Party since 1945* (Allen & Unwin, London, 1960).

49 *Sunday Pictorial*, 5 March 1950, cited in Schneer *op. cit.* p. 193. This was in the context of Labour's newly reduced parliamentary majority.

50 A point made by Lord Brockway in discussion.

51 Cited in Schneer, *op. cit* p. 224.

52 For more detail see David Howell, *The Rise and Fall of Bevanism* (Independent Labour Publications, Leeds, 1981); see also Shaw, *op. cit.*, p. 224.

53 Entry for 1 October 1952 in Janet Morgan (ed.), *The Backbench Diaries of Richard Crossman* (Cape, London, 1981) p. 152.

54 Entries for 28 February-18 March 1952 in *ibid.*, pp. 82–96.

55 *Labour Party Conference Report*, 1952, p. 127.

56 See entry for 23 October, 1952 in Morgan, *op. cit.*, pp. 163–8.

57 See entry for 29 January 1953, in *ibid.*, p. 197.

58 *Labour Party Conference Report*, 1958, p. 19. Shaw *op. cit.*, pp. 53–5.

59 The six were Shinwell, Jennie Lee, Arthur Henderson Junior, Sorenson, Philip Noel Baker and George Strauss. In addition Megan Lloyd George had sat in the 1929 parliament but as a Liberal and Emrys Hughes, although an MP only from 1946 had been centrally involved in the ILP's pre-disaffiliation controversies through his work on *Forward*.

60 See Shaw, *op. cit.*, chs. 11–13.

Bibliography

Manuscript sources

Lord Balfour of Burleigh and Lynden Macassey, *Report of the Commission of Enquiry into Industrial Unrest in the Clyde District*, Cmd 8136.

Census for Scotland, 1911, Parliamentary Papers, 1912–1913, vol. III.

Clyde Shipbuilders' Association, Minutes.

Helen Crawfurd, 'Memoirs', ms autobiography (Marx Memorial Library).

Emrys Hughes, 'Rebels and Renegades', ms autobiography, (National Library of Scotland, Dep. 176, Box 10, ff. 1–2).

Glasgow Trades Council, Minutes.

Independent Labour Party, Glasgow Federation, Minutes.

Independent Labour Party, National Administrative Council, Minutes and Papers.

Independent Labour Party, Francis Johnston Correspondence.

Labour Party National Executive Minutes.

Ministry of Munitions, Internal Files.

North West Engineering Trades Employers' Association, Minutes.

Report of an Enquiry by the Board of Trade into Working Class Rents, Housing and Retail Prices . . . in the Principal Industrial Towns of the United Kingdom, Parliamentary Papers, 1908, vol. 108.

Socialist League Collection, International Institute of Social History, Amsterdam.

Arthur Woodburn, Typescript ms (National Library of Scotland, ACC 7656/4/3).

Contemporary newspapers and periodicals

Athenaeum
Commonweal
Communist International
The Democrat
Engineering

BIBLIOGRAPHY

Forward
Glasgow Commonweal
Glasgow Eastern Standard
Glasgow Herald
Glasgow Observer
Govan Pioneer
The International
Justice
Labour Annual
Labour Leader
The Miner
New Leader
Plebs
Scottish Co-operator
Socialist Review
Socialist Torch
The Times
The Worker

Contemporary printed political material

Glasgow Trades Council
Annual Reports
Independent Labour Party
Annual Conference Reports
Labour Party
Annual Conference Reports
Labour Party: Scottish Advisory Council
Annual Conference Reports

Books and pamphlets

Adams, R.J.Q., *Arms and the Wizard: Lloyd George and the Ministry of Munitions* (Cambridge Mass., Harvard University Press, 1978).

Addison, C., *Four and a Half Years: A Personal Diary from June 1914 to January 1919* (Hutchinson, London, 1934).

Arnot, R. Page, *A History of the Scottish Miners* (Allen & Unwin, London, 1955).

Attlee, C.R., *The Labour Party in Perspective* (Victor Gollancz, London, 1937).

Bell, Tom, *Pioneering Days* (Lawrence & Wishart, London, 1941).

Brockway, Fenner, *Inside the Left: Thirty Years of Platform Press, Prison and Parliament* (New Leader, London, 1942).

Brockway, Fenner, *Bermondsey Story* (Allen & Unwin, London, 1949).

Brown, Callum, *The Social History of Religion in Scotland Since 1730* (Methuen, London, 1987).

Brown, Gordon, *Maxton* (Mainstream, Edinburgh, 1986).

Brown, J., 'From Radicalism to Socialism: Paisley Engineers 1890–1920' (*Our History*, 71, London, 1979).

Burgess, Keith, *The Challenge of Labour* (Croom Helm, London, 1980).

Cage, R.A. (ed.) *The Working Class in Glasgow, 1750–1914* (Croom Helm, London, 1987).

Campbell, Calum, 'The Making of a Clydeside Working Class: Shipbuilding and Working Class Organisation in Govan' (*Our History*, 78, London, 1986).

Campbell, Roy H., *Scotland Since 1707: The Rise of an Industrial Society* (John Donald, Edinburgh, 1985).

Castells, Manuel, *The City and the Grassroots: A Cross-Cultural Theory of Urban Social Movements* (Edward Arnold, London, 1983).

Challinor, Raymond, *The Origins of British Bolshevism* (Croom Helm, London, 1977).

Clarke, Peter, *Lancashire and the New Liberalism* (Cambridge University Press, Cambridge, 1971).

Cline, C.A., *Recruits to Labour* (University Press, Syracuse, NY, 1963).

Cohen, G.A., *History, Labour and Freedom: Themes from Marx* (Oxford University Press, Oxford, 1988).

Cole, G.D.H., *British Working Class Politics* (Methuen, London, 1941).

Connell, J., *Glasgow Municipal Enterprise* (Labour Leader, Glasgow, 1899).

Crossick, Geoffrey, *An Artisan Elite in Victorian Society: Kentish London 1840–1880* (Croom Helm, London, 1978).

Crow, Duncan, *A Man of Push and Go: The Life of George Macaulay Booth* (Rupert Hart-Davis, London, 1965).

Cunningham, Hugh, *The Volunteer Force: A Social and Political History, 1859–1908* (C.R. Hay, London, 1975).

Dalton, Hugh, *Memoirs Volume 2: The Fateful Years 1931–45* (Muller, London, 1957).

Dangerfield, George, *The Strange Death of Liberal England* (Constable, London, 1936).

Davidson, Roger, *Whitehall and the Labour Problem in Late-Victorian and Edwardian Britain* (Croom Helm, London, 1985).

Davies, Paul, *A.J. Cook* (Manchester University Press, Manchester, 1988).

Donnachie, Ian, Harvie, Christopher and Wood, Ian, S. (eds), *Forward!*: *Labour Politics In Scotland 1888–1988* (Polygon, Edinburgh, 1989).

Dowse, Robert, *Left in the Centre: The Independent Labour Party 1893–1940* (Longmans, London, 1966).

Englander, David, *Landlord and Tenant in Urban Britain 1838–1918*

(Clarendon Press, Oxford, 1983).

Flanagan, J.A., *Wholesale Co-operation in Scotland* (SCWS, Glasgow, 1920).

Foster, John and Charles Woolfson, *The Politics of the UCS Work-In* (Lawrence & Wishart, London, 1986).

Gallacher, William, *Revolt on the Clyde* (Lawrence & Wishart, London, 1936).

Gallacher, William, *Last Memoirs* (Lawrence & Wishart, London, 1966).

Gallacher, William and Campbell, John, *Direct Action* (Glasgow, 1919).

Gallagher, Tom, *Glasgow The Uneasy Peace: Religious Tension in Modern Scotland* (Manchester University Press, Manchester, 1987).

Gilbert, Martin (ed.), *Plough My Own Furrow* (Longmans, London, 1965).

Gordon, Eleanor, *Women and the Labour Movement: Scotland 1850–1914* (Oxford University Press, Oxford, 1990).

Gray, Robert Q., *The Labour Aristocracy in Victorian Edinburgh* (Oxford University Press, Oxford, 1976).

Gray, Robert Q., *The Aristocracy of Labour in Nineteenth Century Britain, c. 1850–1910* (Macmillan, London, 1981).

Gregory, Roy, *The Miners in British Politics 1906–1914* (Clarendon Press, Oxford, 1968).

Hannan, John, *The Life of John Wheatley* (Spokesman, Nottingham, 1988).

Harris, J., *William Beveridge* (Oxford University Press, Oxford, 1977).

Harrison, Martin, *Trade Unions and the Labour Party Since 1945* (Allen & Unwin, London, 1960).

Hinton, James, *The First Shop Stewards' Movement* (Allen & Unwin, London, 1973).

Hinton, James, and Hyman, Richard, *Trade Unions and Revolution: The Industrial politics of the Early Communist Party* (Pluto, London, 1975).

Hobsbawm, Eric and Ranger, Terry, *The Invention of Tradition* (Cambridge University Press, Cambridge, 1983).

Hoggart, Richard, *The Uses of Literacy: Aspects of Working Class Life* (Chatto & Windus, London, 1957).

Holford, John, *Reshaping Labour: Organisation, Work and Politics in Edinburgh in the Great War and After* (Croom Helm, London, 1988).

Holton, Bob, *British Syndicalism: 1900–1914, Myths and Realities* (Pluto, London, 1976).

Howell, David, *The Rise and Fall of Bevanism* (Independent Labour Publications, Leeds, 1981).

Howell, David, *British Workers and the Independent Labour Party 1888–1906* (Manchester University Press, Manchester, 1983).

Howell, David, *A Lost Left: Three Studies in Socialism and Nationalism* (Manchester University Press, Manchester, 1986).

Hunt, E.H., *British Labour History 1815–1914* (Weidenfeld & Nicolson,

London, 1985).

Hutchison, Ian, *A Political History of Scotland 1832–1924: Parties Elections and Issues* (John Donald, Edinburgh, 1986).

Jowett, Fred, *The ILP Says No to the Standing Orders of the Labour Party* (ILP, London, 1932).

Joyce, Patrick, *Work, Society and Politics. The Culture of the Factory in Later Victorian England* (Harvester, Brighton, 1980).

Kendall, Walter, *The Revolutionary Movement in Britain 1900–1921* (Weidenfeld & Nicolson, London, 1969).

Kirkwood, David, *My Life of Revolt* (Harrap, London, 1935).

Knox, William (ed.), *Scottish Labour Leaders 1918–1939: A Biographical Dictionary* (Mainstream, Edinburgh, 1984).

Knox, William, *James Maxton* (Manchester University Press, Manchester, 1987).

Leventhal, F.N., *The Lost Dissenter: H.N. Brailsford and His World* (Clarendon Press, Oxford, 1985).

Lowe, David, *Souvenirs of Scottish Labour* (Holmes, Glasgow, 1919).

Lowe, Rodney, *Adjusting to Democracy: The Role of the Ministry of Labour in British Politics, 1916–1939* (Oxford University Press, Oxford, 1986).

McCallum, R.B. and Readman, Alison, *The British General Election of 1945* (Oxford University Press, Oxford, 1947).

Macassey, Lynden, *Labour Policy – False and True* (Thornton Butterworth, London 1922).

MacFarlane, Leslie J., *The British Communist Party: Its Origin and Development until 1929* (MacGibbon and Kee, London, 1966).

McGovern, John, *Neither Fear Nor Favour* (Blandford Press, London, 1960).

MacIntyre, Stuart, *A Proletarian Science: Marxism in Britain, 1917–33* (Cambridge University Press, Cambridge, 1980).

McKenzie, Robert, *British Political Parties* (Heinemann, London, 1963).

McKibbin, Ross, *The Evolution of the Labour Party 1910–24* (Clarendon Press, Oxford, 1974).

McLean, Iain, *The Legend of Red Clydeside* (John Donald, Edinburgh, 1983).

McNair, John, *James Maxton: The Beloved Rebel* (Allen & Unwin, London, 1955).

McShane, Harry and Smith, John, *No Mean Fighter* (Pluto, London, 1978).

Marquand, David, *Ramsay MacDonald* (Jonathan Cape, London, 1977).

Martin, Roderick, *Communism and the British Trade Unions 1924–1933: A Study of the National Minority Movement* (Clevedon Press, Oxford, 1969).

Marwick, Arthur, *Clifford Allen: The Open Conspirator (Oliver and Boyd, Edinburgh and London, 1964).*

Matsumura, Takao, *The Labour Aristocracy Revisited: The Victorian Flint Glass Makers, 1850–80* (Manchester University Press, Manchester, 1983).

Maxton, James, *Twenty Points for Socialism* (Glasgow, 1925).

Maxwell, W., *The History of Co-operation in Scotland: Its Inception and Leaders* (Co-operative Union, Glasgow, 1910).

Melling, Joseph, *Housing, Social Policy and the State* (Croom Helm, London, 1980).

Melling, Joseph, *Rent Strikes: Peoples' Struggle for Housing in West Scotland 1890–1916* (Polygon, Edinburgh, 1983).

Middlemas, Keith, *The Clydesiders: A Left Wing Struggle for Parliamentary Power* (Hutchinson, London, 1965).

Middlemas, Keith, *Politics in Industrial Society* (Deutsch, London, 1979).

Miliband, Ralph, *Parliamentary Socialism. A Study in the Politics of Labour* (Merlin, London, 1961).

Milton, Nan, *John Maclean* (Pluto, London, 1973).

Morgan, Janet, *The Backbench Diaries of Richard Crossman* (Cape, London, 1981).

Morgan, K.O., *Keir Hardie: Radical and Socialist* (Weidenfeld, London, 1975).

Owen, F., *Tempestuous Journey: Lloyd George His Life and Times* (Hutchinson, London, 1954).

Paton, John, *Left Turn: An Autobiography* (Secker & Warburg, London, 1936).

Paton, John, *Proletarian Pilgrimage* (Routledge, London, 1935).

Pelling, Henry, *A Short History of the Labour Party* (Macmillan, London, 1961).

Pelling, Henry, *The Origins of the Labour Party, 1880–1900* (Oxford University Press, Oxford, 1965).

Pelling, Henry, *Popular Politics and Society in late Victorian Britain* (Macmillan, London, 1968).

Pimlott, Ben, *Labour and the Left in the 1930s* (Cambridge University Press, Cambridge, 1977).

Pimlott, Ben (ed.), *The Political Diaries of Hugh Dalton* (Jonathan Cape, London, 1986).

Pribicevic, Branko, *The Shop Stewards' Movement and Workers' Control* (Blackwell, Oxford, 1959).

Price, Richard, *Masters, Unions and Men Work Control in Building and the Rise of Labour, 1830–1914* (Cambridge University Press, Cambridge, 1980).

Price, Richard, *Labour in British Society* (Croom Helm, London, 1985).

Reid, Fred, *Keir Hardie: The Making of a Socialist* (Croom Helm, London, 1978).

Reynolds, Jack, Laybourn, Keith, *Labour Heartland: A History of the Labour Party in West Yorkshire During the Inter-war Years 1918–39* (Bradford

University Press, Bradford, 1987).

Reynolds, Sian, *Britannica's Typesetters: Women Compositors in Edwardian Edinburgh* (Edinburgh University Press, Edinburgh, 1989).

Rowbotham, Sheila, *Friends of Alice Wheeldon* (Pluto, London, 1986).

Rubin, Gerry, *War, Law and Labour: The Munitions Acts, State, Regulation, and the Unions 1915–1921* (Clarendon Press, Oxford, 1987).

Sanger, Margaret, *An Autobiography* (Dover, New York, 1971).

Savage, Michael, *The Dynamics of Working Class Politics: The Labour Movement in Preston 1880–1940* (Cambridge University Press, Cambridge, 1987).

Saville, John, *The Labour Movement in Britain* (Faber, London, 1988).

Scanlon, John, *Decline and Fall of the Labour Party* (Peter Davies, London, 1932).

Scanlon, John, *Cast Off All Fooling* (Hutchinson, London, 1938).

Schneer, Jonathan, *Labour's Conscience: The Labour Left 1945–51* (Unwin Hyman, London, 1960).

Scott, W.R. and Cunnison, R., *The Industries of the Clyde Valley during the War* (Oxford University Press, Oxford, 1924).

Shaw, Eric, *Discipline and Discord in the Labour Party: The Politics of Managerial Control in the Labour Party, 1951–87* (Manchester University Press, Manchester, 1988).

Shinwell, Emanuel, *Conflict Without Malice* (Oldhams, London, 1955).

Smout, T.C., *A Century of the Scottish People 1830–1950* (Fontana, London, 1987).

Stedman Jones, Gareth, *Outcast London: A Study in the Relationship between Classes* (Oxford University Press, Oxford, 1971).

Stevenson, D.M., *Municipal Glasgow: Its Evolution and Enterprises* (Glasgow, 1914).

Taylor, A.J.P., *English History, 1914–1945* (Clarendon Press, Oxford, 1965).

Thompson, E.P., *William Morris: From Romantic to Revolutionary* (Merlin, London, 1977).

Walker, Graham, *Thomas Johnston* (Manchester University Press, Manchester, 1988).

Webb, Sidney and Beatrice, *The History of Trade Unionism* (Longmans, London, 1911).

Wertheimer, Egon, *Portrait of the Labour Party* (Putnams, London, 1929).

Wheatley, John, *The New Rent Act: A Reply to the Rent Raisers* (Glasgow, 1920)

Wheatley, John, *Socialise the National Income* (Glasgow, 1929).

Williams, Francis, *Fifty Years March. The Rise of the Labour Party* (Oldhams, London, 1951).

Winter, Jay, *Socialism and the Challenge of War: Ideas and Politics in Britain, 1912–18* (Routledge & Kegan Paul, London, 1974).

Wrigley, Chris, *David Lloyd George and the British Labour Movement* (Harvester, Brighton, 1976).

Articles

Alderman, R.K., 'The Conscience Clause of the Parliamentary Labour Party?', *Parliamentary Affairs*, 19, 1966, pp. 224–32.

Blewett, N., 'The Franchise in the United Kingdom 1885–1918', *Past and Present*, 32, 1965, pp. 27–57.

Brady, Barbara and Black, Anne, 'Women Compositors and the Factory Acts', *Economic Journal*, 9, 1899, pp. 261–6.

Brotherstone, Terry, 'The Suppression of *Forward*', *Scottish Labour History Society Journal*, I, 1969, pp. 5–23.

Cook, C., 'Labour's Electoral Base', in C. Cook and I. Taylor (eds), *The Labour Party* (Longmans, London, 1981), pp. 84–99.

Damer, Sean, 'State, class and Housing: Glasgow 1885–1919', in J. Melling (ed), *Housing, Social Policy and the State* (Croom Helm, London, 1980).

Davidson, Roger, 'The Myth of the Servile State', *Bulletin of the Society for the Study of Labour History*, XXIX, 1974, pp. 62–7.

Davidson, Roger, 'War-Time Labour Policy 1914–1916: A Re-Appraisal', *Scottish Labour History Society Journal*, 8, 1974, pp. 3–20.

Englander, David, 'Landlord and Tenant in Urban Scotland: The Background to the Clyde Rent Strikes, 1915', *Scottish Labour History Society Journal*, 15, 1981, pp. 4–14.

Foster, John, 'Scotland and the Russian Revolution', *Scottish Labour History Society Journal*, 23, 1988, pp. 3–14.

Foster, John, 'Strike Action and Working Class Politics on Clydeside, 1914–1919', unpublished paper, Paisley College, 1989.

Fraser, W.H., 'Trades Councils in the Labour Movement in Nineteenth Century Scotland', in Ian McDougall (ed.), *Essays in Scottish Labour History* (John Donald, Edinburgh, 1978).

Gallagher, Tom, 'Protestant Extremism in Urban Scotland 1930–1939: Its Growth and Contraction', *Scottish Historical Review*, LXIV, 1985, pp. 143–67.

Gallagher, Tom, 'Red Clyde's Double Anniversary', *Scottish Labour History Society Journal*, 20, 1985, pp. 4–14.

Hall, Stuart, and Schwarz, Bill, 'State and Society, 1880–1930', in Mary Langan and Bill Schwarz (eds), *Crises in the British State 1880–1930* (Hutchinson, London, 1985).

Harvie, Christopher, 'Labour and Scottish Government: the Age of Tom

Johnston', *Bulletin of Scottish Politics*, 2, 1981.

Hinton, James, 'The Clyde Workers' Committee and the Dilution Struggle', in Asa Briggs and John Saville (eds), *Essays in Labour History 1886–1923* (Macmillan, London, 1971).

Hinton, James, 'The Suppression of the *Forward*: A Note', *Scottish Labour History Society Journal*, VII, 1973, pp. 24–8.

Howard, Christopher, 'Expectations Born to Death: Local Labour Party Expansion in the 1920s', in Jay Winter (ed.), *The Working Class in Modern British History: Essays in Honour of Henry Pelling* (Cambridge University Press, Cambridge, 1983).

Irving, R.J., 'New Industries for Old? Some Investment Decisions of Sir W.G. Armstrong, Whitworth & Co. Ltd., 1900–1914', *Business History*, XVII, 1975, pp. 162–9.

Kellas, James, 'The Mid-Lanark By-Election (1888) and the Scottish Labour Party (1888–1894)', *Parliamentary Affairs*, XVII, 1965, pp. 318–29.

Kline, P., 'Lloyd George and the Experiment with Businessmen in Government', in K.D. Brown (ed.), *Essays in Anti-Labour History* (Macmillan, London, 1974).

Knowles, K.G.J.C. and Robertson, D.J., 'Differences Between the Wages of Skilled and Unskilled Workers, 1880–1950', *Bulletin of the Oxford University Institute of Statistics*, April 1951, pp. 107–27.

Knox, William, 'Religion and the Scottish Labour Movement c. 1900–39', *Journal of Contemporary History*, 23, 4, 1988, pp. 609–30.

Lancaster, Elizabeth, 'Shop Stewards in Scotland: The Amalgamated Engineering Union Between the Wars', *Scottish Labour History Society Journal*, 21, 1986, pp. 26–33.

McClelland, Keith and Reid, Alastair, 'Wood, Iron and Steel: Technology, Labour and Trade Union Organisation in the Shipbuilding Industry, 1840–1914', in Royden Harrison and Jonathan Zeitlin (eds), *Divisions of Labour: Skilled Workers and Technological Change in Nineteenth Century England* (Harvester Press, Brighton, 1985), pp. 151–84.

McGoldrick, Jim, 'Crisis and the Division of Labour: Clydeside Shipbuilding in the Inter-War Period', in Tony Dickson (ed.), *Capital and Class in Scotland* (John Donald, Edinburgh, 1982).

McKibbin, Ross, 'Why Was There No Marxism in Great Britain?', *English Historical Review*, XCIX, 1984, pp. 295–331.

Marwick, Arthur, 'The Independent Labour Party in the Nineteen-Twenties', *Bulletin of Historical Research*, XXXV, 1962, pp. 62–74.

Matthew, H.C.G., McKibbin, R., and Kay, J.A., 'The Franchise Factor in the Rise of the Labour Party', *English Historical Review*, XCI, 1976, pp. 723–52.

Melling, Joseph, 'Clydeside Housing and the Evolution of State Rent Control,

1900–1939', in Joseph Melling (ed.), *Housing, Social Policy and the State* (Croom Helm, London, 1980).

Melling, Joseph, ' "Non-Commisioned Officers": British Employers and their Supervisory Workers, 1880–1920', *Social History*, V, 2, 1980, pp. 183–221.

Melling, Joseph, 'Scottish Industrialists and the Changing Character of Class Relations in the Clyde Region', in Tony Dickson (ed.), *Capital and Class in Scotland* (John Donald, Edinburgh, 1982), pp. 61–142.

Melling, Joseph, 'Clydeside Industry and the Building of Class Politics, 1750–1971', *Bulletin of the Society for the Study of Labour History*, 52, 1987, pp. 54–8.

Melling, Joseph, 'Industry, Labour and Politics', *Business History*, XXXI, 1989, pp. 114–19.

Melling, Joseph, 'Clydeside Rent Struggles and the Making of Labour Politics in Scotland, 1900–1939', in Richard Rodger (ed.), *Scottish Housing and State Policies* (Leicester University Press, Leicester, 1989), pp. 54–88.

Melling, Joseph, 'The Servile State Revisited: Law and Industrial Capitalism in the Early Twentieth Century', *Scottish Labour History Society Journal*, 24, 1989, pp. 68–85.

Morris, R.J., 'Skilled Workers and the Politics of the "Red Clyde" ', *Scottish Labour History Society Journal*, 18, 1983, pp. 6–17.

Morris, R.J., 'Urbanisation and Scotland', in W. Hamish Fraser and R.J. Morris (eds), *People and Society in Scotland, 1830–1914* (John Donald, Edinburgh, 1990).

Oldfield, Adrian, 'The Independent Labour Party and Planning 1920–26', *International Review of Social History*, XXI, 1976, pp. 1–29.

Phillips, G., 'The British Labour Movement Before 1914', in Dick Geary (ed.), *Labour and Socialist Movements in Europe before 1914* (Berg, Oxford, 1989).

Price, Sylvia, 'Riverters' Earnings in Clyde Shipbuilding, 1889–1913', *Scottish Economic and Social History Journal*, 1, 1981, pp. 42–65.

Reid, Alastair, 'Dilution, Trade Unionism and the State in Britain during the First World War', in Steven Tolliday and Jonathan Zeitlin (eds), *Shop Floor Bargaining and the State* (Cambridge University Press, Cambridge, 1985).

Reid, Alastair, 'Glasgow Socialism', *Social History*, 11, 1, 1986, pp. 98–97.

Reid, Fred, 'Keir Hardie's Conversion to Socialism', in Briggs, Asa and Saville, John, *Essays in Labour History 1886–1923* (Macmillan, London, 1971).

Reynolds, Jack and Laybourn, Keith, 'The Emergence of the Independent Labour Party in Bradford', *International Review of Social History*, XX, 1975, pp. 313–46.

Rodger, Richard, 'The Building Industry and the Housing of the Scottish Working Class', in Martin Doughty (ed.), *Building the Industrial City* (Leicester University Press, Leicester, 1986).

Saville, John, 'The Ideology of Labourism', in R. Benewick, R.N. Berki and B. Parekh (eds), *Knowledge and Belief in Politics* (Allen & Unwin, London, 1973).

Schwarz, Bill and Durham, Martin, ' "A Safe and Sane Labourism": Socialism and the State 1910–24', in M. Langan and B. Schwarz (ed), *Crises in the British State: 1880–1930* (Hutchinson, London, 1985).

Smith, Joan, 'Labour Tradition in Glasgow and Liverpool', *History Workshop Journal*, 17, spring 1984, pp. 32–56.

Smith, Joan, 'Class, Social Structure and Sectarianism in Glasgow and Liverpool 1880–1914', in R.J. Morris (ed.), *Social Structure in Nineteenth Century British Cities* (Leicester University Press, Leicester, 1986).

Trebilock, Clive, 'War and the Failure of Industrial Mobilisation, 1899 and 1914', in Jay Winter (ed.), *War and Economic Development* (1975).

Treble, J.H., 'The Market for Unskilled Male Labour in Glasgow, 1891–1914', in Ian McDougall (ed.), *Essays in Scottish Labour History* (John Donald, Edinburgh, 1978).

Vestri, Paolo, 'The Rise of Reformism', *Radical Scotland,* April–May 1984.

Willis, Paul, 'Shop Floor Culture, Masculinity and the Wage Form', in John Clarke, Charles Critcher and Richard Johnson (ed), *Working Class Culture: Studies in History and Theory* (Hutchinson, London, 1979).

Winter, Jay, 'A Note on the Reconstruction of the Labour Party in 1918', *Scottish Labour History Society Journal*, 12, 1978, pp. 63–9.

Yeo, Stephen, 'A New Life: The Religion of Socialism in Britain, 1883–1896', *History Workshop Journal*, 4, 1977, pp. 5–56.

Zeitlin, Jonathan, 'The Labour Strategies of British Engineering Employers, 1890–1922', in Howard Gospel and Craig Littler (eds), *Managerial Strategies and Industrial Relations* (Heinemann, London, 1983), pp. 25–54.

Zeitlin, Jonathan, 'From Labour History to the History of Industrial Relations', *Economic History Review*, XL, 2, 1987, pp. 159–84.

Unpublished theses

Brown, Gordon, 'The Labour Party and Political Change in Scotland 1918–1929: The Politics of Five Elections', Ph. D., Edinburgh University, 1981.

Cooper, Samuel, 'John Wheatley, A Study in Labour History', Ph.D., Glasgow University, 1973.

Corr, Helen, 'The Gender Division of Labour in the Scottish Teaching Profession, 1872–1914, with particular reference to elementary school teaching', Ph.D., Edinburgh University, 1984.

Durham, Martin, 'The Origins and Early Years of British Communism, 1914–1924', Ph.D., Birmingham University, 1982.

Howard, Christopher, 'Henderson, MacDonald and Leadership in the Labour Party, 1914–1922', Ph.D., Cambridge University, 1978.

Kinloch, J.A., 'The Scottish Co-operative Wholesale Society 1868–1918', Ph.D., Strathclyde University, 1976.

McKinlay, Alan, 'Employers and Skilled Workers in the Inter-War Depression: Engineering and Shipbuilding on Clydeside 1919–1939', D.Phil., Oxford University, 1986.

McLean, I.S. 'Labour in Clydeside Politics 1914–1922', D.Phil., Oxford University, 1971.

Marwick, Arthur, 'The Independent Labour Party, 1918–1932', M.Litt., Oxford University, 1960.

Smith, Joan, 'Commonsense Thought and Working-class Consciousness: Some Aspects of the Glasgow and Liverpool Labour Movements in the Early Years of the Twentieth Century', Ph.D., Edinburgh University, 1980.

Smyth, James, 'Labour and Socialism in Glasgow 1880–1914: The Electoral Challenge Prior to Democracy', Ph.D., Edinburgh University, 1987.

Weekes, Brian, 'The Amalgamated Society of Engineers 1880–1914: A Study of Trade Union Government and Industrial Policy', Ph.D., Warwick University, 1970.

Index